BEAR CHILD

D1366600

BEAR CHILD
The Life and Times of Jerry Potts

RODGER D. TOUCHIE

Heritage House

VICTORIA • VANCOUVER • CALGARY

Heritage House Publishing Company Ltd.
#108 – 17665 66A Avenue
Surrey, BC V3S 2A7
www.heritagehouse.ca

Library and Archives Canada Cataloguing in Publication

Touchie, Rodger, 1944–
    Bear Child: the life and times of Jerry Potts/Rodger D. Touchie.

Includes bibliographical references and index.
ISBN 1-894384-63-6

    1. Potts, Jerry, 1840?–1896. 2. Frontier and pioneer life—Canada,
Western. 3. Indians of North America—Canada, Western—History.
4. Northwest, Canadian—History—1870-1905. 5. Scouts and scouting—
Canada, Western—Biography. 6. Métis—Canada, Western—Biography.
7. Northwest, Canadian—Biography. 8. Montana—Biography. 9.North West
Mounted Police (Canada)—History. I. Title.

FC3216.3.P68T69 2005   971.2'01'092   C2005-904909-X

Cover design: Nancy St.Gelais and Frances Hunter
Book design and layout: Darlene Nickull
Editors: Karla Decker and Elaine Jones
Proofreader: Audrey McClellan

Printed in Canada

Heritage House acknowledges the financial support for its publishing program
from the Government of Canada through the Book Publishing Industry
Development Program (BPIDP), Canada Council for the Arts, and the British
Columbia Arts Council.

BRITISH
COLUMBIA
ARTS COUNCIL

We acknowledge the support of the Province of British Columbia
through the British Columbia Arts Council

The Canada Council | Le Conseil des Arts
for the Arts | du Canada

In tribute to
Gene Touchie,
a man who made his own march
from New Brunswick to Ottawa
during the Great Depression to join
the Royal Canadian Mounted Police

and

Patricia,
a soulmate in life.

Contents

Acknowledgements

First and foremost, I would like to thank Hugh Dempsey for his many wonderful books and meticulous research related to the Aboriginal ways of life on the Canadian prairie. Time and again I found myself delving into his work, rereading his detailed accounts, and generally gaining insight into aspects of the obstacles facing the Blackfoot Confederacy in the last half of the 19th century. His most recent book, *Firewater: The Impact of the Whiskey Trade Upon the Blackfoot Nation*, was particularly helpful.

Lesley Wischmann, biographer of Alexander Culbertson, went out of her way to clarify aspects of Fort McKenzie life at the time Jerry Potts (Bear Child) was born. Staff at both the Glenbow Museum and the Montana Historical Society provided timely input to all requests, including the latter's file of unpublished biographical information on Andrew Dawson, a key influence in Jerry Potts' upbringing.

This project started through conversation with Sharon Basque, whose late husband, Garnet, had published an entertaining book called *Jerry Potts: Paladin of the Plains*. Sharon allowed me access to all files and photographs that supported the writings from their commissioned author, Bernard Fardy. That book did not include source information, but much of his account was verified as both accurate and insightful. Excerpts of Mr. Fardy's phraseology are included and noted in this book, while other descriptions inspired me to seek more information on the scenes he portrayed.

On occasions when time seemed a rare commodity and progress was slow, inspiration came from the fine novelists Fred Stenson and Guy Vanderhaeghe. Stenson's *The Trade* and Vanderhaeghe's two widely applauded works, *The Englishman's Boy* and *The Last Crossing*, were perfect respites from the many non-fiction accounts of the people and events that defined the history of both the Upper Missouri and the Canadian West.

As for the historians, rather than paraphrase their observations after reading books listed in the bibliography, I have often attempted to incorporate the quotes of other writers into the flow of this narrative. Exploring their historic interpretations of events and people and gaining some understanding of the dynamics of the western frontier in 19th-century North America has been a fascinating process.

In current times the collective Aboriginal peoples of the Alberta-Montana border country prefer to be known as the Nitsitapii as opposed to the European term Blackfoot. Likewise, rather than Blood, Peigan and Blackfoot for the individual main tribes, current generations use Kainai, Pikani and Siksika to identify themselves in many cases. While this book, for the most part, adopts the classic European terms, to recognize the distinctive spellings used by the Pikani tribes who traditionally wintered both above and below the Medicine Line—north and south of the 49th parallel—I have used the spelling "Peigan" (also called Apatohsipkani today in southern Alberta) for those north of the border, and "Piegan" or "South Piegan" (also called Amsskaapipikani today) for tribes in what was then the Montana Territory. "Assiniboine" has been used throughout in preference to "Assiniboin."

Some names can be confusing. Mountain Chief was a South Piegan tribal leader with lodges near the Marias River. Chief Mountain is a landmark peak near the border in the Rockies. The honorary name Chief Mountain was bestowed upon the author S.H. Middleton by Blood chiefs in the 20th century.

While much of my research is based on information garnered from the United States, I have chosen to adopt Canadian spellings for words such as "honour," as the book is to be published first in Canada. Also, as I am not a fan of revisionist history, I have used the word "Indian" in its historical context, as well as "Aboriginals" and "Natives" in references to the First Nations peoples of Canada and Native Americans.

And finally, this book was never intended as a scholarly study of Bear Child/Jerry Potts, and my use of secondary resources has been extensive. It is through the many wonderful books that have been written about 19th-century frontier history in North America that I have developed a keen interest in those times, and it is upon that literature that I have greatly relied to develop this story. In places, to connect the narrative, I have had to resort to conjecture, based as completely as possible on a review of available facts. I feel confident that none of this speculation distorts history as it has been presented.

This story covers much of the 19th century, and as an aid to the reader a timeline has been inserted near the end of the book, before the endnotes.

I wish to thank all of the staff within the three Heritage Group publishing programs (Heritage House, TouchWood Editions, and Rocky Mountain Books) for picking up the slack while I took time to research and write this book. Vivian Sinclair, Linda Martin, and Karla Decker were particularly helpful along my circuitous path, Marlyn Horsdal provided much constructive advice and Elaine Jones helped immensely with the fine tuning. Long-time colleague Darlene Nickull was most helpful in defining the final layout.

Rodger Touchie
June 2005

Preface

Historical studies of North America have failed, in the main, to compare the fascinating and remarkably dissimilar evolutions of two of the continent's cultures as they occurred in the second half of the 19th century. In particular, these developments took place in an area that has become modern-day Montana and Alberta, on both sides of the "Medicine Line," that invention that defined the border shared by the United States of America and its northerly neighbour, the Dominion of Canada.

More than 50 years after the Americans and British signed a peace treaty ending the War of 1812, Canada was no longer a group of colonies but an exuberant young country still trying to grasp the magnitude of its vast northwestern territory. A joint commission had been delegated by both countries to march along the 49th parallel and survey a border from east of the Red River to the Rockies. The boundary that they charted, marked only by a single line of metal columns, earthen mounds, and stone cairns constructed at regular intervals, was a concept unfathomable to the nomadic Aboriginals who had roamed these lands for thousands of years, knowing only the constraints imposed by rival tribes. Gathering in their winter camps or chasing the buffalo during the long hunting season, the Blackfoot Confederacy was an alliance of tribal groups whose traditional territory occupied both sides of the new Medicine Line border that would so affect their lives. While this political invention would provide them with a northern haven from some of the aggressive military tactics of the U.S. Cavalry, their fate nevertheless marched west on four white horses in the form of disease, firewater, greed, and starvation.

The beginning of the great decline can be traced back to well before the smallpox epidemic of 1837, but it was this event that sounded the death knell for the Indian way of life along the Upper Missouri River and across the Canadian prairies.

It is often said that with death comes a new birth, an observation apropos to this story. Bear Child, the name he was given by his Blackfoot brothers, or Jerry Potts, as he is best known to historians, was born in the shadow of that great epidemic. Of mixed blood, he lived and learned the ways of two opposing cultures. Ultimately, he would serve each of them well.

When I first undertook this project, I had the simple motive of filling a gap in a series of books that Heritage House has published profiling some of the individuals and events that played a large part in history as it unfolded on the Canadian prairie in the 1870s. It was a time of cultural clashes, when a few men in red coats brought a new form of justice to the proud and often-suspicious Native peoples who hunted the buffalo wherever it roamed. The buffalo herds (more properly called bison) and their eventual disappearance are at the heart of this story. Those who hunted the buffalo ranged from legitimate hero to mercenary scoundrel, all fodder for writers of both fiction and non-fiction bent on documenting the epic struggles of this era. With good reason, they have chosen to recognize well-known Native leaders such as Crowfoot, Red Crow, and Sitting Bull, and Mounties like Macleod, Steele, and Walsh. While these men and a host of other Aboriginal and White leaders are more than deserving of such study, my editorial tasks and ongoing reading kept pointing to one little-recognized character who always seemed to be on hand at a steady series of events.

At first look, Jerry Potts seemed little more than a supporting player in the defining events of his time. Yet, able to earn his keep as an interpreter with a limited knowledge of English and assorted Indian dialects, he came to understand the western frontier as well as any man. The circumstances of his birth and the diverse influences of both the Blackfoot and White fur trade cultures during his formative years confirm that he, possibly more than any other man of his times, was moulded by the triumphs and tragedies that occurred on both sides of the Medicine Line.

Although he is most familiar to us as Jerry Potts, I have concluded that his soul was that of a Blackfoot warrior and his heart belonged to the Blood and Peigan peoples he stayed close to all his life. Bear Child's biography is not without its gaps, and historians have developed various speculations to fill the void. My research has helped me understand why some accounts of the man's youth have been distorted, and at least one first-hand account has led to this confusion. This book is not, by any means, a definitive study of the subject, but I hope the story generates an expanded interest in the deeds of this small man who made such a big difference.

Although his life did not begin until 1838, Bear Child's full story spanned most of the 19th century, taking root when the man who would be his father opted to leave Pennsylvania to try his luck in the West. The depiction of his journey to the Upper Missouri is based largely on research into a similar, well-documented expedition that had left the same state only a few years earlier.

Jerry Potts' importance in Canada's historic narrative has been understated; in the United States, where he spent most of his first 35 years, he has been almost completely ignored. In those early years he became a survivor, sporadically under the spells of both good men and bad, learning through raw experience his own code of justice. Raised amid two male-dominated cultures—the Missouri River fur trade and the Blood Indian camps near the Medicine Line, both environments of enterprise, ego, and the regular conquest of might over right—he was enough like every other entrepreneur in Montana that his unique talents as scout, trader, hunter, and interpreter were viewed as little more than useful commodities.

After 1873 and a serendipitous event in his life, he became part of a distinctly Canadian experiment that saw a stubborn band of disillusioned recruits in ragged red tunics licking their wounds and nursing their remaining horses at a campsite near the Medicine Line. Over the next decade, with his Bear Child persona costumed in the attire of a man known to his new employers only as Jerry Potts, he would help make the experiment work and aid the stable, peaceful assimilation of the Blackfoot peoples into a multicultural Canadian West.

This story is largely rooted in events and motivations that originated in the Wild West trading town of Fort Benton on the Upper Missouri at a time when lawlessness ran rampant. Ironically, it was here, under dire circumstances, that two lead officers of the fledgling North West Mounted Police force came seeking supplies, counsel, and guidance to sustain their men and livestock through the severe Canadian winter that lay ahead. As fate would have it, only a day before these officers arrived at the door of the town's main supply house, a lone "breed" rode into town from his camp on the Marias River with a string of ponies in tow, intent on quickly selling the animals for a fair price, then drinking his fill of whiskey. The binge was short-lived.

Prologue

Dusk was setting in when the shot rang out. It was unmistakable, only slightly muffled by the walls of the palisade. Seconds later came the yelling, the calls for help, the doctor, White men's curse words everywhere.

In the shadows near the stables, a young Native woman cowered and drew her son near. It was not her place to join the melee. Whatever the problem, anger ruled the air. This was a matter for the traders only. The child wrestled to get free, his curious black eyes drawn to the din near the fort's walls. Crooked Back let him turn to face the sounds, wrapped her arms around his waist and rocked her Jeremiah. Andrew would come soon; he would tell her what had happened, and whom the firewater had hurt this time.

As quiet returned, except for the orders being barked by the boss man, she released the boy and watched his wobbly steps toward a lone man walking her way. Andrew? No, it was Thank You. Most called him Merci, but Andrew said "Thank You" was his English name. Mercy? Merci? The White words were hard to understand sometimes. Mercereau was the man's actual name, but nobody called him that.

The pigeon-toed toddler raised his hand toward the approaching man, who took it in passing and turned the child back to his mother. Slowly the two drew closer, and she beckoned her son back to her. Thank You bent low, steered the boy into her arms, and then removed his hat. It was a gesture of respect, one she rarely saw.

"Andrew," the Frenchman said. "Il est mort."

U.S. POLICIES IN THE 19TH CENTURY
REGARDING NATIVE PEOPLES

Thomas Jefferson set the fate of the American Native peoples on its destructive course when he first addressed the incompatible ambitions of the United States government and the Amerind cultures that lived to the west of the original 13 states. In the decade preceding his two-term presidency (1801-09), Jefferson helped introduce the "factory system" as a means to assimilate the more docile tribes into his vision of a civilized society. Factories were to be government-managed trading forts that would first attract tribesmen to settle near the goods and services provided and then encourage the Aboriginals to adopt the ways of their so-called benefactors.

Jefferson's plan was to drive all non-conforming chiefs west of the Mississippi River if they did not abide by his grand scheme.

The border was considered temporary because the learned Jefferson, who classified the Indians as "hunter-gatherers," believed that they could not be contained or civilized if they were allowed to have hunting grounds. He knew that the settlement drive west would be endless, and all Indian lands would gradually shrink to reservation size.

East of the Mississippi, Jefferson set out to acquire all Native-owned lands through a three-pronged strategy. Special favours were bestowed upon chiefs who signed over their people's land claims. Protection from both White bullies and other tribes was provided in exchange for title to the land. Finally, through either withdrawal of trade privileges or a unilateral declaration of hostilities, Jefferson directed the army to conquer the enemy.

During Jefferson's term the Ohio Valley and east shore of the Mississippi became federally owned, thus surrounding many tribes that lived west of the Appalachian Mountains. Gradually they were enticed to sign away their land until they were completely confined to reserves. In 1808 Jefferson's lone action to secure land across the Mississippi came when the Osage people ceded title to 50,000 square miles in return for protection from the Sioux.

Even then, however, the factory system was proving unworkable, doomed because the government-sponsored forts were prohibited from using whiskey in trade. Private traders moved into the wilderness and conducted business with total disregard for the law. Vile concoctions of alcohol-laced firewater remained the most effective way to earn large profits. Meanwhile, tribal groups unwilling to conform to Jefferson's vision escaped farther west only to run up against the fierce resistance of another territorial entity, the Blackfoot Confederacy.

Although the factory system was abandoned in 1822, laws that restricted liquor sales to Natives remained on the books, and in 1832 new legislation banned liquor anywhere in "Indian country." The only real effect was to give an advantage to those willing to defy unenforceable laws.

Chapter 1

The Lure of Fur

It was one of his greatest undertakings and would ultimately define the destiny of his country. Thomas Jefferson's $15,000,000 purchase of the Louisiana Territory from Napoleon in 1803 brought under his control lands between the Mississippi River and Rocky Mountains that would eventually become 13 new states in the Union.

While the shrewd acquisition, only 27 years after the country was formed, marked the end of the beginning for the developing United States of America, it also spelled the beginning of the end for the Indian way of life west of the Mississippi. Proud warriors of many tribes who lived in the mountains or roamed the Great Plains were unaware that the lands they had occupied for countless generations had been bought and sold by distant self-appointed masters. Nor could they foretell that eight bloody, disease-filled decades hence, the last remaining chiefs would succumb to the military power of the U.S. bluecoats.

After persuading Congress to fund Meriwether Lewis and William Clark's exploration of the newly acquired lands, Jefferson laid out his own agenda for the unexplored territory. For the first time he was able to grasp the entire length of the Missouri as it was now depicted on Aaron Arrowsmith's 1802 update of his original map of North America. By 1806, when Lewis and Clark filed their findings, three of the U.S. president's five objectives had been accomplished. The expedition had mapped its route, reached the Pacific, and established U.S. claims to the Oregon Territory, countering the looming encroachment of the British fur traders. (Alexander Mackenzie and Alexander Mackay had reached the more northerly Pacific coast in 1793.) Jefferson's fourth directive, that his emissaries befriend the Natives, had proven less successful. The Lewis party's shooting of two Piegan horse thieves along the Upper Missouri helped identify the blue-eyed invaders from the east as new enemies to the Blackfoot Confederacy.

The final element in Thomas Jefferson's strategy was to cultivate a climate that would advance his country's fur trade while turning back the poachers who were stealing down from the British-controlled prairies. Jefferson's wishes were fulfilled through the aspirations of the man who would become America's first millionaire. John Jacob Astor founded the American Fur Company (AFC) shortly before Jefferson retired to his Monticello plantation. Astor pleased his political ally even more in 1811 when he established a subsidiary, the Pacific Fur Trading Company, to build Fort Astoria at the mouth of the Columbia River in Oregon and establish the American presence that Jefferson sought.

Astor's fort on the west coast was but one of many entrepreneurial moves into the new territory. When seeds of opportunity were planted in the minds of adventurers by accounts of the Lewis and Clark expedition, and stories of the riches to be made in the fur trade became the idle chatter of dreamers, a small stampede of opportunists ensued. By the time Astor reached Oregon, several small alliances and dozens of independent trappers were operating on the Lower Missouri, pushing ever farther into the Plains country of the northwest. Until then, much to Thomas Jefferson's dismay, the only trade in areas he thought should be part of his United States had been conducted by French and Spanish independents or the far-reaching Hudson's Bay Company (HBC). By then the HBC was a 160-year-old enterprise and undisputed master of the vast Canadian fur trade across the great northern prairie, through the Rockies and along the mighty rivers that drained into the Pacific Ocean.

Although John Jacob Astor was firmly established south of the Great Lakes, the War of 1812, with the British forces intent on protecting their remaining North American colonies, put a serious crimp in his efforts to establish his fur-trading capital

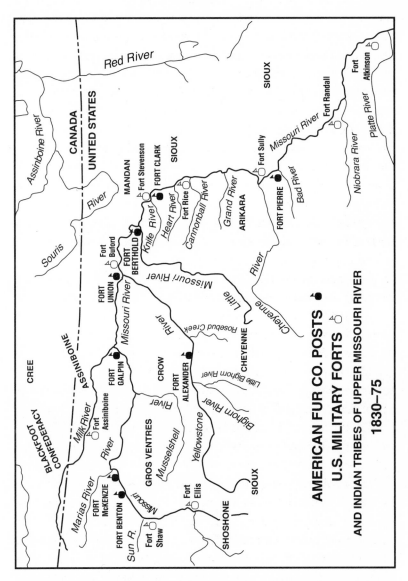

AMERICAN FUR CO. POSTS ●

U.S. MILITARY FORTS △○

AND INDIAN TRIBES OF UPPER MISSOURI RIVER

1830–75

Aside from Fort Atkinson, most of the early stockades were built by fur traders who used the Missouri as their main means to expand trade with the Blackfoot Confederacy as well as other tribes.

of Fort Astoria. In 1813 his attempt to compete with British fur interests on the Pacific coast ended when Astor's fort was occupied by the legendary Nor'Wester Alexander Henry, after Henry's men surrounded the palisade. Although it was portrayed as a negotiated settlement, these North West Company operatives virtually dictated the terms of purchase to Astor's representative, Duncan McDougall, who effectively sold out Astor for a third of the value of the furs on hand. The pliant Scot thereafter served his new masters as chief factor under the British flag.

After regrouping around his established Great Lakes enterprise and basing his expansion plan in St. Louis, Astor's success west of that city more than made up for any temporary setback. Astor had the financial clout to acquire the competition; he spawned a network of trading forts, invested in a wealth of trading inventory, and made astute choices of partners to solidify his position as America's wealthiest entrepreneur.

By this time, Astor's right-hand man, Ramsay Crooks, who was only 23 when he joined the 1810 expedition to Astoria, was becoming a significant force in the fur-trading industry. Under Astor's tutelage, and with the aid of a Missouri senator named Thomas Benton, he spearheaded the demise of Jefferson's so-called factory system, opening the gates to private enterprise in the expansion of the fur trade. Crooks completed two negotiations in particular that made the AFC and its successors the dominant force in the Missouri fur trade for as long as the industry continued to flourish. In both cases Crooks was purchasing both assets and managerial talent.

With the AFC's purchase of Bernard Pratte & Company came Pierre Chouteau Jr., a hard-edged man of cunning and guile whom Crooks immediately put in charge of the Missouri trade. Crooks also persuaded the leader of a small, determined band of ex-Nor'Westers, then known as the Columbia Fur Company, to join Astor. Kenneth McKenzie, who had emerged as the driving force at Fort Tecumseh, led the consolidation with Astor and the formation of a new AFC subsidiary operation known as the Upper Missouri Outfit.

Trade architects Astor and the aptly named Crooks had their ambitious tandem in place. "Chouteau was ruthless and

After the War of 1812 it was John Jacob Astor (left) who retained the vision of a fur empire in the western U.S. that could compete with the British firms to the north, but it was the ambition, ruthlessness, and energy of Pierre Chouteau Jr. that drove the fur trade up the Missouri and ultimately into the land of the Blackfoot Confederacy. Chouteau died at age 76, in 1866, only months after selling Fort Benton.

unscrupulous and not above resorting to gunplay to have his way. McKenzie, while more affable and genial, was no less determined."[1] These attitudes meshed well with the AFC's ethical code, or lack thereof. "Another distinctive characteristic of the company was its lawlessness—not a flagrant disregard of fundamental moral codes, but the kind of arrogance that ignores regulations which appear to the regulated as ill-judged and inconvenient."[2]

At the age of 19, Kenneth McKenzie had arrived from Scotland. A decade later he was a dominant force on the fur trade frontier. Historian Hiram Chittenden later wrote of McKenzie's rise to power in the fur trade that "[he] was universally feared but respected," and "correspondence with [his subordinates] shows diplomatic skill of no mean order, and he could with equal facility praise well doing, administer mild censure in a way to rob it of all bitterness, or bear down with merciless weight upon him who deserved it."[3]

With Pierre Chouteau Jr. and Kenneth McKenzie his partners and allies, John Jacob Astor was ready to expand his eastern empire beyond the Missouri. Chouteau and McKenzie made a formidable team. The former was an experienced but cautious field general, aware of both the dangers and the profits that were to be had 2,000 miles upriver from his St. Louis headquarters. The latter was a frontline soldier, unique in the blend of durability, diplomacy, and deftness that he brought to the enterprise.

The astute McKenzie well knew the potential that lay to the west, but he also knew that this would eventually require winning co-operation from the fierce Blackfoot Confederacy that ruled those lands. And every indicator showed that the inhospitable Blackfoot had proven themselves a major obstacle to any independent mountain men who had entered their realm. As McKenzie embarked upon his new mission, however, the Blackfoot tribes were still far to the west, well beyond his immediate concerns.

In 1828 McKenzie was ready to unleash his Upper Missouri Outfit into the Rockies, take on the independents, and capture market share by whatever means it took. Chouteau, however, won the ear of Astor, outlining the risks that ranged from severe winter conditions to Indian uprisings and citing a dozen ways in which frontline impetuousness could spell disaster. McKenzie contained himself, settling for a less ambitious plan. With one of his trusted allies, veteran trader James Kipp, in command, he dispatched the keelboat *Otter* to build his first Missouri fort in the land of the Mandan tribes he had already befriended.

Things went his way that first winter as both independent mountain men and Indian hunters promised to trade their pelts the following spring. A successful season and the knowledge that even greater bounty lay farther upriver in the lands of the legendary Blackfoot tribes propelled McKenzie onward.

The location that eventually became the hub of AFC trading on the Upper Missouri for almost two decades was called Fort Union. It was built by Kenneth McKenzie, who not only selected its strategic location but also made it his personal base for as long as he remained in the fur trade.

Fort Union, whose cottonwood stockade enclosed more than an acre of land, remained the headquarters for the Upper Missouri Outfit until 1865, when encroaching homesteaders and the Civil War brought an end to the era. Prominent in most early depictions like this Karl Bodmer painting are the flagpole and the home of Kenneth McKenzie.

LAYOUT OF FORT UNION

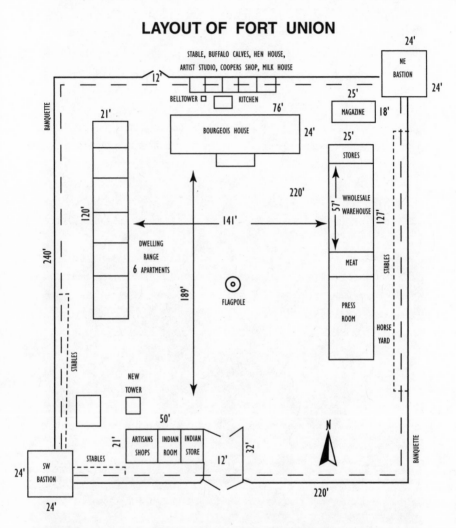

This schematic illustrates the placement of the original buildings and the double front gate that faced the Missouri River. The gate design allowed Natives access to the trading window of the "Indian room" without breaching the security of the fort itself.

Astor and Crooks made it clear that they would back Chouteau and McKenzie and use any method required to dominate the western fur trade. "They were to 'écraser toute opposition.' And smash the opposition they did ... McKenzie expanded into the country to the west, cajoling or threatening the free traders into joining his company," thus reducing the Rocky Mountain Fur Company to a minor irritant. "It was not long before McKenzie had earned himself the title 'King of the Missouri' and he lived up to it. At his headquarters in Fort Union he lived in the lap of luxury, eating the best food, drinking quality wines and brandies, and smoking fine cigars. He dressed his Indian mistresses in the latest styles from St. Louis and reigned supreme on the upper Missouri."[4]

Once, when told that an Indian attack on a band of his trappers had resulted in the men escaping but all of their horses being captured, he ranted, "Damn the men! If the horses had been saved it would have amounted to something."[5]

McKenzie found that the Rocky Mountain Fur Company and its grizzled mountain men like Jim Bridger, Joe Meek, William Sublette, and James Beckwourth would not easily succumb to pressure. Ever the charmer when there was an advantage or profit to be gained, the King of the Missouri devised a new plan. He was well aware that the free spirits of this small company gathered for their annual rendezvous upstream from Fort Union on the Yellowstone River to exchange their fur inventory for supplies and trading goods. In 1833, McKenzie appeared in their midst with an olive branch of peace and new overtures of co-operation.[6] At a lavish reception, he treated his competitors to roast beef and mutton, cheese, bacon, and butter. Before, during, and after the feast, he regaled them with spirits and cigars lit by Assiniboine maidens. Later that year the Rocky Mountain Fur Company fell apart and Astor finally had his monopoly.

Ironically, it was the moonshine from his private still that would tarnish McKenzie. Separating fact from legend is challenging, as the fur trade was full of larger-than-life characters and as many yarns as pelts. Controversy surrounding Kenneth McKenzie had one constant, however—whiskey. Whiskey in Indian Territory was forbidden by an act of Congress, and when word got out about the Fort Union contraband, the political uproar created a much-publicized embarrassment for Astor and Crooks. McKenzie was widely rebuked for flouting the laws of the land, and he became a scapegoat for what had long been a common practice. In the arena of *caveat emptor* where barter was the means of enterprise, no laws had ever succeeded in limiting what commodities would be exchanged. There were open markets and black markets, and whiskey was bound to rule the fur trade for decades to come.

Like many men from many countries who were part of that frontier in the early 19th century, Andrew Potts was leaving behind bad memories and few prospects in his homeland. An educated man, he reputedly suffered a professional setback while studying medicine. Whether it was at the urging of his Edinburgh family or solely of his own accord is not known, but Andrew chose to start a new life across the Atlantic, in Pennsylvania. Arriving in early 1832, at a time when New York and Philadelphia were cities of equal size, he encountered a vibrant world that was in the midst of quadrupling its population to over 23 million souls in less than 50 years. From Boston to Baltimore, this eastern seaboard was a mix of Old World establishment, nouveau riche, and seething masses of immigrants anxious for a better life.

Potts' choice was Philadelphia, home of the Liberty Bell, where William Pitt had built the country's first brick home 150 years earlier. Since then Pitt's planned community on the banks of the Delaware River, along with the nearby cities of Northern Liberties and Southwark (then ranked sixth and seventh in population in the U.S. and both now part of Philadelphia), had represented the gateway to the west.

It was in this "City of Brotherly Love" that *The Cent*, the nation's first penny paper, appeared. *The Cent* and a similar publication in New York, publisher Benjamin Day's upstart newspaper *The Sun*, represented an entrepreneurial trend that would inspire a new age in journalism and an onslaught of inexpensive dailies focussing on human-interest stories of appeal to the masses. Other cities soon had their emulators, dispensing descriptions of the spectacular meteor showers in the skies over Alabama, or of women in Philadelphia forming an anti-slavery society. Particular interest was shown in a young inventor's new pistol: Samuel Colt had unveiled the first revolver, a multi-chambered device that would become a symbol of the American West.

By all accounts, Andrew Potts had not come to America for an urban life but to seek frontier adventure. For a young man with wanderlust there were several options. To the south was the state of Virginia, the genteel breeding ground of four of the country's six past presidents. To the north, beyond the great Niagara cataracts, lay the colony of Upper Canada, still far too British for the likes of most immigrants who had crossed an ocean to escape the class distinctions of their homeland. And to the west were the expansion lands, where new agrarian settlements were rapidly squeezing the remaining Native people into ever smaller spaces so that crops could be produced to feed the growing population in the original 13 states.

Although Andrew Potts reached America about 18 years after Lewis and Clark reported on their western discoveries, very few settlers had crossed the Mississippi yet. Fear-mongering and sensationalism in the penny papers had presented distorted impressions of what lay beyond the settled lands; even the views of learned men, based on the second-hand reports of a few isolated observers, dampened enthusiasm. The all-too-common stories of rampant brutality by Indians reinforced most homesteaders' reluctance to venture too far west. Ill-informed but influential politicians like Daniel Webster, the Whig "Boston man" who rejected the Jefferson vision for the West and condemned policies of expansionism, discredited the land beyond the "shining mountains" as a "vast, worthless region of savages and wild beasts, of deserts, of shifting sands, and whirlwinds and prairie dogs," claiming, "I will never pledge one cent from the public treasury to place the Pacific coast [nearer] Boston than it is now."[7]

Potts started his western trek beside the Delaware, along the Bethlehem Pike, the country's oldest road, which connected Philadelphia to the Moravian settlement of Bethlehem, at the time home to 1,000 settlers. Quite possibly he was near that community when two distinctive gentlemen came his way in 1832. The two, Prince Maximilian of Wied and Karl Bodmer, a 24-year-old artist retained by the German aristocrat, spent close to a month near Bethlehem that summer.

Having departed Rotterdam seven weeks earlier, the two Europeans sailed into Boston's harbour on July 4 aboard the American brig *Janus,* as cannon fire celebrated the 56th anniversary of U.S. independence. After a brief visit to New York, where a plague of cholera had broken out, the prince hastened to Philadelphia, leaving Bodmer and a personal servant to follow with the luggage. The energy of this youthful city on the Delaware impressed Prince Max, as the newspapers would dub him, but his main goal was to visit the museum of Titian Peale, an artist-naturalist known to have been part of an exploratory expedition in the far west of the continent 14 years earlier. Peale received him and shared his knowledge and a collection of illustrations painted in the West by his companion, Samuel Seymour. Aside from this, Prince Max could find no publication that portrayed the Aboriginals that so intrigued him. Maximilian was an experienced naturalist who had studied the tribes of Brazil on a previous adventure, and he found himself appalled at the attitudes of even the learned men he had encountered in this new land. "It is incredible how much the original American race is hated and neglected by these foreign usurpers," he wrote in his diary.[8]

With luggage still missing and the dreaded cholera infestation spreading around Philadelphia, the prince, Bodmer, and his manservant, David Dreidoppel, who was also a competent taxidermist, travelled north. On July 24, Maximilian, who had served during the Napoleonic Wars, found himself near Bordentown and the 300-acre estate of Joseph Bonaparte, the exiled elder brother of the French emperor. The next day they arrived at Bethlehem. There they lingered for a month collecting flora and fauna to be shipped back to Germany. In mid-August Prince Max took the stage west to Harrisburg, where health issues led him to rest, study the region's vegetation, and visit some of the colonies of Germans and other nationalities that had chosen the Allegheny Mountain foothills and valleys as their Utopia. Next came Pittsburgh, where they again lingered, absorbing local ways and venturing often into the surrounding countryside. All in all, the prince and Bodmer spent almost three months in Pennsylvania before boarding a steamboat to descend the Ohio River. While it is unlikely they made the acquaintance of Andrew Potts during that stay, their prominence would most likely ensure that the educated Potts would have read of their presence or their grand plan to follow the footsteps of Lewis and Clark.

Maximilian and his small entourage moved through Ohio to Indiana, where they wintered before going on to St. Louis in the spring of 1833. It would be the following summer before they returned east. In June of 1834, Congress passed a law making all lands west of the Mississippi, other than Arkansas Territory and the states of Louisiana and Missouri, Indian Territory, a no man's land where the Sioux and other displaced tribes driven west would have to fend for survival in the traditional lands of the Blackfoot Confederacy. In July of that year, *The Sun* announced the return to New York of a German scientific expedition, organized by Prince Maximilian of Wied. The party had reached the end of the civilized world, and after wintering at one of the American Fur Company forts, it had descended the Missouri to St. Louis and made its way east, leaving others to crate samples and prepare them for an overseas voyage. The homeward journey hugged the Great Lakes, visiting Cleveland and Buffalo. Bodmer sketched Niagara Falls before they descended the Hudson to New York.

In response to curious newspaper reporters, they told of their many discoveries and sang the praises of their western host, the American Fur Company, and of Astor's successor, Pierre Chouteau Jr., who had recently introduced steamboats and extended navigation up the Missouri as far as Fort Union. Under the care of Chouteau's protegé, 25-year-old Alexander Culbertson, another transplanted Pennsylvanian, the two European gentlemen had barged upriver from Fort Union to spend five summer weeks at

Fort McKenzie, one painting and the other gathering artifacts and recording the habits of the Natives they encountered.

According to the papers, the prince was a slight man, his toothless mouth commonly sporting a brier-root pipe. He did not impress the muscular, six-foot Culbertson, who would later write, "His favourite dress was a white slouch hat, a black velvet coat rather rusty from long service, and probably the greasiest pair of trousers that ever encased princely legs."[9]

The mixed impressions may have been mutual, since Culbertson apparently won little recognition or praise from his royal guest. In the prince's diary, that respect was reserved for Alexander Harvey, a ruthless, barrel-chested trail-blazer who, at the instruction of his American Fur Company boss, had literally carried the diminutive prince ashore and out of harm's way on more than one occasion. On July 14, 1834, after a brief business trip to Philadelphia, the prince and Bodmer sailed from New York, never again to set foot in America.

If Andrew Potts had left his homeland in hope of finding a new land of personal freedom in America, he had discovered a paradox. While the United States Congress was accepting slave ships in its ports and was banishing the country's Aboriginals from their homelands, on August 1, 1834, his native country, Great Britain, had abolished slavery throughout its empire, including the Canadas. In America, tolerance was a fickle concept. Pennsylvania citizens grew uneasy as race riots erupted, and some of Philadelphia's European workers tried to drive the "Negroes" out of town.

Mere months later, on January 30, 1835, in Washington's Capitol rotunda, a deranged house painter named Richard Lawrence aimed two pistols at Andrew Jackson, becoming the first American to try to kill his president. In May 1835 another New York penny paper, Gordon Bennett's *Herald*, was launched. Among the early tragedies noted in this and other papers was the total destruction by fire of the *Assiniboine*, only the second steamboat to reach inland as far as Fort Union on the Missouri. The paper recalled the previous year's *bon voyage* to Prince Maximilian and noted that with the burning of the *Assiniboine* went all the samples collected and readied for shipment to the German scientist—the only man of such reputation to have visited Fort McKenzie, Fort Union, and Fort Clark. By year-end the big *Herald* story was Texas' declaration of independence from Mexico and the full-scale civil war in that future state.

By this time, Potts was again feeling restless. What spurred him toward St. Louis remains unknown, but it was most likely the newspaper accounts of the day that made him aware of the fur trade and the opportunities it might offer. Certainly other Pennsylvanians were known to have made their way to the distant forts of the American Fur Company. In 1832, native son and renowned artist George Catlin was aboard the *Yellowstone*, the first paddlewheeler to reach Fort Union, where he disembarked, intent on recording his impressions of the "noble races melting away."[10]

While Pierre Chouteau Jr. was on the maiden voyage of the Yellowstone *in 1832, he ordered a new Fort Pierre to be constructed to replace flood-ravaged Fort Tecumseh. In mid-June the sidewheeler became the first steamboat to reach Fort Union, greatly enhancing the AFC's trading power and opportunity to drive farther upriver into Blackfoot country.*

THE PRINCE AND THE ARTIST

In 1832, Prince Alexander Philip Maximilian of Wied-Neuwied was a 50-year-old retired Prussian army major-general who had won respect among European scientists after publishing the findings of a two-year expedition to Brazil to study natural history. His next quest was to the American frontier, and to document the journey he recruited Karl Bodmer, a young Swiss artist whom he found apprenticing in Koblenz. Maximilian later wrote to his brother of his satisfaction with Bodmer, "I am glad I picked him. He makes no demands and in diligence, he is never lacking."[1]

Their ship left Rotterdam in May 1832, and despite a cholera epidemic along the U.S. seaboard, they made their way from Boston to New York to Philadelphia. There, Maximilian took time to visit Titian Peale, curator of his family museum that housed specimens of earlier expeditions onto the Plains. The Old World party visited various Pennsylvania communities over

Bodmer portrayed Maximilian and himself (right) in more than one setting, but always dressed in their European finery. The battle depicted on page 35, occurring on August 28, 1834, weeks after the artist arrived at Fort McKenzie, was captured in a superb aquatint included in Bodmer's original portfolio as plate 75.

two months before reaching the Ohio River, where they boarded the steamer *Nile*. At Cincinnati, where they changed vessels, the dreaded cholera was killing 40 people per day. Below Louisville, when a fellow passenger suddenly fell ill and died within hours, and feeling ill himself, Maximilian opted to delay his trip and spend the winter at New Harmony, Indiana, the home of "an excellent natural history library and ... two veteran naturalists ... Charles-Alexander Lesuer and Thomas Say ... [They] spent the winter of 1832-33 collecting specimens ... and in learned conversation."[2]

In March 1833 they resumed their 2,000-mile trek to St. Louis, where retired explorer and cartographer William Clark advised Maximilian to abandon any overland plans and accept the hospitality of Pierre Chouteau Jr., Kenneth McKenzie, and the American Fur Company. They prepared to join the inaugural spring voyage of the *Yellowstone* up the Missouri. Bodmer was only the second artist of note to head deep into Blackfoot country, George Catlin having returned to St. Louis aboard the *Yellowstone* on its last trip of the previous autumn. At Fort Pierre, Maximilian and Bodmer disembarked to spend a week ashore while the *Yellowstone* loaded a cargo of 7,000 buffalo hides to take back to St. Louis. The prince's small entourage then joined

100 *engagés* aboard the *Assiniboine* on a two-week journey to Fort Clark, then on to Fort Union, where they heard the welcoming clamour of the fort's cannon on June 24, 75 days after boarding the *Yellowstone*.

Shallow waters above Fort Union were conquered by the keelboat *Flora*, whose crews poled and dragged their craft upstream in alternating two-hour shifts for five weeks.

When the *Flora* made Fort McKenzie in early August, they were greeted by the original fort manager or bourgeois, David Mitchell, and 1,000 Blackfoot Indians. On August 28, with trading finished and many of the lodges dispersed, the fort's occupants were awakened by unfamiliar war cries. Manning the ramparts, they saw a force of 600 Cree and Assiniboine invaders assault the camp of 20 Blackfoot tipis outside their stockade. It took steady rifle fire from the fort and the help of more Blackfoot riders from the surrounding hills to stave off the attack. Karl Bodmer became, on that day, the only artist to capture first-hand a battle scene between Blackfoot warriors and their attackers.

Maximilian adapted well to the fur trader personalities he encountered. "He established genuine friendships," wrote one biographer, "with such varied people as ... hardbitten frontier entrepreneurs Kenneth McKenzie and Pierre Chouteau Jr. On the Missouri River journey he won the comradeship of trading post managers James Kipp, David Mitchell ... these men often married women of prominent Indian families and they became Maximilian's entrée to their wives' people."[3]

After they returned to Europe, Bodmer's art eventually illustrated the three-volume English edition of Maximilian's treatise, first published in 1843. His *Travels in the Interior of North America in the Years 1832, 1833 and 1834* was reissued, unabridged, by the Arthur H. Clark Co. in 1906.

After the retirement of American Fur Company founder John Jacob Astor in 1834, a new mystique grew around the rough-and-ready Pierre Chouteau Jr., the successor fur baron who was driving his trading empire farther west into the hostile lands of the Blackfoot. Big-city editors always had room for news from the frontier, especially if it came through transient scholars like Bodmer and Maximilian, who were curiosities in their own right. Their expedition was topical not only for New York papers like *The Sun* and the newly founded *Herald,* but also for the five-year-old *Pennsylvania Inquirer* and most of the seven other dailies in Philadelphia. While the papers had no photos to aid the imagination, it was through written accounts in these sources that Andrew Potts and any other restless young man learned that if they wanted to escape to the edge of civilization, it could be found at a place called Fort McKenzie.

Less than two years after Bodmer and the prince returned to Europe, Andrew Potts set out to retrace their western route. He made his way to St. Louis and started the riverboat leg of the 1,600-mile river journey from the mouth of the Missouri River into the realm of the American Fur Company.

Chapter 2

The Missouri

When Andrew Potts left the St. Louis waterfront aboard the *Diana*, he was crossing the Mississippi for the first and last time. Entering the mouth of the Missouri, he was on the first upriver boat of the 1836 season, a steamboat laden with merchandise bound for Fort Pierre, Fort Clark, and Fort Union, under the command of Master C.M. Halstead. It was the second year that Halstead and his *Diana* had served the needs of the Upper Missouri Outfit and its AFC parent entity. Potts, the young Scot, had been hired in the St. Louis offices of Pierre Chouteau Jr. to serve as an AFC clerk at distant Fort McKenzie, in the vanguard of the relentless advance into the lands of the Blackfoot Confederacy.

In St. Louis he had found but one similarity to Philadelphia. The north-south streets in the booming community of 15,000 were numbered from the town centre while the east-west corridors were named after trees. The influx of newcomers was spreading out rapidly from the core village of about 800 primarily French and Spanish inhabitants who were living there when Jefferson acquired the territory only 32 years earlier. Pierre Laclede Liguest, who had won a trade monopoly in the area from the then-ruling Spanish, had christened the original trading fort St. Louis in the 1760s. Laclede trained his two stepsons, Auguste and Pierre Chouteau, in the ways of the business, and their ensuing success made them one of the leading families in St. Louis by the 1790s. Forty years later Pierre Jr. was the dominant family entrepreneur.

Following in the footsteps of his father, who had first traded with the Natives of Kansas in the early 1790s, the teenaged Pierre Jr. worked as a clerk and trader before opening his St. Louis store in 1813 with his brother-in-law, Bartholomew Berthold, as his partner. Two decades later he had his own established trade network that surpassed all the competition.

Chouteau was not a man to sit idle or ignore new trends in his marketplace. Since the fur trade had begun, European tailors and milliners had demonstrated an unquenchable appetite for beaver pelts, to the ongoing benefit of Astor and his business partners west of the Mississippi. But for two successive years shipments of beaver pelts had fallen below those of buffalo, the magnificent beast known to inhabit only the great western plains. Pierre Jr. knew that he would have to find a way to make the tribes of the Blackfoot Confederacy dependable trading partners. The tentacles of the American Fur Company had now spread beyond Fort Union, where his partner and the company's senior bourgeois Kenneth McKenzie had established a grand manor. (The AFC term "bourgeois" was synonymous with "manager," or the HBC term "factor.") Continued success depended on younger men like his latest recruit, Andrew Potts, who would join senior trader Alexander Culbertson and his small group of clerks and traders at Fort McKenzie.

It was mid-April when Potts began what would probably be a 75-day journey upriver to his first destination of Fort Union. He had received some training before his departure and had carefully studied one of the larger invoices of goods that had been broken into three identifiable packets for the main forts. The Fort Pierre shipment was loaded last and would be unloaded first. It represented about a third of the inventory and was more than twice the number of packages destined for Fort Clark. Potts took some comfort in knowing that this left more than half of the supplies and trade goods to go with him all the way to Fort Union —if the Missouri water levels co-operated and Captain Halstead could get them that far.

Potts studied the manifest and noted that Fort Union alone would receive 24 kegs of twist tobacco in four different varieties. A variety of beads—black, blue, red, yellow, and white—weighed in at 2,980 pounds for Fort Union alone. There were pistols and axes and 100 guns with barrels measuring up to 42 inches. Iron kettles, tin plates, iron spoons, bundles of blankets and bolts of cloth and one violin bow were noted. The Fort Clark invoice included large barrels of alcohol, a commodity nowhere to be seen on the Fort Union lists. For Potts, the calico shirts and Marseille vests were understandable, but what were wampum moons, hair pipes, and Indian awls?

The sternwheeler that carried Potts onto the Missouri was a charter. The loss of two of the company's vessels in recent years had convinced Chouteau that staying out of the shipping business was prudent on the Missouri. Chouteau's *Assiniboine* had spent the winter of 1834 trapped on the riverbed near the mouth of the Poplar River, forcing the company to build a fort there simply to protect its craft from curious Natives. Dislodged from the sand the following spring as the river rose, the steamboat again went aground near the mouth of the White Earth River until new storm waters freed it and allowed it to descend the river to Fort Clark. As eastern papers reported, Prince Maximilian's extensive collection was stowed aboard Chouteau's steamboat before it continued its ill-fated journey to a final mishap farther downstream at the mouth of the Little Heart River (near modern-day Bismarck, North Dakota).[1] By 1836, when Andrew Potts made his journey, there was no trace of the *Assiniboine* hull that had burnt there only two years earlier. Fighting against the river current of the Missouri slowed the boat's progress, but tedium was rarely a factor. All river men knew that Big Muddy, as it was known, was not only the longest river in the country but by far the most difficult to navigate. When they ran aground, all hands were enlisted to unload part of the cargo onto a flatboat procured from the nearest fort. With lightened draft, men sent ashore with ropes in hand, and the pilot's maneuverings, the boat came free and the journey continued.

They passed their first Indian agency at Bellevue, in the land of the Omaha people, and 10 days later reached Fort Lookout, the agency of the Yankton and Teton branches of the Sioux Nation.

At the new Fort Pierre, two miles upriver from the original Fort Tecumseh that had been salvaged from the flood plain five years earlier, Potts got his first sense of Indian country while eying the raised burial scaffolds that dotted the riverbank. Near the fort were camps of Sioux families, while traders gathered around the fort entrance, fully aware that with the ship's arrival they could soon exchange their mounds of buffalo robes for the White man's goods.

After a few days under the tutelage of the local bourgeois, Jacob Halsey, Potts returned to his cramped space on the *Diana*. Contentedly he noted that Halsey had moved from clerk to bourgeois in only a few short years. Two weeks later they made Fort Clark, where two villages of Mandan Indians were camped near the palisades. A large collection of tipis sat on a steep bluff less than a quarter mile from the palisades. Other tribes were also there to trade. Potts watched an advance party of painted warriors ride in from the west, much as Prince Max had observed only three years earlier when he had written in his journal, "tall and handsome men ... The haughty Crows rode on panther skins, with red cloth under them ... mounted warriors with diversely painted faces, feathers in their long hair, bows and arrows slung across their back, and with a musket or spear in their hands."[2]

Captain Halstead had the cargo quickly ashore and allowed little time to dawdle. Potts could not tell if all the alcohol destined for Fort Clark had been unloaded. It seemed odd for Clark to get substantial alcohol and Union to get none. The lightened load eased *Diana*'s draft and the river level held as they covered the final leg of their journey in less than a week. Potts calculated that since leaving St. Louis, they had averaged over 26 miles per day including their stops.

The first thing Potts saw at Fort Union was a large Stars and Stripes flying from a massive pole in the centre of the fort. In the foreground a substantial bastion guarded the closest corner of the stockade. When he disembarked and made his way to the fort, a large front gate that apparently folded in half had been propped open to enhance the welcome. Above, he noted a gatehouse that had been crafted to match the nearby corner bastion. He judged the gate to be at least two-and-a-half times his height and almost as wide. Next his eye was drawn to the flagpole; it stood 60 feet high, surrounded by an octagonal, fenced vegetable garden. Atop the pole, the massive flag they had seen from the river loomed even larger, now stirred by the afternoon wind. Beyond the pole stood the house Potts had heard described time and again on his long journey up the river. He had seen nothing like it—a massive wooden house at least 80 feet wide and two floors high. As he faced this rustic palace, there were rows of buildings on his right and left and he could see the top of a second bastion, diagonal to the one that protected the river gate.

It was here that Potts first met the legendary Kenneth McKenzie.

Not only as a fellow Scot, but as a man of education and ambition, Andrew Potts would have been a welcome addition to the mixture of humanity that McKenzie encountered in his frontier life. The bourgeois, who was closer to the end than the beginning of his fruitful career, had entered the trade via the established realm of the North West Company, the Montreal-based fur-trading syndicate whose voyageurs had opened up the lands that would become the Canadian West. When the HBC had induced the North West owners to merge their enterprises, some disgruntled underlings like McKenzie himself, feeling betrayed by this event, had gone south to form their own operation, the Columbia Fur Company that later attracted Astor and Crooks.

McKenzie had established his beloved Fort Union 200 miles upriver from his previous headquarters at Fort Tecumseh (near St. Pierre, South Dakota), using hand-built, cargo-laden keelboats to navigate the ever-shifting Missouri shallows. "The keelboats were marvels ... products of an evolution that was colored by bitter experience and the blood of the adventurers who had devised them."[3] They drew only four feet of water and were stabilized by a solid keel that ran the 75-foot length of the boat. For much of the journey in the Missouri shallows, two columns of voyageurs would plant long poles on the silted riverbed and then march toward the stern along *passe avants*, narrow walkways on each side of the craft, their poling slowly winning the battle against a ceaseless current.

At other places, where the river narrowed and deepened, the same men were let ashore, harnessed to a *cordelle*, a long rope attached to an angled mast that allowed the line to clear brush and snags. Determined and tireless, they trudged onward until a new obstacle called for more ingenuity.

By the time Potts arrived at Fort Union, McKenzie had been there for eight years and was enjoying some returns for his efforts to trade with the Blackfoot tribes, the suspicious nations who ruled the headlands of the Missouri. Basing the location on Aboriginal travel patterns recorded by Lewis and Clark and a confidence that river craft could navigate that far up the Missouri in the spring, McKenzie had positioned Fort Union near the mouth of the Yellowstone on a site that allowed him to set up trade with the Assiniboine from the north, the Crow who came down the Yellowstone, and the Sioux in the Dakota Territory who were being pushed west by soldiers and settlers. They and other tribes, like the Chippewa, Mandan, and Hidatsa, would camp along the river near the fort and barter their beaver pelts. Even bands of Cree and Métis were coming down from the north, seeking an alternative to the Hudson's Bay Company.

Despite the growth of the Astor-founded empire, the HBC remained the fur industry's dominant force in North America. Originally chartered to trade furs in the vast wilderness of rivers that drained north and east into the great bay that Henry Hudson had discovered in 1610, it had expanded across North America to the Pacific. In 1821 the HBC and North West Company had joined forces under the HBC banner, but Kenneth McKenzie was no HBC man. Effectively he became American out of necessity, following a post-War of 1812 act of Congress that banned foreigners from trade in American territory.

In contrast to the fragmented industry to the south, the new northern alliance gave the HBC trading empire 53 active chief factors to supervise trade operations from the immense prairie to the forts of the Pacific coast. While Fort Union was the American Fur Company's most western outpost in the Dakotas, the HBC domain stretched to Fort Vancouver above the mouth of the Columbia River, not far from where Astor's foray into this region had proven unsuccessful. There, despite their distance from the

The Assiniboine and Crow that travelled to Fort Union, as depicted here in a John Mix Stanley rendering, remained peaceful traders for decades. It was the nomadic Sioux race being pushed farther west and the ever-warring Blackfoot tribes that followed the buffalo down from Canada that provided the greatest resistance to White civilization.

eastern markets, Chief Factor James Douglas and his wife, Amelia, were firmly ensconced. Whereas McKenzie was most likely feeling quietly thankful that a single literate man like Andrew Potts had decided to join the crude brigade of the Upper Missouri, James Douglas was welcoming groups of missionaries—Anglicans by sea and Presbyterians by land—intent on bringing civility to the far reaches of the British Empire.

Once Kenneth McKenzie set up permanent residence in the United States along with those disgruntled operators who followed him, he represented an experienced band that had the know-how and fortitude to build the American Fur Company's wealth. At the peak of its operation in the 1840s, Fort Union was home to a hundred men, many with Indian wives and families to feed. Through the years McKenzie expanded the original fort with a palisade of foot-thick, 20-foot-high pickets with bastions on the southwest and northeast corners. Together with cannons on a lower level and sentries posted above, these two stations protected the 240-by-220-foot perimeter. This was a community of hunters, carpenters, blacksmiths, bartenders, sutlers, and gunsmiths who lived in close quarters in the shadow of the substantial residence of 29-year-old Kenneth McKenzie. They entered every winter season aware of their isolation and knowing it would be spring before any new supplies would arrive.

By this stage of the fort's history the residents could at least thank McKenzie for one of his more ambitious visions. The ever-restless McKenzie had gone down to St. Louis in August 1830 with a new proposal for Chouteau and Astor: build a steamboat that could reach Fort Union, a small, rugged ship that could drive northward after the spring melt, bringing supplies and trade goods and then getting the haul of winter furs back to St. Louis by June. After some initial reluctance on their part he got his wish in the form of the *Yellowstone*. With his partners committed to this substantial investment, McKenzie had returned upriver to Fort Union, anxious to lure the Blackfoot nations to trade in the south. Based on hearsay alone, McKenzie anticipated resistance when he sent a wizened mountain man named Jacob Berger and a party of five upriver in an effort to make contact with the nomadic Canadian tribes. He fully expected never to see them alive again.

The Blackfoot legend had grown steadily, ever since word spread throughout the territory that hostile Indians had stripped mountain man John Colter naked and forced him to run for his life. Then they killed eight of trader Andrew Henry's party when he tried to build a stockade near the three forks of the Missouri. Every year thereafter, fearless White traders entered their territory, and only small remnants of their scalps were ever seen again.

Thus the bourgeois was elated the next spring when Berger's group and a number of Blackfoot chiefs arrived at the gate of Fort Union. While McKenzie would later bask in this achievement, taking much of the credit for Berger's remarkable deeds, it was the mountain man who deserved the plaudits. It was he alone who had wintered in a South Piegan village above the Marias River and won the trust of the Confederacy. McKenzie's house, the grandest structure west of the Mississippi, hosted a select group of the most important chiefs while he impressed his guests with the manor's eight genuine glass windows, gifts of food and tobacco, and promises of generous trade terms if they would allow the construction of another fort closer to their homeland. Under a treaty most likely penned by Berger, the White traders and Natives "may hail each other as brethren, and smoke the calumet in friendship and security."[4]

In the late summer of 1831 McKenzie sent his trusted partner James Kipp west to the mouth of the Marias to build a trading fort. Kipp struggled against a shallow Missouri, finally reaching his destination in mid-October. His two dozen voyageurs and traders started construction of what they would call Fort Piegan while curious tribesmen watched from a distance. Kipp communicated that they would be ready to trade in the new year, and in the spring of 1832, he and his cargo of 6,400 beaver skins rode the Missouri's current down to Fort Union.

When they got there the fort was abuzz with the pending arrival of the *Yellowstone*. The steamer had failed to navigate the shallow waters beyond the Niobrara River the previous year, but eventually reached Fort Tecumseh after offloading much of its cargo. A higher spring runoff in 1832 allowed the boat past Fort Tecumseh, and McKenzie's vision of fur-laden canoes descending from the land of the Blackfoot and powerful paddlewheelers ascending the Missouri from St. Louis was about to be realized.

Aboard the *Yellowstone* was a very satisfied Pierre Chouteau Jr., who had just witnessed the christening of an expanded Fort Tecumseh with its new name, Fort Pierre. Chouteau would win accolades from Astor and the eastern newspapers for the remarkable feat of taking the *Yellowstone* so far inland, but for McKenzie there was a more practical benefit. He took great comfort in the Indians' reaction to "the monster who walked on water ... and the respect it brought him." Newspapers like the *Missouri Republican* wrote, "Indians declared that the Hudson's Bay Company could no longer compete with the Americans and concluded thereafter to bring all of their skins to the latter [where] the Fire Boat walked on the waters."[5]

Since the fur trade's inception in the United States, the ambitions and fortunes of men like Astor, Chouteau, McKenzie, and the many underlings in their ranks were based on the profit to be made through trade with the Native tribes of the immediate west. Astor's wealth was already legendary by the time he reached the Missouri. By then, only scant numbers of beaver, marten, deer, bear, otter, and lynx remained east of the Mississippi compared to the populations roaming the foothills of the Great Divide. At the time the *Yellowstone* reached Fort Union, fur prices ranged from three-dollar bearskins to the five dollars per pound paid for prized lynx. Buffalo was a novelty at six dollars per robe.

When Astor filled the hold of one of his ships with two-dollar kegs of gunpowder in London and dispatched the ship southeast through the Gulf of Mexico to New Orleans, then offloaded his cargo onto a company steamboat bound for St. Louis, he was well on his way to making another small fortune. At first the 10-pound kegs were allotted to keelboats, unloaded, and stored at company forts until they were eventually carried inland, where they were measured in one-pound parcels on Indian trading blankets.

At a time when beaver hats were still the rage in New York and London, the Indians gladly handed over a tanned adult skin to gain the gunpowder. Astor's ships would soon be hauling 100-pound bales of fur back across the Atlantic. There, 10 beaver pelts that the original $2 kegs of gunpowder had yielded would sell for the equivalent of $140. Allowing 25 percent to cover shipping and related costs, Astor would take a 5 percent handling fee and 50 percent of net profits. When all was said and done, each $2 keg put $56 in his pocket, and his partners would split another $48 to apply to their expanding network of forts.

The successful opening of Fort Piegan, where James Kipp amassed thousands of beaver pelts through the winter, drew the attention of their northern competitors in the persons of the imposing six-foot-four Dr. John McLoughlin, the Fort Vancouver-based boss of the HBC, and his ally on the prairies, Chief Factor John Rowand, who ruled the Saskatchewan district for 30 years. McLoughlin, known among the Natives as White-Headed Eagle because of his fierce grey eyes and silver mane, was always aware of the AFC's encroachment into his domain and urged Rowand at Fort Edmonton to counter the AFC advance up the Missouri. Rowand thought he had persuaded some of his long-time Blood trading partners to chase off the American interlopers, but Kipp had won the war party over with significant gifts of whiskey. Both McLoughlin and Rowand were former Nor'Westers who may have well known the talents and passions of Kenneth McKenzie, their former junior partner.

Despite McKenzie's and Kipp's small victory, Fort Piegan had a short life. With the spring melt, after Kipp had paddled east with his bounty of beaver pelts, the Blackfoot, who resented the infringement on their hunting grounds, quickly razed the walls of the fort. Whether its reduction to ashes was due simply to anger over the whiskey flow drying up or was encouraged by McLoughlin and Rowand is unclear.

Construction soon started on Fort McKenzie on the slight rise that separated the Teton River from the north bank of the Missouri at a site six

Dr. John McLoughlin's domain covered a vast area from California to Alaska and east to Nebraska and Fort Edmonton. For over two decades he ruled like a feudal lord before siding with American interests as settlement spread west. He resigned from his Fort Vancouver post and is today known as "The Father of Oregon."

miles upriver from the remains of Kipp's fort. McKenzie recruited respected trader David D. Mitchell and a force of 60 men to take on the job, and they erected the 140-foot-square perimeter around what would become one of the American Fur Company's most lucrative trading posts over the next 10 years.

In all of McKenzie's years of dealing with different tribes, he had never encountered as much innate hatred and suspicion as he found among the Blackfoot. His success at pacifying these people and gaining their acceptance of both the original Fort Piegan

KING OF THE MISSOURI

Kenneth McKenzie was born in Inverness, Scotland, in 1801. He was "a relative of Alexander Mackenzie, who made the first journey across the continent ... north of the Spanish possessions," reaching the Pacific in 1793.[4]

Kenneth went to Canada as a teen and started a life of adventure, working first for some of the eastern fur houses and later for the North West Company. The merger of that company with the HBC in 1821 left him low on the totem pole, and at age 21 he became a founding partner of the Columbia Fur Company. Six years later, as president, he agreed to end the growing battle with Astor's empire and became the northern master of trade on the Missouri.

Stories about McKenzie's eccentricities abound. He ordered a coat of mail from England, custom-made to his instructions, and had a rifle made to his specification that would fire six rounds; he also had die-cut gold medals bearing the

Called "King of the Missouri" by the rough-and-ready mountain men of the American northwest, Kenneth McKenzie ran the American Fur Company with the "fist of a tyrant and the tastes of a dandy."[8]

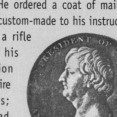

countenance of J.J. Astor that he used for trade with the Blackfoot chiefs. For the Indians, these discs became as prestigious as scalps and medicine bonnets, worthy of greater esteem than captive squaws or livestock. Of McKenzie's regal stature, clerk Charles Larpenteur wrote, "Imagine my surprise ... to find myself in the presence of Mr. McKenzie ... the king of the Missouri: and from the style in which he was dressed, I really thought he was a king."[5]

Historian Hiram Chittenden described McKenzie as "the ablest trader that the American Fur Company ever possessed."[6] As bourgeois he was the "Almighty" in a lawless land, "holding supreme power ... He could cast a man out, rob him of his wages ... shoot him. Or he could, if he so desired, be kind, considerate, fair. The Bourgeois' first duty was to guard his company's investment. Furs were more important than men."[7]

and the new Fort McKenzie was one of his greatest diplomatic accomplishments. After placing Alexander Culbertson in charge of the new fort, McKenzie watched him quickly take hold of his responsibilities and expand the trade to the point that another clerk was mandatory. And in response, Chouteau had sent another young Scot out to his front lines.

Whether Andrew Potts would claim McKenzie as a personal mentor is unknown, but he, like many of the White men who came west, abided by a key dictum in the frontier philosophy of his new leader. McKenzie's experience among the northern tribes while he was with the North West Company had taught him the most effective way to gain co-operation from the Indians: setting guns, whiskey, and trade goods aside, the key to opening up the West was marriage. McKenzie openly encouraged his men, first at Fort Union and then at Fort McKenzie, to follow the precedents set farther north by many of the HBC Scots and most of the North West voyageurs. They were the sires of the original mixed-blood offspring who would proudly adopt the Métis identity in the century to come. Bartering for or accepting a father's gift of a young Indian woman could bring a trader an instant bond with a particular tribe. Paying heed to his new in-laws and making them preferred trade partners could encourage both peace and prosperity. Andrew Potts was not long at Fort McKenzie before he embraced local custom and adopted his own "country wife."

In the aftermath of the burning of Fort Piegan, McKenzie and Mitchell were able to establish a peaceful understanding with the Blackfoot, Blood, and Piegan chiefs, convincing them that it was their sole intent to make the new Fort McKenzie a permanent trading post where the Indians could bring their furs—so long as the chiefs could control their warriors and not attack the fort.

By 1832, the King of the Upper Missouri was used to dictating his own terms. He had already run afoul of the courts for acting willfully against his competitors, and when he heard that Congress had passed new laws prohibiting liquor importation into Indian Territory, he decided it was time for drastic action.

Because the American Fur Company relied on the large riverboats to get their goods to Fort Union, and government inspectors reviewed their cargo farther downriver at Fort Osage, the new law made trade whiskey a scarce commodity along the Missouri. Meanwhile, a competing band of independent traders was carting pure alcohol overland, with neither licences nor the assurance that it was for personal use. Astor, Crooks, Chouteau, and McKenzie were defiant. "I have no alternative," Astor wrote Crooks in St. Louis, "if I want to stay in business but to violate the law." As he had done many a time before, Astor turned a blind eye while his tacit message was relayed to Fort Union.[6]

Facing competition that had a distinct advantage, McKenzie solved the problem through corn and connivance. He brought in bits and pieces of metal that, when deftly assembled, gave him the Upper Missouri's first distillery. He reported to Crooks that "our manufactory flourishes admirably. The Mandan corn yields badly but makes a fine sweet liquor ... Do not load the boat too heavily at St. Louis, that a few hundred bushels of corn may be placed on board."[7] Once the still was in operation, pride overcame discretion and McKenzie showed off his prize possession to the wrong people. Always a gregarious host, McKenzie entertained two of his competitiors after the summer traders' rendezvous of 1833 but refused to provide them adequate whiskey for their planned descent of the Missouri. The irked pair turned tattlers at Fort Leavenworth by reporting McKenzie's new enterprise to Henry Ellsworth, the resident Indian agent. The resulting furor reached all the way to Washington, and the next spring the still was decommissioned.

In the summer of '34 McKenzie, who had hosted Prince Maximilian of Wied during his expedition, found himself at odds with Chouteau over the still and other business decisions and responded to his reprimand by taking extended leave and visiting the prince in Europe. While McKenzie was crossing the Atlantic, John Jacob Astor made his final exit from the Missouri fur trade when he sold out all of his interests in the Upper Missouri Outfit to Pierre Chouteau Jr. and his partner, Bernard Pratte.

McKenzie only returned from his voluntary exile in the fall of 1835. The following spring he was again head of the Fort Union community that greeted the good ship *Diana*. By this time the novelty of a ship at the fort had diminished to the point that Captain

Halstead's arrival marked the beginning of what one diarist would call a relatively uneventful year at Fort Union. Charles Larpenteur commented that, compared to the eventful seasons that had preceded it, the year was quiet and routine. "The Indians came and went. Liquor was smuggled in."[8]

Larpenteur's diary did shed some light on the ways of Kenneth McKenzie and how he responded to new competition. The last upstart competitors that McKenzie faced were mountain men William Sublette and Robert Campbell, who had first established Fort William three miles east of Fort Union, across the river from the mouth of the Yellowstone. Their misguided intent was to compete with the AFC through the winter season of 1833. This operation was soon the victim of the king's fervent countermoves as he outbid the newcomers at every turn. Sublette's only coup may have been as an informer. It was widely speculated that he had been the complainant who made the authorities aware of McKenzie's still in a last desperate act to survive. Once Sublette recognized that their efforts were fruitless, he reluctantly sold out to Pierre Chouteau Jr., who had the nearby stockade disassembled and much of the wood hauled to Fort Union for new corrals. In ensuing years some AFC employees housed their families in the deserted Fort William. And then came turmoil.

Coincident with Captain Halstead urging his steamboat upriver on the eve of the summer solstice of 1836, Fort William was afire. Serious differences had arisen between the most prominent clans that lived there—the Deschampses and Remses. Gunfire got the best of the former and they were cremated amidst the flames that consumed all that was left of Fort William's outbuildings. Historian R.G. Robertson wrote of the Remses' ruthless victory: "When the Deschampses took cover at Fort William, some of their attackers kept them pinned down with rifles, while others set the buildings ablaze. Like the Deschampses, Fort William came to a fiery end."[9]

In the acrid scent of burnt flesh that lingered near the riverbank as they passed, Andrew Potts and his fellow passengers got their first whiff of Missouri justice.

Potts' orientation to Fort Union lasted only as long as it took to transfer trade goods onto the craft that would carry on upriver. During his brief exposure to the king, the new AFC clerk absorbed all the advice that McKenzie offered but also listened closely to men like Larpenteur who could describe what lay ahead at Fort McKenzie. That stockade was smaller than the half-hectare Fort Union and there was nothing to match the grand manor. After learning that fort founder David Mitchell had moved on to a government job and given way to a new bourgeois, he could only take encouragement from knowing that he would work for another Pennsylvanian, Alexander Culbertson.

Culbertson, Chouteau and McKenzie's protegé, had first arrived at Fort Union in 1833 aboard the *Assiniboine* and demonstrated trader skills that had earned him his recent posting hundreds of miles farther upriver. He had proven himself an effective diplomat at Fort McKenzie, earning the trust of Blackfoot and Piegan chiefs. Heeding the philosophy of marriage of McKenzie and others, Culbertson briefly took as his first wife a young Indian girl, but it was his second liaison with a Blood woman that would strongly impact White relationships with the Blackfoot Confederacy over ensuing decades. In 1840 Culbertson entered into one of the most successful of frontier affiliations when he took Nayoyist-siksina' (Holy Snake, or Natawista Iksana), the teenaged daughter of the respected chief Two Suns, as his wife.

Culbertson was nearing the end of his first three-year contract managing Fort McKenzie when Andrew Potts arrived in the region. Their relationship would prove all too brief.

Chapter 3

Four Years of Turmoil

Before he left Fort Union, if Andrew Potts felt comfortable enough with his new surroundings to venture outside the palisade and visit the camp of 25 Assiniboine shelters on the nearby flatlands, he would have been drawn to one large tipi that stood out from the rest. No doubt the home of the tribal chief, the outer skin was adorned with painted bear figures on each side of the entrance. The bear, Potts would learn, was a symbol among the Plains tribes of spiritual power, strong medicine to take into battle or protect against sickness.

Potts' first clerk duty was to monitor the transfer of supplies, packages of beads, and other trading goods from the *Diana* directly to the keelboat *Flora*. The river trek from Fort Union to Fort McKenzie would take until August, covering 500 miles in about five weeks if the water flow held. By the time Potts boarded the 60-foot boat, it was packed to the gunwales, its 16-foot-wide deck offering little space for its occupants. The crew and other hirelings destined for Fort McKenzie numbered over 40. They either shared a forward cabin or clambered ashore at night to make camp if it was deemed safe to do so. Aft, a second small cabin, one that had been occupied by Prince Max, Bodmer, Dreidoppel, and two other paying passengers three years earlier, was limited to two berths. An exposed iron grate at mid deck, atop the central hold, served as their only kitchen.

The long summer days and average progress of less than two miles per hour allowed Potts ample time to study the landscape. The voyage involved strenuous poling on most stretches, with separate shifts of 16 men toiling for two hours at a time and then resting while their counterparts took over.

Memorable among the shoreline discoveries for all was the day the pilot pulled ashore and let passengers climb to a 15-foot-high cairn of intertwined elk antlers, a monument that grew with the offerings of each hunting party that passed its way. Believing that such an act would benefit the hunt, Blackfoot and Assiniboine warriors had contributed more than a thousand racks to form a unique elk horn pyramid.

Almost a month into the journey, the landscape changed dramatically as the *Flora* entered a stretch of the river where the natural beauty heightened with every mile. One day there were white, building-like mountaintops highlighted by the sun; a few days later, as the river narrowed, sandstone outcroppings sculpted by nature into pillars, pulpits, and pointed towers closed in on both sides. Then, near the end of their 30th day, the landmark of Citadel Rock welcomed Potts to the land of the Blackfoot. They were five days away from his new home.

If Andrew Potts' goal in fleeing his homeland was to seek obscurity in America, he certainly accomplished that objective when he ended up in Fort McKenzie. The fort's White male inhabitants and their Indian women shared rustic shelters in an area of less than 20,000 square feet within the perimeter walls. When they stood at the main gate, they were 225 feet from the water, looking down on the murky river with its ever-shifting muddy bed. The fort was surrounded by a picturesque prairie and stood on the north side of the river, easily accessible to the Blackfoot traders who came south from the Canadian hunting grounds.

The surrounding country marked the territorial lands of the Blackfoot Confederacy of tribes as well as the Cree, Crow, Assiniboine, Sioux, and Gros Ventres. All these peoples abided by their treaties with Kenneth McKenzie as far as the fort was concerned, but gave no assurances about peace among themselves. Nor did solo mountain men fare well. Disappearances and rumoured scalpings of independent traders were regular events. In the first year of Fort McKenzie's operation, the Blackfoot were thought to have killed more than 50 White trappers. When Andrew Potts arrived in 1836, the Upper Missouri was very dangerous country.

While Potts learned his new job at Fort McKenzie, he saw less and less of the fort's master, Alexander Culbertson, who was soon to assume more respon-sibility at Fort Union and Fort Leavenworth. Kenneth McKenzie had announced plans to retire and Culbertson was the heir apparent. Potts was new to the fur trade and certainly junior to the likes

Alexander Culbertson's career on the Missouri was one of triumph and tragedy, his proudest achievements aided greatly by his Blood Indian wife, Natawista, or Holy Snake. She was instrumental in the success of treaty talks at Fort Laramie in 1851, and later with her Blackfoot peoples on the Missouri in 1855. The couple is pictured here with their young child Joe.

of Alexander Harvey, who by then had been in the employ of the American Fur Company as a hunter and trader since 1830. With Culbertson away much of the time, the fate of Fort McKenzie was more often than not left in Harvey's hands.

Harvey had come to Fort McKenzie in 1833, escorting Prince Maximilian on the personal instruction of Pierre Chouteau Jr. At six feet tall and 200 pounds, he towered over his guests and left a lasting impression on the diminutive Maximilian, who recalled him in his memoirs. Prince Max wrote that he was able to pick up the whole carcass of an elk and carry it off on his shoulders. Harvey had great endurance and strength, cared for nothing or no one, and was said to be without fear.

In 1837 Andrew Potts and Alexander Harvey shared an experience that would forever change the West. While junior clerk Potts went about his daily routine, Culbertson sent Harvey to Fort Union to meet the late June arrival of a steamboat laden with both passengers and the all-important cargo that was key to the AFC's trading season. That year's steamboat bore the name *St. Peter's*, and in its wake came a summer of devastation. This *St. Peter's* was an apostle of death, stopping first at Fort Clark, where three ailing passengers were taken ashore, and then unknowingly spreading the smallpox virus to the Hidatsa and Mandan hillside villages. Of 1,400 Mandans, only 10 percent survived: "By the time the epidemic had run its course, the Mandans ceased to exist as a nation."[1]

When the *St. Peter's* reached Fort Union on June 24, the first blanket-wrapped person carried ashore was the fort's temporary bourgeois, Jacob Halsey, formerly of Fort Pierre. An anxious Alexander Harvey, intent on escaping the dreaded virus, ordered his cargo of trade goods to be loaded as quickly as possible. Soon his keelboat crew was poling its way against the steady Missouri current. They passed the confluence with the Milk River and then the Musselshell River before Harvey realized that they had not escaped their brief encounter with the *St. Peter's* unscathed. When two severe cases of smallpox were found on board, he decided that he had no choice but to hole up near the mouth of the Judith River until the infection had passed. Word was sent to Culbertson at Fort McKenzie, but the bourgeois had his own problems. Camped outside the stockade were 3,500 impatient Blackfoot awaiting the trade goods they had quickly come to covet. Their threats to burn the fort if the goods were delayed any longer left Culbertson in a no-win predicament. Reluctantly he sent orders for Harvey to continue his journey.

At Fort McKenzie the trading was done, the whiskey was drunk, and the invasive and invisible virus quickly spread. By the time the various tribes packed their travois and broke camp, two of Harvey's voyageurs were dead. It could be that Culbertson's fateful decision to disperse the trade goods had merely expedited the inevitable, but both the fort's small community and all tribes that drifted north and west ended up paying a grave price. Before the raw cold of November set in at Fort McKenzie, 27 men and women had died; the weakened survivors finally gave up on grave digging, and corpses were simply deposited in the river.

Culbertson, Harvey, and Potts survived the winter, but there was more death to come. When fewer Blackfoot traders than usual appeared in the spring, the Fort McKenzie leader rode out in search of his clientele only to discover village after stench-filled village of bloated corpses. The few people who remained alive were starving, their dogs and the wild coyotes living off the limbs of the dead.

Across the entire prairie, whole tribes of the Blackfoot Confederacy were decimated. It would not be the last time this plague took its toll, but it was the epidemic of 1837–38 that sapped the power of the Piegan, Blood, and Blackfoot warriors forever.

How Namo-pisi made her way to Fort McKenzie is unknown. Did she wander into the fort amid the epidemic, or did Andrew Potts find her in one of the devastated camps in the spring of 1838? More likely she was already sharing his bed and helping him bury the dead and tend to the sick. That she both escaped death that awful winter and bore their son while surrounded by a pall of gloom seems miraculous. Namo-pisi, or Crooked Back, as the Whites called her, was a daughter of the Black Elks band, one of the Blood lodges that shared the hunting grounds above the Medicine Line. As was the custom in the fur forts, the children of these frontier marriages were often given biblical names—in this case, Jeremiah.

Jerry Potts was not much more than two years old when the violent world he was born into touched him personally. Historian Hugh Dempsey described it this way: "In 1840, while young Potts gurgled happily in his moss bag, his father dispensed trade goods through the stockade wicket at the fort. One day a French-Canadian engagé named Mercereau ejected a troublesome Piegan Indian known as Ah-pah or One White Eye."[2] He may have demanded more than usual for his furs or perhaps made some remark about Mercereau's Shoshone wife, but whatever the cause of the altercation, Mercereau threw the belligerent Piegan out of the fort. Ah-pah, his ego bruised, was bent on revenge. He skulked back to the fort and lurked in the shadows as dusk turned into night. It was Mercereau's job each evening to lock the wooden shutters on the barred wickets, and the Piegan planned to be close at hand when he did so. The encounter was not to be. Inside the post, Mercereau was tending to another chore and it fell to Andrew Potts to lock the fort up for the night. When Potts' profile appeared behind the bars of a wicket, the half-blind Ah-pah fired his musket point-blank into the young Scot's face.

Whether it was Harvey or Mercereau, the intended victim, who conveyed the tragic message of her husband's death to Crooked Back is unknown. Anger over the incident was widespread. The Piegans had liked and respected their White brother-in-trade, and when Ah-pah's own tribe learned of the cowardly act, they promptly closed his remaining good eye and made sure that the traders saw his corpse.

Culbertson was away from Fort McKenzie at the time of the tragedy but present or not, he could have done little to alter the fate of Crooked Back and her two-year-old boy. They also became casualties of the murder. Now without a husband, the Blood mother was left on her own. During this period of initial contact between the Whites and the Blackfoot Confederacy, the Indians proudly followed their traditional ways, confident that they could at any time wipe out the few traders at Fort McKenzie. While they were not averse to trading daughters or wives to Whites or other tribes if the trade was a good one, the wives of White men were not readily welcomed back into their tribes unless they had a sponsor willing to adopt them and their children. Left to her own resources, Crooked Back had to survive as best she could.

Whether Andrew Potts' young widow had any option or was simply taken as a convenient bedmate by the man loosely identified as her son's second father matters not. He has been described as "a man with a somewhat distasteful reputation and ... a proclivity for Indian women ... who reluctantly accept[ed] her young child as his 'son.'"[3] That man was none other than Prince Maximilian's frontier hero, Alexander Harvey.

Harvey's legacy would prove to be more that of a villain than a hero. One respected Culbertson biographer, familiar with the makeup of Fort McKenzie during its brief history, could never reconcile her subject's tolerance of Harvey's antics. Based on details surrounding Andrew Potts' murder, she speculated that the evil Harvey could have "arranged the murder of Potts simply to get Crooked Back."[4] Since the event occurred in the shadows of the smallpox epidemic, she surmised that "Harvey wanted her and took her. The Indian women in the post had been decimated in the smallpox epidemic ... I don't know how scarce women would have

This engraving after Karl Bodmer projects the potent image of the Blackfoot warrior with his horse and rifle—master of the northern plains.

been, but almost certainly more scarce than men like Harvey would have wanted."[5]

By all accounts Andrew Potts had been a quiet, well-liked man and a well-meaning father. Harvey must have had some redeeming qualities as well to have had the career that he did, but there is no doubt that he could be as mean, ruthless, and savage as any trader in the West. "On one occasion when a Blackfoot stole a pig from the fort, he pursued the Indian and shot him in the leg. He strolled up to the wounded man, passed a pipe, and invited him to have a smoke." The Blackfoot accepted the pipe while his assailant spoke of the beautiful country they shared and encouraged the man to take one last look as "Harvey coolly put a gun to his head and pulled the trigger."[6]

In 1841, Pierre Chouteau Jr. handed command of Fort McKenzie over to the notorious Francis A. Chardon. Chardon was not the choice of his immediate boss, Alexander Culbertson, but was another character of questionable virtue whom Chouteau seemed to take a shine to. Sharing a deep hate for all Indians, Chardon and Harvey got along famously.

However, there were other bourgeois, clerks, and engagés (hired boatmen and labourers) within Chouteau's company who had seen enough of Alexander Harvey. His appalling demeanour strained the tolerance of even the roughest and readiest men he associated with, so much so that they complained to the head office in St. Louis. When the owner of the American Fur Company summoned him to St. Louis to answer for his outrageous conduct, Harvey left Fort McKenzie with the winter freeze fast approaching and travelled the length of the Missouri in a canoe with nothing more than his rifle and a dog.

Chouteau was so impressed by this feat that he granted the trapper a plenary indulgence and sent him back upriver the following spring. Along with Harvey went diarist Charles Larpenteur, to whom Harvey boasted, "I never forgive or forget."[7] The whiners who had called for his discipline would soon be getting a taste of their own. "It may be years but they will all have to catch it," he vowed.[8] When they reached the Upper Missouri posts of Clark, Union, and McKenzie, Harvey sought out the men who had tried to get rid of him and severely beat every one he could find. Isadore Sandoval, a Spaniard who had earned a spot on Harvey's hit list, became an implacable enemy and some time later, when these combatants were jointly sent downriver to Fort Pierre with a load of furs, the consensus of those who knew them was that only one would return.

Surprisingly, both did make it back to Fort Union, but one evening, liquor doing most of the talking, Sandoval began to parade around the post with his rifle, loudly boasting that he was going to kill Harvey. The next day all of the clerks and engagés were ordered to start preparing an order of goods for Fort McKenzie. When Sandoval did not show up, Harvey and Culbertson, who was by then the bourgeois of the post, went to look for him. They found the Spaniard in a sutler's store, still suffering from the previous day's overindulgence. Harvey baited him, asking what he had meant by all his loud talk. Sobered, Sandoval tried to ignore Harvey, who challenged him to step outside to settle the grudge. Harvey strode outside and waited. Legend has it that when Sandoval did not appear, his challenger strutted back inside and said, "You won't fight me like a man so take this!" Lifting his rifle, Harvey shot the Spaniard in the head. He then invited any of Sandoval's friends to take up the gauntlet for him, but none would. Soon he was back at Fort McKenzie.

Author R.G. Robertson paints a gruesome portrait of Harvey and Chardon. "In the winter of 1843–44, two of the most Blackfoot-hating men ever to work for the American Fur Trading Company ... were together at the McKenzie fort. Francis Chardon was the bourgeois and Alexander Harvey was his senior trader," he wrote. "In January a party of Bloods murdered a black bondman named Reese. Swearing revenge Chardon hatched a plot with Harvey ... whereby they would kill the tribe's chiefs when they next came to trade."[9]

In February their chance came. Harvey loaded his cannon with grapeshot and aimed it into the trading area as the fort gate opened to receive a group of Blood Indians anxious to trade. With the gate locked behind them, one warrior sensed a trap, raised the alert, and was soon clawing his way up the stockade, bent on escape. Harvey's blast killed three and wounded two as Chardon shot the chief down from his attempted ascent. Robertson writes, "With the wounded Indians writhing on the ground Harvey went from one to another, slitting their throats, and lifting their scalps. After he finished he slowly licked the blood off his dirk."[10] With all the Natives dead or escaped, the murderers shared the trade goods left behind and prepared for a celebration. For Crooked Back and the other wives of the engagés there was one final insult: Harvey forced them to dance around his mound of blood-crusted scalps.[11]

Their devious attack had long-lasting effects. The Blackfoot not only stayed away from the fort, but were hostile to any AFC trader who ventured too far afield. They took all their robes and pelts to the rival Union Fur Trading Company at Fort Cotton, a few miles upriver. Eventually Pierre Chouteau Jr.'s ill-chosen tandem was forced to abandon Fort McKenzie. As a parting gesture, Harvey and Chardon left the fort in flames and moved downriver to the mouth of the Judith River, where the renegade bourgeois established his namesake post, Fort Chardon.

Culbertson had been attending to matters at Fort Laramie during the chaos at Fort McKenzie and had then returned to his home base at Fort Union. When he came upriver after wintering there, he fired Chardon and embarked on another diplomatic mission to restore relations with the Blackfoot chiefs. Culbertson, acting as Chouteau's emissary, destroyed the ill-conceived Fort Chardon and directed his *engagés* to stow all recoverable supplies from the fort in their keelboat. He instructed them to pole the goods beyond the McKenzie ruins (thereafter known as Fort Brulé or Brulé Bottoms) as far as they could and he would establish a new fort as far into Blackfoot country as the river allowed.

No record exists of Crooked Back's whereabouts during this period, but it is certain that whether or not Alexander Harvey was absent from Fort McKenzie, only a fool would mess with his chattels. After the fort was razed, mother and son may have sought refuge with Crooked Back's Blood relatives. Both were proven survivors, and they would soon resurface in a more pleasant environment.

Within another two years, those who wanted to get rid of Harvey decided to do it themselves, and this time they succeeded. His depredations had become so vile that they set out to murder him. Some historical accounts suggest that none other than Alexander Culbertson led this movement. Culbertson had broad responsibilities, and although he was officially the bourgeois at Fort McKenzie at the time of the smallpox epidemic, as well as on the day that Andrew Potts was killed, he only spent about a third of his time there, usually during winter. When he was not there, the man he reluctantly left in charge was his senior clerk and trader, Alexander Harvey.

He wasn't present to witness or stop Harvey's murderous cannon attack in 1844, but he knew what the man was capable of: he was close by when Harvey had ended Isadore Sandoval's life. If Culbertson, the respected diplomat, was now leading a vigilante movement to eliminate Harvey altogether, it was based on total frustration and may even have had the tacit approval of Pierre Chouteau Jr. himself.

When Harvey's enemies finally acted on a plan to kill him, he fought his way out of the ambush against overwhelming odds but left the Upper Missouri in 1845, ending any contact with Crooked Back and then-seven-year-old Jerry Potts. Given that the boy would grow up to be a very observant man, it is likely that as a child he had been cognizant of Harvey's reputation and deeds. Had he learned anything from Alexander Harvey? Of that there is little doubt: enemies of Jerry Potts, like those of his first stepfather, were guaranteed punishment.

Of young Jerry Potts' time with Harvey, one historian has written, "He became a quick-witted, independent boy. Fortunately, his natural intelligence helped to make up for his physical disadvantages caused by Harvey's neglect. His bowlegs and stunted growth were probably a result of generally poor nutrition and frequent periods of starvation …"[12]

The Alexander Harvey story finally ended in 1854 at Fort William when Harvey succumbed after a brief illness at the age of 45. But this was not before he'd enjoyed some success competing against the Chouteau empire. In 1846 he recruited a gang of American Fur Company malcontents who banded together with him to form Harvey, Primeau & Company. Backed by St. Louis outfitter and Chouteau adversary Robert Campbell, Harvey resurrected Fort William as his trading base near the mouth of the Yellowstone River, a stone's throw from the AFC's Fort Union. His energy and ambition served him well, and over the next few years he attained a measure of the power and riches he had craved his entire life.

History would focus on his cruelty, though few accounts seem to credit him for his most devastating act in the late summer of 1837 when he delivered smallpox to Fort McKenzie. After his death his body made one last trip down the Missouri to St. Louis where, tongue-in-cheek or otherwise, someone saw fit to lay him to rest beneath the epitaph, "Here lies a brave, honest, and kindhearted man."[13]

Chapter 4

Last King of the Missouri

In 1845 Jerry Potts was about seven years old and again without a father. Had he any sense of the future, he might have recognized that Harvey's departure left him much better off. That autumn, the American Fur Company acquired the Union Fur Company, taking over its outposts, including Fort Cotton, upriver of the Fort McKenzie site. With an alternate site in mind, Alexander Culbertson dismantled Fort Cotton and used the timber to rebuild a palisade on the east bank of the Missouri. He called his folly Fort Lewis: because there was no nearby ford in the river to accommodate arrivals from the west, Culbertson's traders faced many complaints. The fort was again disassembled and floated downriver to its final site on the opposite bank. Here, firewood and lodgepole timber were readily available and there was room for different tribes to make their own camps. Briefly known as Fort Clay, this newest pride of the AFC was rechristened Fort Benton. Despite the lingering ill feelings that followed the murderous actions of Alexander Harvey and Francis Chardon a few miles downriver amid the ashes of old Fort McKenzie, this new trading post prospered. Some Blackfoot warriors would never trust Whites again, but they realized that they needed the White man's trade goods and weapons if they were to remain as strong as their enemies. After personally relocating to Fort Union, Culbertson appointed another Scot as the manager of the AFC's new post. An educated and gentle man, Andrew Dawson was a fur trade veteran who would earn himself a regal sobriquet before the inevitable decline of the fur trade made him the "last King of the Missouri."[1]

After Harvey's departure from the Upper Missouri, Jerry Potts probably survived solely by his wits, a fort urchin eating scraps left by the traders, possibly welcomed occasionally into the tipis of his mother's people in the camps outside the fort. Some historians believe that Crooked Back withdrew to her own Blood band and left her son in the care of the White men, assured by a few among them that they would teach the son of Andrew Potts their ways. Survival, not the luxury of choice, was the reality of frontier life. A lesser probability is that Harvey took the boy downriver to Fort Union or Fort Clark before abandoning him.

Andrew Dawson was one of the best things that ever happened to Jerry Potts. Dawson, in his kindly way, took a fatherly interest in the orphan and cared for him as if he were his own son. The attentive Scotsman taught young Jerry all the values he had not learned from Harvey. Under Dawson's guardianship, Potts received a semblance of education and, more importantly, used the wits that had kept him alive to glean the ins and outs of the fur-trading business. In his travels with his foster father, he learned to speak several languages, including the three Blackfoot dialects plus Cree, Crow, Assiniboine, and a smattering of Sioux.

Various attempts to document Potts' youth have led to a mixed record of speculation and hearsay. However, it is safe to say that, in some ill-defined sequence, he experienced both the White and Blood cultures. By 1850, the 12-year-old boy is thought to have made his first journey north to the Belly River in today's southern Alberta to rejoin his mother's people. That province's long-time archivist and author Hugh Dempsey has provided the most respected accounts of Jerry Potts' early life.

Dempsey paints Dawson as a paternal mentor to the child he had taken in. "It was under his patient guidance that the young boy learned English and the many lessons that separated him from most of the mixed-bloods on the frontier. In the next decade, Potts learned much about the fur trade, Indian languages, and the ways of both [cultures]. When he reached his late teens he was on his own but still retained close ties with his foster father."[2]

Dawson himself seems cut from much the same cloth as Alexander Culbertson, who remained his direct superior within the American Fur Company. He was trained as a lawyer in Edinburgh, but shunned a law practice and left, after a brief administrative career, for the New World. He sailed to New Orleans, then up the Mississippi to St. Louis, arriving with less than the proverbial dollar in his pocket. The next day he began work for the thriving enterprise of Pierre Chouteau Jr.

Seeing first-hand the flow of trading goods and the profits that traders made, Dawson offered his services the following year to carry important dispatches to Chouteau's forts. He travelled with another Edinburgh transplant, Robert Morgan, until they saw their first "red men." One evening when Dawson returned from a hunting foray, he found a note from Morgan and a horseless camp. Fearing what lay ahead and possibly trying to induce Dawson to follow him, Morgan had headed back to St. Louis with their animals and supplies. "Do as you please," he wrote Dawson.[3]

Andrew Dawson chose to go on, living off berries and little else. He arrived at Fort Pierre six weeks later, his dispatches intact and his family heirloom sword at his side. It was not long before he went on to Fort Clark as a clerk and began his rise through the company's ranks. Both resourceful and daring, he made regular trips between Clark and Fort Union.

Dawson soon settled at Fort Clark, where he sired a son named Andrew with a Sioux Brule woman, and a son named James with respected scout Pierre Garreau's daughter, whom he married. Later in life, James would leave the only first-hand account of his father's life, in which he described some of Dawson's adventures.

"Upon one occasion when Indians were hostile and travel dangerous, Dawson, traveling alone, carried an old copper kettle from Fort Clark to Fort Union, ostensibly to have it repaired, but really to furnish visible excuse for the trip, which was to carry company dispatches having to do with the American Fur Co.'s competition with the Hudson's Bay Co."[4]

Dawson first met Alexander Culbertson at Fort Union. In 1854, because of excessive demands on his own time, Culbertson promoted Dawson to take over Fort Benton as chief trader. One

Andrew Dawson ruled Fort Benton at a time when a shift in European fashion taste from beaver to silk, and declining stocks of that animal, eroded the level of trade at Fort Union. Demand for the buffalo robe shifted the entire focus of trade to the gateway of Montana, and Fort Benton quickly rose in stature.

news story in the *Fort Benton Journal* of March 11, 1854, suggests that the move upriver was not without tragedy. The terse obituary simply said that Mr. Dawson's wife had died and was interred in the back of the fort.

Dawson's legend grew as he continued his solo wanderings through the Missouri watershed. One morning he woke to find himself "surrounded by fifteen Indians. Among them was one he had befriended, but he pretended not to recognize him and saluted them all ... making up his mind that a brave front was his only show for life. He was most agreeably surprised to see them make friendly overtures ... On finding out to which fort he was going they made signs that they were going that way also ... Dawson was allowed to enter the Fort, where he at once explained how the Indians had surprised him but were peaceably disposed. They told the interpreter that they had planned to take him by surprise at daybreak and see what he would do, and when he had shown such a brave and fearless front to them and was ready to die or be tortured, they concluded that he was a brave warrior. Had he run ... or shown a disposition to fight, they would have killed him at once."[5]

During his time at Fort Benton, Andrew Dawson became a full partner with the other fort bourgeois and made enough of an impression as a founder of the territory that he was immortalized in a massive oil painting that now hangs in the Montana State Capitol building. Given that he only lived in the territory for a decade, this recognition shows his impact on the community.

During 10 years of travel across the West as part of a railway survey crew, John Mix Stanley sketched many of the trading forts. This view of Fort Benton in 1853 shows its placement on the west side of the river, with a suitable ford for Natives from the north and east in the foreground.

Among the Blackfoot visitors to the fort, Dawson gained a reputation as a medicine man. "On many occasions when sickness struck the Indians he was ready with his medical advice and medicine chest. On one occasion a noted Indian chief ... who had shown much enmity to him became ill after gorging himself ... Dawson, seeing what the matter was, gave him a strong emetic. The Indian vomited bone after bone, after which he was much relieved, and ever after was one of Dawson's best Indian friends."[6]

Throughout his tenure at Fort Benton, Dawson won the loyalty of many men who were loners by nature. One such man was free trader Charles Chouquette, who operated independently of the fur company and was suspicious of its managers until he met Andrew Dawson. The chief trader saw in Chouquette a capable, dependable trapper whom he recruited into his employ. There was mutual admiration and Chouquette later recalled that "Dawson outfitted and helped many in distress and many prospectors he grubstaked, and on many occasions assisted the Jesuit priests when they were robbed by Indians, and greatly assisted them in many of their missions." Another time, according to Chouquette, "Charley Thomas had been employed by LaBarge & Co. ... and having sold out to

Dawson they owed Charley $300." Charley was left high and dry, it seems, but "Dawson paid this amount and ever after had Charley in his employment."[7]

Dawson's role at Fort Benton and his reputed benevolence in the community are helpful in understanding how he might have adopted the fatherless half-Scottish boy and taught him as he would his own sons. Based on what is known, Potts probably spent time at Fort Clark or Fort Union with Andrew Dawson, and after Dawson moved to Fort Benton, young Jerry was encouraged to visit Crooked Back's people and learn the ways of the Blackfoot culture. Thus the adolescent's world covered the length of the Upper Missouri and Marias rivers, all the way north to the Belly River homeland of the Bloods. If not as a child then certainly as a teenager, Jerry Potts spent several moons immersed in Blackfoot culture, and compared to the misfortunes that had befallen him and his mother during their "fort" lives, the open prairie offered salvation and enlightenment.

The communal nature of the Blood people and their willingness to embrace the son of Namo-pisi, teach him their way of life, and allow him to grow in stature based solely on his own merits left Jerry Potts with a lifelong affinity for the Blackfoot society. His brave deeds, heart, and determination won him the name by which the Blackfoot Nation would forever know him: Kyî-yo-kosi or Bear Child. Dempsey describes it as "an honoured and respected name that had been handed down through several generations of Blackfoot."[8]

As a young teen, Jerry Potts was introduced to the rituals of the Sun Dance and thereafter he became devoted to the religious traditions of his mother's people. He shared the Blackfoot respect for the power of dreams and had a lifelong reliance on the strength of his medicine bag.

At Fort Benton one night while under the tutelage of Andrew Dawson, Potts' instincts reverted to the Blackfoot ways. He had a dream that strongly suggested a cat that was living in the post could protect him from evil. He woke immediately, prepared to search every corner of the post until he found his cat. When he found it sleeping in the early morning sun, young Bear Child killed, skinned, and tanned it. For the rest of his life he wore the hide as the dominant element of his medicine.

FORT BENTON

On Christmas Day, 1850, Alexander Culbertson stood before his new adobe building, four years after its first stockade was built, and officially proclaimed the trading post's new name: Fort Benton. It was named in honour of Thomas Hart Benton—the man who had helped John Jacob Astor put an end to government controls of the fur trade 28 years earlier. Benton was a firm supporter of presidents Jackson and Polk, and a strong proponent of the popular Manifest Destiny doctrine that defined White America's political aim of conquering and developing the West. The fort was dedicated after Benton's long career as a Missouri senator ended in electoral defeat. Fort Benton was the only White settlement in what, 14 years later, Abraham Lincoln would proclaim the Montana Territory.

Culbertson and his esteemed wife, Natawista Iksana, daughter of a respected Blood chief, soon left the comfortable agent's quarters at Fort Benton for a new home at Fort Union, a move necessitated by his broadening responsibilities. The new factor, Andrew Dawson, oversaw the replacement of all log buildings, except the substantial barn, with adobe ones, a process that was completed in 1859. Two blockhouses on diagonal corners of the fort sported flagpoles and lookout stations, and the fort's 14-inch-thick walls were designed to withstand a siege that never came. A two-storey building housed trades on the lower level and *engagés'* sleeping quarters above. The blacksmith and carpenter shops were essential for the constant reshoeing of pack animals and for constructing the flat-bottomed mackinaw boats, built every winter to float mounds of buffalo robes downstream.

In 1862 the first steamboat to arrive made Benton the world's farthest inland port, 3,485 miles from the Gulf of Mexico. After the decline of the southern herd of buffalo, the American Fur Company sold the structure to competitors in 1864. The fort gradually fell into a state of disrepair that left it too dilapidated to house a garrison when the U.S. military took over in 1870. Even so, until the railways came west in the 1880s, Fort Benton remained Montana's most important city and a critical transportation link to the east. Today it is the county seat of Chouteau County.

As a youthful warrior, Bear Child came to view some of the traditional enemies of the Blackfoot with a unique perspective. With Dawson's encouragement he visited Crow and Assiniboine camps, observing them not as adversaries but in peaceful settings. He also moved freely between Blood or Piegan camps and the American Fur Company post at Fort Benton, all the time remaining loyal to and ever respectful of his foster father.

Andrew Dawson took a third wife while at Fort Benton, a Gros Ventre woman who gave birth to a son, Thomas, in the adobe home that Dawson had built. Baby Thomas came a few months after his father had suffered a serious fall in the winter of 1858. Plunging through an open trap door into a basement, he had lain there half-conscious through the night. Dawson was found by his clerks in the morning, almost frozen to death. The robust trader never recovered full use of his legs and within six years was totally crippled.

Jerry Potts maintained as much affection for Dawson as he had for any White man. He spoke highly of him in later life and they continued to work together as long as Dawson was able.

By the time of Dawson's fall, Potts was a capable interpreter who, unlike any of the White traders, could enter the Blackfoot world both trusted and welcome. He was skilled with weapons and brave to a fault. In spite of his rough upbringing, meanness was not a part of his makeup—until he was challenged. Then young Jerry could take care of himself anywhere. And as was the case with anybody who spent time in and around Fort Benton, he had become well acquainted with the town's foremost commodity—whiskey.

In 1862, Dawson was no doubt of two minds when he heard that his protegé, travelling on company business, had killed a man in a confrontation at Charles Galpin's new fort on the north bank of the Missouri, 12 miles upstream from where it met the Milk River. The fact that his foster son could leave a main-street gunfight unscathed must have offered some solace; that he was unable to find a more peaceful solution to a barroom argument probably provoked despair.

Potts, then 23, stood an unimposing five feet six inches, his torso perched with a permanent lean over his right leg. He can be pictured "in his moccasins on stubby, bowed legs that had been moulded around the belly of a horse. His rounded, sloping shoulders always gave him the appearance of standing with a slouch. A straight-nosed, angular face stretched tight with swarthy, bronzed skin was punctuated with piercing black eyes that told little of the thoughts behind them. A black, drooping moustache framed his tight-lipped mouth."[9] He favoured a White man's buckskin jacket and wore "the leggings and moccasins of the Blackfoot, his shell belt hung with a sheathed scalping knife and beaded *parfleche*."[10]

Potts was almost taciturn, easy to discount. The gunfight at Galpin's fort was described thus: "A French Canadian named Antoine Primeau learned that the unimposing Potts was not to be fooled with. Unfortunately, Primeau learned too late. As a result of a drunken quarrel the two men stepped out into the street to settle their differences ... Potts shot Primeau dead ... The incident established his reputation as a fighter among the rough frontiersmen of the upper Missouri country and few men would rile him, especially when he was drinking."[11]

Primeau was the only White man that Potts ever killed.

After some time in a bar, Potts' favourite exhibition involved a partner, his mixed-blood pal George Star, whom he had befriended at Fort Benton. The two Métis were kindred spirits and it was one of the very few real friendships Potts made early in his lifetime. Whenever they got together at Fort Benton they would celebrate the event with a game of cards and a bottle of red-eye. Having fortified themselves with rotgut, they would saunter into the street, face each other at 20 paces, and try to trim each other's moustache with lead. They performed this stunt many times, always inebriated, but neither man was ever touched by a bullet. Potts knew it was simply good shooting, but his Blackfoot brothers believed he had supernatural powers that they attributed to his medicine.

Already a respected marksman, Potts became even more proficient with bow and arrow and a crack shot with a rifle. He also became an excellent tracker and honed what in later years would prove to be an almost supernatural sense of direction. Bounded on the north by the North Saskatchewan River, on the south by the Missouri, on the east by the Cypress Hills, and on the west by the Rocky Mountains, the Blackfoot domain was the best buffalo range of the Great Plains and home of the vast northern herd. Potts travelled the country extensively on the yearly buffalo hunts and soon knew every mile of the route. He also learned the ways of his Blackfoot brothers, the lessons of war—defence against enemy attack, the glory of bravery, the art of attack, and the thrill of revenge.

Once Jerry Potts became Bear Child, his first allegiance was to the Blackfoot Confederacy. Although he often represented the Whites in matters of trade and negotiation, he always showed a preference for a way of life some distance from the stockades of the White man.

One of his grudging admirers describes Potts' evolution: "Between the sedate, sagacious council tipis of the Blackfoot and the raw, wild trading posts of the Whites, Potts learned the best and worst of both worlds. At Fort Benton he was schooled in the rough and ready ways of the lawless frontier, soon acquiring both the skills and the vices of the frontiersmen. He grew fond of gambling and downright religious about drinking. He also became very skilful with a revolver." Potts' main weakness was "his shameless love of the 'pure' ... he preferred refined spirits but, if they were in short supply, then he was just as fond of the traders' firewater. When he was particularly thirsty, he would guzzle Jamaica ginger, essence of lemon or Perry Davis' Painkiller. In desperately dry times he was even known to drink a palatable potion compounded by a Boston firm for a common female complaint."[12]

During the same summer as Potts' gun duel with Primeau, Andrew Dawson was in Fort Union awaiting the arrival of the *Spread Eagle*, the AFC's latest steamboat, carrying Pierre Chouteau Jr., the retired Alexander Culbertson and his wife, and six dozen newcomers to the Missouri frontier.

When Dawson greeted the ship at Fort Union, it was obvious that his restricted mobility would soon force him to retire. Possibly for that reason, in tribute to his loyal friend, Chouteau christened a new fort being built to compete with Charles Galpin's post as Fort Andrew Dawson. The new fort itself was part of the AFC's relentless strategy to smash all opposition, even though the fur trade seemed to be entering its twilight years.

Different challenges faced Dawson at Fort Benton in 1863. That year a light spring runoff meant the AFC paddlewheelers could climb the Missouri only as far as Fort Union, almost 400 miles shy of Fort

Benton. In addition, the Sioux war chief Red Cloud and his warriors were trying to wipe out the White presence along the Bozeman Trail in Wyoming and southern Montana.

Despite his bad legs and the threat of Sioux unrest, the ever-spirited Dawson refused to be intimidated. He knew the success of his winter trading season depended upon securing the downriver supplies, and overland was his only option, so he decided to lead a small brigade and fetch the freight himself. The best of his employees rode with him, including chief clerk Matt Carroll, brothers Jim and Bob Lemon, Joe Cobell, and, to guide and scout for them, Jerry Potts. Only clerk George Steell was left to man the trading business. Jerry Potts must have known when he set out with the crippled Dawson in the autumn of 1863 it was likely they were sharing one last adventure. And Andrew Dawson had reason to be proud of the foster son at his side.

The main problem that faced the crew was that they would have to return, with their invitingly laden wagons, on established trails that ran straight through hostile Sioux country. No doubt outnumbered, the party would be an attractive target.

The wagon train started out for Fort Benton on the morning of October 23, 1863. Three days later, near a bend in the Missouri called Ash Point, Potts spotted a large band of horsemen headed in their direction. He deftly picked out trappings that marked them as Sioux, and therefore trouble, and signalled back to Dawson to circle the wagons. The Sioux war party pulled up out of rifle range, as if determining a plan of attack. The Whites checked their weapons and waited. Finally, a big, powerful-looking warrior rode out from the ranks of his companions and slowly approached the wagons. Using sign language, he explained that he came in peace and wanted to talk with the leader of the White men, shake hands with him, and smoke the pipe.

Matt Carroll had spent many years in Montana trading among the Sioux, and he was certain that Red Cloud was determined not to end hostilities until he had won his war. Carroll's warnings convinced Dawson that the warrior's platitudes could not be trusted, but the bourgeois reminded his men that the American Fur Company sought to gain the trade of all tribes, including the hostile ones.

While their contribution to the state was fleeting at best, both Andrew Dawson and his boss, Pierre Chouteau Jr., have a permanent place in the Montana State Capitol building. This 168-by-102-inch oil painting portrays the two (Dawson standing) against a backdrop of Fort Benton. State counties are named after both men.

Carroll agreed to meet the Sioux warrior, but, sure that the man was planning some treachery, he unholstered his pistol and tucked it into the back of his belt. Carrying his rifle, he stepped over a wagon tongue and watched intently as the Sioux dismounted and laid down his rifle. Carroll put his down also. As the two came face to face the band of Sioux began to shuffle forward slowly.

Extending one hand in peace, the Sioux warrior used his other to snatch a hidden scalping knife from beneath his buckskin shirt. But before he could thrust the blade, Carroll had shoved his cocked six-gun into the painted face.

"Now, dog," Carroll said, "you are shaking hands with a White man. Go! Tell your people that a White man gave you your life—that the palefaces know how to kill and how to spare their enemies. Go now, and ask your medicine men if they cannot send a better warrior to meet a White man."[13]

The disgraced warrior began his retreat as the row of Sioux horses inched closer. Carroll stood his ground while his adversary signalled his friends to halt, apparently in tribute to the White's bravery. They retired without attacking.

As Potts followed at a distance to confirm the Sioux departure, the wagon train reassembled. Dawson, Carroll, and the other drivers continued on to Fort Benton without further incident. It was experiences like this that prepared Jerry Potts for the great challenge that lay ahead in a country that was yet to be born—Canada.

This trading season would be Andrew Dawson's last. He had spent almost 18 years as a steadying influence in a volatile world that was about to get worse. The buffalo was on the verge of disappearing, and Civil War casualties and deserters were growing in number. But even more significantly, the paralysis in his lower limbs had steadily worsened over the six years since his terrible fall. The much-loved trader, respected by his employees, his competitors, and the Blackfoot tribes, made plans to return to his family in Dalkeith, Scotland. With him would go his eldest son, James, and his youngest, Thomas. Andrew was put in the care of his long-time friend Robert Morgan, who had opted to trade farther north with the Canadian Métis at Fort Garry.[14]

Dawson handed over his business interests to his clerks of recent years, Matt Carroll and George Steell, and advanced them some money to operate. He vowed to come back to Fort Benton once his legs had improved and check on his investment. The paraplegia never dampened his perpetual determination, but his intentions remained unfulfilled.

Although he never saw it for himself, a final tribute to Dawson's civility came in mid-1864 when the frontier he had ruled gained official status in Washington as the Montana Territory and a county was named in his honour.

This sketch of "Old Fort Benton" appeared in M.A. Leeson's illustrated, 1,367-page, two-volume opus History of Montana 1739-1885 *and depicted the original community in its simplest form, before the AFC's sale of its local assets and withdrawal from the fur trade.*

There is no record of his last meeting with his foster son, Jerry Potts. However, Andrew Dawson was without doubt the single most significant male influence on the adolescent who would one day prove to be significant in western history.

After settling affairs with his American Fur Company partners in St. Louis and New York, Andrew Dawson and his two sons boarded the steamer *Scotia* and were met in Liverpool by Andrew's brother, Alexander. Shortly afterward, he returned to his birthplace and regaled family and old schoolmates with tales of his adventurous life until his death in the parish of Dalkeith in September 1872.[15]

Both James and Thomas Dawson later returned to North America. Thirteen years after his father's death, Tom made his way onto the western Canadian Plains, possibly visiting his older half-brother Andrew in Manitoba. Tom Dawson held a position as a civilian scout for the North West Mounted Police at the time of the Northwest Rebellion in 1885. After that brief adventure he returned to his Montana roots, living near Glacier Park well into his 90s.

At Fort Benton, a new man came upriver in the spring of 1864 to replace Andrew Dawson. Like his predecessors on many occasions before him, he was forced to abandon the river and carry his goods the last 120 miles by wagon. Isaac Gilbert Baker would prove an astute businessman, adaptable and decisive. He was also a pragmatist who arrived in Fort Benton with 200 barrels of whiskey.

Isaac G. Baker first came to Fort Benton in 1864 as the last AFC manager before the post was sold. He arrived with 200 barrels of whiskey in tow, a symbol of the decade that lay ahead. Able to sustain a reputation for responsible trading in spite of the use of whiskey, his company was the most prominent merchant in Montana throughout Fort Benton's heyday.

In that same year the American Fur Company, no longer attracted to the diminishing returns of the fur trade, sold its adobe fort to the Northwest Fur Company. Baker, seeing a bright future on his own, decided he would rather compete than join the new company. Isaac Baker quickly assumed a leading role in a community about to enter a new era of free trade. Pierre Chouteau Jr.'s powerful monopoly was a force of the past, and in 1865 anyone who had the capital and the courage could barter with the tribes of the Upper Missouri. But trade for what? Had the era of the fur trade run its course? Not for men who went farther afield, beyond the law. Industrialists in the east were still looking for thick, durable leather that could be used to drive the machinery belts of progress. Compared to the buffalo, the hides of domestic cattle were thin and wore too quickly. Out on the sage-covered plains of the West there remained, somewhere, more of the beast whose dried hide was as tough as iron.

It was not the ongoing hunt for buffalo, however, that would spur the new business of I.G. Baker and his competitors. As it had 15 years earlier on California's Sutter Creek, and only 6 years earlier along British Columbia's Fraser River, the word "Gold!" was heard in Fort Benton, and a whole new form of madness soon prevailed.

Chapter 5

The Warrior Years

Gold was first discovered in the Alder Gulch region of southwest Montana in 1864. With the demise of the fur companies, many men who had made their living in that trade caught gold fever and flocked to the area. Not even the threat of Red Cloud's Sioux war party could deter their quest for the motherlode.

When George Steell, one of Andrew Dawson's former chief clerks, decided to seek his fortune in the ore pockets of Alder Gulch, he recruited a young partner and then sought a knowledgeable guide to take him into the unfamiliar country. Knowing well of Jerry Potts' skills and reputation in Blackfoot country from their days together at Fort Benton, Steell asked him if he would lead them toward the Sun and Smith river areas. Potts agreed.

After Steell outfitted the expedition at Fort Benton, Potts led them to a Sun River location where the trio spent several weeks prospecting. Finding nothing of note, they opted to return home across Red Cloud's domain. As they were nearing Fort Benton, 200 screaming Sioux warriors charged out of a coulee.

The three men wheeled their horses and whipped them into a full gallop. It was late in the day and their mounts were too tired to outrun their assailants. The closest place to make a stand was a deserted log cabin two miles up the coulee; Potts decided they should try to get there. Under cover they would have a better chance, but the strategy had one major barrier to overcome: the charging Sioux horsemen were between them and the cabin.

Momentarily hidden from their pursuers by a small rise, Potts suddenly reined up, yelled at his mates to join him, and turned his horse to charge back into the oncoming horde of Sioux. The plan seemed desperate, but Potts was counting on surprise to make the dash through the Sioux lines safely. As the warriors neared, they were met by the charging Whites and the sound of their guns. The plan worked, and after scattering the Sioux, they reached the log cabin.

The entrance to the old sod-roofed house was too low for the horses, so saddles were removed and the animals turned loose. Potts quickly turned the unhinged door on its side across the entrance and reinforced it with some nearby logs.

Within minutes they were surrounded by the Sioux war party, who slid from their ponies and began their assault on the cabin. Precise rifle fire from Potts and the others discouraged any advance. When Potts' rifle was empty he pulled out his revolver, reputedly "dropping six Indians with six shots."[1]

Stunned by this resistance, the Sioux retreated to rethink their attack. As dusk approached, Potts acted first. "Taking his saddle blanket, Potts wrapped it about him in Indian-fashion and slipped into the early evening darkness." After crawling a quarter mile through underbrush, he "strolled cautiously through the Sioux camp ... found the horse herd and selected three of the best runners."[2] Potts then led them quietly to a position behind the cabin where he signalled success to his comrades.

After the three men put the coulee and a sloped rise behind them, Potts yielded to a primitive urge to call out his triumph. As he rode into the night, he let out a blood-curdling Blackfoot war cry for the benefit of the unsuspecting Sioux below.

In Benton, Potts decided that his prospecting days were over. White man's work had disappeared with the American Fur Company, and the country south of the Missouri was just too full of Sioux; it was time for a return to his people. He gathered his few possessions and took the trail that led northwest. Finding refuge in a Piegan camp beside the Marias River, Potts, for the first time in his life, was content to settle down and concentrate on building his own horse herd. His first act of domesticity was to take a young Crow girl as his wife.

On the Marias and on trips north to his Blood relatives on the Belly, Potts embraced the Blackfoot way of life. Dempsey writes: "He began to gain fame as an Indian warrior ... He took part in several battles with enemies of the Blackfoot and brought considerable honour to his mother's tribe."[3]

During this warrior decade Bear Child earned a reputation as being invincible, his medicine strong enough to withstand any attack. Possibly his greatest single coup came when he left the Blood-Peigan camp to cross the Missouri and hunt buffalo. Bernard Fardy provides a colourful account:

One winter's morning he left camp, crossed the frozen Missouri and rode into Benton where he tended to some business. Leaving town, he headed south along Shonkin Creek to hunt buffalo for his camp. While riding along the creek he was suddenly confronted by seven Crow braves. Three of the Indians were armed with bows but the others carried awkward but lethal breech-loading trade rifles. Potts' markings identified him as Blackfoot but he offered no greeting, even though he knew the Crow language and was improving on it through his wife.

Confident because of their numbers, the Crows used sign language to explain that they had a camp a few miles away and that they would like him to visit their chief. Realizing that he had no choice, Potts agreed to go with them. Potts fell in behind the three with bows while the four riflemen followed him.

As they rode along, the Indians behind Potts began to discuss what they should do with the little half-breed Blackfoot. One wanted to take him to their chief but the others preferred taking his scalp now. After some haggling they opted for the scalp. Unaware that Potts was warned, they rode on a while longer.

When Potts heard the metallic click as a rifle cocked behind him, he tumbled from his horse, eluding the bullet that whistled over his head. Rolling in the snow the Métis came up on his knees while levering his repeating rifle.

Before the surprised Crow quartet gained control of their spooked horses Potts triggered off a fusillade of shots that dropped all four into tangled heaps. Wheeling on the three bowmen, he found them desperately fleeing, spurring their horses through the impeding snow.

Potts mounted up and headed back toward Benton where he knew there were camps of both Piegans and Bloods. He described his encounter and the ambush. Within an hour he was leading an anxious war party toward the unsuspecting Crow camp at Shonkin Creek.

Night was coming and the Blackfoot quietly surrounded the Crows and struck suddenly in the last twilight. As the surprised Crows frantically tried to flee, the Blackfoot chased and killed dozens of them. Flushed with victory, Potts' war party finished off the wounded, lifted scalps and rode back to Benton for a victory celebration.

At the trading post the triumphant Blackfoot went wild. They held a great scalp dance in the streets of the town, celebrating with singing, dancing and general hell-raising. The revelry continued long into the night and the terrified citizens of the town locked themselves in their houses and root cellars, fearful that the Indians would go completely crazy and wipe them out. It was probably due to the influence of Potts and other Métis among the party that the Blackfoot were restrained from tearing Benton to pieces.[4]

Word of Potts' bravery and great victory over the Crow won plaudits from the different tribes, and news of Bear Child's feats spread.

A recurring theme among the many stories of Jerry Potts' bravado is his apparent ability to turn his back on enemies in spite of recognizing their intent to murder him. Only months after the great victory over the Crow encampment, Bear Child was hunting with a younger cousin near the Sun River when three Crow horsemen ambushed them. As Potts later recalled, his companion that day was killed with a shot to the chest, while Bear Child quickly alighted and used his mount as a shield. He listened to the three Crow openly discuss a strategy in their own tongue, not knowing that their mixed-blood foe understood every word. They soon decided to offer him freedom if he rode away without his rifle or his cousin's body. Then they would leave their cover and shoot him in the back. Bear Child played their game, knowing it was his best chance for them to show themselves.

He mounted and rode slowly away, his ear ever alert for the cocking of a rifle. When he heard that sound he dove to the ground as a bullet removed his hat. He drew a hidden revolver and killed the shooter. Then he took careful aim and dispatched the other two Crow as they fled. After recovering his cousin's body, he scalped the three Crow and took the blue-steel rifle that had been used against him. He left the corpses to the vultures and returned to his Black Elk band with his cousin's corpse so his family could pay tribute to their dead youth. Potts would later commemorate this event by naming his youngest son Blue Gun after the trophy weapon he had won that day.

Only a year or two after his cousin's death, Bear Child and a band of Piegans were camped on Two Medicine River when they were attacked at dusk by a party of Assiniboines and Gros Ventres. Quickly assessing the situation, Bear Child grabbed his repeater rifle and made his way to a point high above the melee. With deadly accuracy, he deftly turned the tide against the intruders. He never knew exactly how many Assiniboines and Gros Ventres he killed in that exchange, but there were enough witnesses that word of his deeds spread across the Plains and his status as an invincible warrior reached a new level. Soon his full-blood brothers were inviting him to sit in on tribal councils, where his observations on matters dealing with trade, war, and daily community life were often heeded.

Chief status among the Blackfoot was earned through deeds of bravery and the accumulation of wealth. As a result of his prowess in battle and the growing herd of horses near his lodge, Bear Child became a sub-chief among the Piegans. Some families sought out his personal camp and gradually a small band of nine lodges assembled around him. Amid this new clan, homesick for her own people, was Bear Child's 18-year-old Crow wife, Mary. Although her tribe and the Blackfoot were long-standing enemies, such marriages were not uncommon and showed the paradoxical nature of tribal relations. Traditional adversaries could make individual friends or barter for a wife knowing they would later meet on a battlefield.

Jerry Potts' bicultural upbringing meant that he never fully succumbed to the Blackfoot way of life. He would take no part in attacking enemy camps for scalps, nor would he instigate a fight with any Crow or Assiniboine camp willing to respect a truce. Defence or justified retaliation was a different matter. He would willingly and ably join the fight to avenge an attack. Potts also abstained from taking part in raids for horses or booty; the traders had taught him the concept of private property and the law. In the White man's world, the ability to acquire property was the reward for hard work; theft would only lead to harsh punishment. He did not hold with rustling, whether the villain was White or Native. On at least one occasion he played both judge and jury.

W.S. Stocking paid $150 for a grey horse at Fort Benton and took it to his ranch. Within days it was stolen and Stocking, after making inquiries, was directed to a small Piegan camp on the Marias River and the mixed-blood known as Jerry Potts. Hesitant to go there, the rancher waited until Potts made one of his regular trips to Benton. Stocking explained the situation and Potts agreed to help him.

The two men rode to the Marias, where Potts invited his guest into his tipi to wait while he resolved the matter. He wandered around the camp, located the horse, and discreetly asked questions. Back at his tipi he assured Stocking that he was satisfied the matter would best be resolved on a full stomach. Over a feast of boiled "boss ribs," or buffalo hump, Potts explained his strategy to the rancher and, once again adopting his chiefly position, sent for the Piegan who claimed ownership of the horse.

When the man arrived, Bear Child asked him how the grey horse had found its way into their camp and was not surprised to hear that he had bought it from another tribe. Following Potts' suggestion, Stocking asked what the price would be to buy the horse. Potts listened to a long list of about $500 worth of demands ranging from

Along the steep banks and benchlands of the Marias River, clusters of Piegan lodges were spread out during the winter months. These people, who were led by Mountain Chief, became primary targets once they were discovered by the whiskey traders.

cartridges, hatchets, and knives for the man to needles and calico for his wife. Stocking said that he could not pay that much, and Bear Child, having watched the exchange, simply excused the man. Potts assured Stocking that he was now convinced that the Piegan had stolen his grey. The exorbitant demands were out of character and posed only in the hope that he would not prove to be the thief. Both the rancher and Potts knew, however, that they could not challenge the warrior in front of his peers and force him to lose face in the camp. Potts, remaining tactful, invited his guest to share the shelter of his tipi for the night.

Shortly before dawn, Potts slipped from under his robes and made his way toward the horses. Soon he awakened Stocking, handed him the reins of the grey, and, with little more than a nod, bid him adieu.

"Jerry was about the most decent specimen that I ever met with," Stocking later recalled in his memoir *Fort Benton Memories*, "... certainly a remarkable man, one with the sinews of a panther and the heart of a lion."[5] Stocking also noted that by that time Jerry Potts was "a sort of sub-chief ... he had a camp of six or eight lodges ... peopled by his Piegan relatives by marriage." (This assessment was not accurate at the time, as Potts' lone wife was the young Crow girl, Mary. Later, he would take two Piegan wives.)

Potts was 30 when Mary bore a son they named Mitchell, possibly after David Mitchell, who had built the fort where Potts was born and his father had been murdered. Mitchell had gone on to become a respected Indian agent in Montana. Whether it was the added responsibilities of his new son, a homesick wife, or a simple wanderlust is not known but one morning Jerry Potts came out from under his buffalo robes with a yen to re-enter his other world.

On his regular trips to Fort Benton, Potts had seen a dramatic change in the old fur-trading post. More efficient sternwheelers had eventually got all the way to Benton, but the fickle river dictated their schedule. When Andrew Dawson had come back upriver from Fort Union on the *Spread Eagle* in 1862, it was one of only four steamboats to get to Fort Benton that year. The following year only two boats had made it to the Benton docks. A natural stone ridge barrier in the Missouri just above the Fort Benton waterfront insured that steamboats could go no further inland and that this location would always remain the drop-off point for all river cargo. An influx of prospectors, settlers, and U.S. Army recruits spurred an increase in traffic in 1865, when 31 vessels ascended the Missouri all the way to Benton, fast becoming the storage depot and warehouse community for points further west. Although furs were reduced to a minor role in the local economy, a few ambitious traders sought to establish themselves as the new merchant princes of a vast frontier. An influx of humanity arrived in record numbers, seeking gold and anxious to escape the war-torn east. Foodstuffs, building materials, eastern luxuries, and, of course, whiskey, were all in demand. Government constraints on liquor in so-called Indian Territory were no longer enforceable, and it was a land with a powerful thirst.

Beyond stevedoring, bartending, or store-clerking, there was little work to be had around Fort Benton. But as a man with astute tracking skills and knowledge of the lands beyond the Marias and Milk rivers, Potts found himself in great demand by this new breed of entrepreneur. The free traders were pushing deeper and deeper

A SECOND BEAR CHILD

Various historical accounts focus on a Fort Benton event that reveals much about the callous treatment of innocent Natives during the whiskey-trading days. In July 1869, when Jerry Potts was well known to his Blood brethren as Bear Child, a Piegan brave who bore the same name had the misfortune of being in the vicinity with two other Marias River-based tribesmen as word spread of the latest frontier atrocity.

On this day, the body of a fatally injured animal herder, one of two victims of an alleged Indian ambush, was brought into the town, provoking three angry locals to go on a rampage. One of the men, George Houk, "dragged out an elderly Piegan named Heavy Charging in the Brush and murdered him in the street. With him was a 14-year-old boy who was also killed."[9]

The vengeance didn't stop there, as Houk and his cohorts sought more recompense. Bear Child and his two friends were lynched and left to hang with a note pinned to one of their shirts saying, "These are three good Indians." Meanwhile, revellers "marched and fought and sang and screamed until they were hoarse and finally wore themselves out."[10]

There is no record of any remorse shown by the vigilantes or their supporters when local trader Isaac Baker "discovered that the herders had not been killed by Piegans but by River Crows from further south."[11]

Of course retaliation followed from the Piegans despite the best efforts of their leader, Mountain Chief, to contain his braves. Again hatred had its day and the tragic legacy of this second Bear Child was limited to brief mentions in Dempsey's fine book *Firewater* and other historic accounts.

into almost-virgin territory west of the Cypress Hills (near modern-day Lethbridge, Alberta), destined to become known as "Whoop-up" country.

It was only a matter of time before Potts was invited to join a new venture. Knowing his wife and young son would be better off with her own people, Potts agreed to send Mary and baby Mitchell back to the Crow lodges where he had found her.

In the pragmatic way of the Plains, and with winter coming on, Potts sought a new relationship in what seemed a not-uncommon arrangement among the Blackfoot. He took two sisters as his new wives. Bestowing gifts and a string of a few of his better horses upon the South Piegan chief Sitting-in-the-Middle, Potts took his daughters, Panther Woman and Spotted Killer, into his lodge.

By this point in his life, Jerry Potts was a respected and rich man with a substantial herd of fine stock in his corral. While the assortment of markings on their rumps no doubt made some of their former owners suspicious of his trading partners, no one would question Potts' trading acumen. But when Bear Child decided to re-enter the White world once again, he surrendered some of his Blackfoot persona forever. Knowingly or not, he would be abetting a process that would bring the northern tribes of his mother's homeland to their knees.

Chapter 6

The Kainai: Bear Child's People

There are different schools of thought on when and how the Blackfoot Confederacy evolved on the Great Plains. Their formidable Siksika chief, Crowfoot, claimed that they had always been there. Others speculate that the Kainai (Blood), who along with the Siksika (Blackfoot) and Pikani (Peigan/Piegan) made up the powerful confederacy known as the Blackfoot Nation, were of Algonquian origin. It is believed they migrated from the eastern forests in the early 1700s and were the vanguard of the Algonquian tribes who established camps in the woodlands of central Saskatchewan. About the same time, the Cheyenne and Arapaho moved southwest, ultimately helping to establish the Algonquian tribes as the foremost group on the continent. Their nomadic ways gradually took the Blackfoot tribes farthest west, with some camps extending into the foothills of the Rocky Mountains. "There they found themselves fighting with the Crees to the northward, and with the Crows to the south to maintain their hunting grounds [extending] from the Red Deer River south to the Missouri and Yellowstone."[1]

When they arrived on the Plains, according to their own traditions, the original tribe that shared a common language

The Blood medicine pipe, represented in the chapter heading above, symbolizes both the ritualistic nature of the Blackfoot Confederacy and the life of Bear Child. In the many exchanges during his life when Jerry Potts would act as interpreter between tribal chiefs and Whites, it was the passing of the pipe that formalized the beginning of peaceful conversation.

separated into three groups to guard their newly acquired territory. Since Peigan is likely derived from *pegenow*, meaning "muddy water," this tribe probably settled near the South Saskatchewan or one of its tributaries. The Blackfoot name is linked to the colour of their moccasins, burnished by the residue of prairie fires.

The Kainai were known for a tendency to splinter into small groups of one or two families. Legend has it that one visitor to a camp asked to speak to their chief, and everyone claimed to be the head of the tribe. The visitor called them *akainai*, "the tribe of many chiefs." That name was adopted by the tribe until it became more commonly referred to as the Bloods. A tribal history prepared over 50 years ago by S.H. Middleton (honoured with the Blood title Chief Mountain), at the request of Blood Chief Shot-on-Both-Sides, included an attempt to explain the origins of the name "Blood" and, interestingly, brought Prince Maximilian into the story. According to Middleton, "Maximilian of Wied states that before [they] divided into separate bands: The Siksika, Kainai and Peigans were encamped in the vicinity of five or six tipis of the Kutenais ... Though the Peigans opposed it some of the Kainai killed the Kutenai, took their scalps, stained their faces and hands with blood and then returned. Disputes arose in consequence of this cruel action; the [tribes] separated from each other, the murderers receiving the name "the Bloods."[2] Truth or fiction, it is a colourful story.

Population estimates of the three main Blackfoot nations at various times in the 19th century vary. Likewise, opinions differ regarding the strength of these tribes' affiliation with the Sarcee and Gros Ventre, often identified as part of the Confederacy, but speaking a different dialect. These two tribes made up about 20 percent of the warriors that ruled the grasslands east of the Rockies, from the Missouri plains to the north arm of the Saskatchewan River.

Bear Child's mother was of the Kainai or Blood nation, which was known for its fragmented infrastructure of different camps made up of extended domestic families, each with its nominal band leader. These families eventually found their place voluntarily within a hierarchy of subtribes. They had a communal lifestyle and little sense of private property. Their social order was determined by band chiefs, who met often to deal with common issues.

The senior Blood chiefs would then take counsel with head chiefs from the other members of the Confederacy. After acquiring horses from the south and guns from the Hudson's Bay Company traders to the north, the Confederacy grew very powerful and was soon feared by all other tribes around its members. Their raiding and warring traditions were more often than not the cause of hostilities between themselves and the Cree, Assiniboine, Sioux, Crow, Nez Percé, and, eventually, the U.S. Army.

By 1830 the Blackfoot were looked upon by White expansionists in the United States as a real obstacle. For 25 years, after Captain Lewis of the Lewis and Clark 1804–06 transcontinental expedition shot and killed two Blackfoot warriors, the entire Confederacy had treated the Whites as its enemy. This was a true confederation of 15,000 independent, suspicious people proud of their warlike ways, contemptuous of all outsiders, and disparaging toward the gods and goods of the White man.

There was one trade good that commanded their attention, however, and it would spell disaster: firewater.

The Blackfoot way of life depended on the buffalo, and they hunted it by different methods, depending on the country in which they found themselves. If steep cliffs were nearby, the Bloods would herd the buffalo toward the jump, driving the animals over the bluffs and finishing them off below with spears and arrows. Another method was the surround, whereby the men stalked the herd on foot and quietly downed the best animals while the passive herd grazed and milled about. The run, which pitted horse, rider, and arrow against the thundering buffalo, was the third method—and the one preferred by the Bloods, horsemen that they were.

While tribal custom has often sought to keep their rituals private within the various Blackfoot tribes, much about their ways has been shared with White confidants over the years, especially among the Kainai in southern Alberta. Deeply religious, the Bloods, who made their homes between the Belly and St. Mary's rivers, worshipped the sun, moon, stars, and the powers of animals. From these deities they derived their medicine, which was carried in a medicine bag and consisted of sacred objects that conferred power or magic on the wearer. Their rituals and ceremonies included prayers and great feasting and dancing. They formed a circle to smoke the pipe that, to all Blackfoot tribes, was not a sign of peace, but rather a religious gesture whereby they acknowledged the presence of the Great Spirit and asked his blessing for the occasion at hand.

The Blood ceremonies paid homage to Napi Naató si, or the Creator Sun. Legend said Napi Naató si delivered to them, through a young woman, sacred bundles and ceremonial rites to guide their spiritual life. The most important day of every year was when all the Blood people congregated on the plains below the slopes of the Belly Buttes (Mookowanssini) to perform and celebrate the Sun Dance. Here young men came of age, sliced buffalo tongues were offered up to Napi Naató si, and the "real people" (as the highly confident Blood tribesmen had always called themselves) rejoiced in their communal acts of faith.[3]

Many Spotted Horses, head of the Many Fat Horses band, took Jerry Potts' mother, Crooked Back, into his lodges after she left Fort McKenzie and returned to her people. Potts was about 17 at the time this chief signed the American Blackfoot treaty, and it is quite plausible that Jerry (soon to become Bear Child) joined the Blood entourage on their return to a winter camp on the Belly River.

In this setting, under the leadership of band chief Many Spotted Horses, Crooked Back and the Blood band that she called her family welcomed young Jerry Potts into their lodge and taught him their ways. He joined the annual pilgrimage to Belly Buttes, listened to the legends, and learned why warriors young and old ascended into the shadows of Chief Mountain and climbed its slope in search of inner strength.

Chief Mountain, young Jerry had been told, was a sacred place to the Kainai people. It honoured a war chief who had lost his life in battle. After his body was returned to his lodge, his young wife, inconsolable and mad with grief, spent days roaming the camp, blindly calling his name. Then one day, clutching her baby, she climbed the mountain and threw herself and her child onto the rocks below. Tribesmen carried her husband's body to her and buried the entire family at the base of what became Ninaiistako, or Chief Mountain.[4]

The flat mountaintop could be seen from many locations, and it became one of the main landmarks Jerry Potts used to confirm his bearings as he travelled the prairie. He, like many Blood warriors, had climbed the slopes and rested his head on a buffalo skull, questing for visions and dreams that would help guide him in his daily life.

The Sun Dance ritual also had a profound effect on Bear Child. One year, when the whole Blood nation had gathered its tipis at Belly Buttes, a sacred Sun Dance lodge was built amid endless feasting and dancing. Here secret ceremonies were conducted to demonstrate the will and strength of the tribe's warriors, in which the young braves would prove their courage and endurance through flagellation and self-mutilation. Some would cut slits across their chests, suspend themselves from ropes tied to the lodge poles, then dance to the entrancing beat of drums until they pulled themselves free of the ropes. Some would string a heavy buffalo to their backs and drag it until their own flesh was torn open. And some would tie one end of a rope around their torsos and the other end to a horse. Clinging to the rope's taut length, they would allow their bodies to be towed through the dust.

In addition to sun worship, the Kainai "also had a lesser, mysterious, more homely deity who they called *Napi*, the Old Man."[5] Any natural mystery they did not understand was attributed to Napi. One river that magically sprang out of the foothills of the Porcupine Hills became The-River-the-Old-Man-Played-On. It was near a ford of this river, where the Blackfoot's traditional trail north crossed, that many of the great Sun Dances were held.

In the Blood camp warring and raiding were considered honourable ways to earn respect. Raids for scalps and horses were attended by great ceremony, all participants painted and dressed in their finery for a celebratory dance.

On the battlefield the highest honour was given to a man who wrested a gun from an enemy; this was counted as a bloodless coup. Wresting a medicine shield, bow, or war bonnet from an adversary ranked close behind. Next was taking a scalp, and finally stealing horses.

The Bloods followed this way of life for more than 100 years before it was disrupted by the coming of the White man. And when the missionaries of different Christian faiths preached their gospel, it was not always met with favour. One Blood chief told Archdeacon S.H. Middleton, "We listen to your words about your Ten Commandments ... Long before you Holy White Men ... came here, we had five laws of our own; ... we keep our five better than you keep your ten." It was "a code of morals and ethics almost Spartan in its simplicity."[6]

Firstly, the Bloods "always demanded a life for a life. Two—theft; the thief had to restore the stolen goods. Three—adultery; an ear was cut off for the first offence, both ears and added punishment for subsequent offences; Fourth—cowardice; the person was clothed in woman's garb ... Fifth — treachery; ... shot at sight."[7]

Before the men of cloth, the first to make their presence felt were the Hudson's Bay Company's rugged Scottish traders and their voyageurs, who swept onto the prairies in search of commerce. Led by tough, penny-pinching factors, whose progress and success were measured only by trade and profit, the HBC managers were far more experienced and sophisticated in their dealings with the Aboriginals than were the traders to the south. Blankets, foodstuffs, utensils, tools, and guns were the main barter goods. Only twice a year, at the end of the two main hunting seasons, was liquor available at the fort for Natives who arrived with their beaver or buffalo pelts. In the vast territory that predated Canadian expansion, the HBC was the law and it was through its management that firewater played only a small role in the fur trade.

In the western U.S. the American Fur Company contained the situation for almost 30 years, although competition from independents became an excuse to join the whiskey trade. Many of the AFC's transgressions have been documented, but compared to what lay ahead, Kenneth McKenzie's Fort Union moonshine and the occasional wagonload of rotgut that got by government officials were insignificant.

For the Blackfoot way of life, the worst was yet to come. The events that unfolded between the Upper Missouri and South Saskatchewan rivers in the two decades after 1864 would almost destroy their culture. Ironically, one of the key factors in this decimation was the attempt to bring law and order to the Montana Territory in 1864.

To an extent, at that time the future of the United States was in doubt. Political will was pushing and tugging all peoples in different directions. The year 1863 had started with President Lincoln freeing all the slaves in the Union. Two months later, freedom of choice was put on hold when Lincoln signed his Conscription Act, forcing all able men to enlist in his army. On the same day, Congress banished all Natives from the state of Kansas.

By July 4, 1863, 40,000 bodies were rotting in the cornfields around Gettysburg, and Robert E. Lee's Confederate Army was shattered. The madness continued through 1864, as the ruthless General William Sherman wreaked havoc on Georgia, burning Atlanta to the ground and taking Savannah on Christmas Eve. Less than four months later, on April 9, 1865, Commander-in-Chief Ulysses Grant and his president enjoyed a hollow victory, as food rations were served to the starving, grey-coated "Johnny Rebs," many with tears in their eyes as they saw the last of their anguished general, Robert E. Lee. The next week Abraham Lincoln was assassinated, and America would never be the same.

The overspill of cruelty and resentment that lies at the end of a civil war seeped into the West. With the value of life greatly diminished, a new type of settler crossed the Mississippi—one with little tolerance for any Aboriginal that stood in his way.

Extending army posts into the Dakota and Montana territories was both a military and political solution for the brain trust of Washington. Protection of settlers meshed well with a patronage plan that would provide successful army officers with both job security and new battles to fight. The demise of the American Fur Company and the arrival of the U.S. Cavalry at Fort Benton marked the beginning of a new era. Many fort owners were most happy to sell their declining palisades to the military, often at a nice profit.

And although the army was intended to protect both Whites on their homesteads and Natives on their reservations, America's Manifest Destiny policy was about to rear its head in the form of devil-may-care whiskey traders and the dark side of entrepreneurship.

Chapter 7

The Whiskey Scourge

To say that Bear Child succumbed to the whiskey trade may be too harsh a judgement. But in the five years after Fort Benton established its own brand of law and order in 1864, Potts managed to adapt along with the ever-changing town. Able to pass seamlessly between two different worlds, he found his way as horse trader, hunting guide, interpreter, or dependable scout. But Jerry Potts was no stranger to whiskey, and he and his pal, George Star, were regular customers in the saloons of Fort Benton by the mid-1860s. To a certain extent, whiskey drinking separated men from boys, and Jerry and George threw back their share of Double Anchor whiskey and lined up with the men.

Whiskey was never far away from any celebration or most arguments in Fort Benton, and it took on new importance as a commodity after Isaac Baker and Tom Power came to town. Baker had arrived at the fort as the last American Fur Company chief trader, but had left the fur trade behind once the original Fort Benton was sold, and had invested in a boatload of inventory in the spring of 1866. He opened the first significant general store on the town's main street and also wholesaled to independent wagon owners who bartered goods with the Blackfoot and Crow. Within a year Baker had his first outpost among the Piegans on the Marias River, and about the same time he welcomed to town a man who would become his chief competition. Tom Power adopted his own way of conducting business, but they agreed that the frontier was

Two years after Baker's store opened, Tom (left) and John Power started the Fort Benton enterprise that greatly expanded the import of whiskey via Missouri riverboats. Tom would eventually fund construction of Fort Whoop-up north of the Medicine Line.

big enough for both of them and became friendly rivals. In his dealings over time, Power demonstrated the flexibility of his ethics. Records suggest that the Indian agent of the day, George Wright, became a regular supplier of stock to local stores, using inventory from the federal government's annuity goods, earmarked for the Blackfoot community, to pay off personal debts.[1]

The reciprocity of this cozy arrangement related to Wright's vision. His eyesight seemed to fail regularly if a wagon of whiskey was seen heading in the direction of a Blackfoot camp.

Given the vast quantities of whiskey that managed to flow upriver, it was quite amazing how little was recorded on the books of the town's leading merchants.

Ship captains on the Missouri steadily increased their cargoes of both legitimate and contraband whiskey as restrictive laws became increasingly unenforceable. One Indian agent wrote his commissioner, "Every year since steamboats first came [to Fort Benton] trading has been carried on by officers ... whiskey and ammunition being the main articles traded for robes."[2]

In 1867, 43 different steamboats left St. Louis for the upper river forts, delivering full slates of passengers and 8,000 tons of freight, only a quarter of which went to the military. The human influx was further abetted by the direct line from Chicago to the new railhead located at Sioux City on the Missouri. Steamers starting from this point could cut six weeks off the round-trip time to St. Louis. The biggest problem all captains faced was the growing hostility of Sioux raiding parties, who targeted river travel in their growing resistance to the White invasion. The average boat burned 24 to 30 cords of wood per day to keep the boilers going and that meant teams of men had to go ashore to cut firewood. Knowing this routine, the Sioux made it their favourite point of attack.

On July 1, the same day that four former British colonies to the north completed their peaceful formation of the Dominion of Canada, General William Sherman announced a new plan to contain the Sioux peoples on a reservation west of the Missouri and north of Nebraska. The next month a reservation that approximately matched the modern boundaries of South Dakota was defined "for the exclusive use of the Sioux nation of Indians."[3] With an estimated 10,000 Whites using the Missouri River during the travel season, Sherman also ordered General Alfred Terry, commanding officer of the Department of Dakota, to build a series of army posts beyond the recently completed Fort Buford to the Sun River in Montana. Buford was at the mouth of the Yellowstone River near the rapidly deteriorating Fort Union that, by then, was also government property.

The fort that had been Kenneth McKenzie's pride and joy suffered a final ignominy in August when the kitchen was razed and the wooden walls carried to the steamboat *Miner* to burn as fuel along the journey to Fort Benton. In the words of one writer, "The postwar wave of immigration lapped at the edges of the river country ... and gave every indication that the Manifest Destiny had lost none of its vigor. By the spring of 1868 a new rush of homesteaders was underway."[4] At this same time, Fort Benton's two main traders, Baker and Power, plus a number of smaller outfits with whiskey at the ready, were trading on the Marias River. Much to their surprise, a Piegan chief they encountered had no use for them. At least three competing trade wagons were sent packing before Isaac Baker's traders made a final plea for co-operation to the respected Piegan head, Mountain Chief. The chief was resolute in his stance and as they left, he told them not to stop until they got to Fort Benton.[5]

Anxious to keep the fire-water away from his braves, he visited the fort and explained to a federal official that his village would bring robes to the fort if they wished to trade. "We want the new traders to act like the old men who traded long ago," he said. "We do not wish these pale faces to come to our villages ... There is nothing in common between us."[6]

That was not the first time Mountain Chief had spoken to government authorities about whiskey. Earlier that summer, after visiting the Benton Indian agent to report unwanted whiskey traders on his reservation, the Piegan elder was roughed up and run out of town by rowdy locals. The agent protested the treatment, but neither the local justice nor the sheriff would act. Having suffered other indignities that year, the Piegans had had their fill of insults and avenged their chief by stealing 80 horses from a mining community.

In October 1855, Alexander Culbertson, acting as an agent of the government, and his wife, Natawista, were instrumental in getting the Bloods and other Blackfoot chiefs to sit in a treaty council at Fort Benton aimed at assuring peace among the tribes and providing safe passage for the Northern Pacific Railroad survey crews to work their way west.

It was ironic that the town of Fort Benton was actually expanding across lands defined as part of the Blackfoot reservation in the original treaty signed in 1855. The treaty process the federal government embarked upon in the 1850s did little to delay the inevitable stampede of White immigrants onto Aboriginal lands. In 1851 alone, Washington representatives signed 18 treaties in

The Bloods' head chief at the time of the treaty was Natawista's brother, Seen From Afar (left), sketched here by treaty attendee Gustavus Sohon. He drew portraits of many of the chiefs who attended the Fort Benton treaty talks, including Mountain Chief (right), who would later be blamed for almost any ill deed that occurred north of the Upper Missouri River.

the new state of California, which was being overrun with gold seekers. That same year, Alexander Culbertson hosted the Upper Missouri delegation at the sitting where the Fort Laramie treaty was endorsed by the Lakota, Cheyenne, Arapaho, Crow, Mandan, Arikara, Assiniboine, and Gros Ventres. Designed to divide the prairie into separate tracts for the various nations and end intertribal warfare, the treaty also allowed for roads and military forts to be built by the government. Each tribe was to receive an annual stipend of $50,000 worth of supplies. Forts and connecting roads were built, but the system quickly fell apart. Officials, not understanding the Native hierarchy, soon found that chiefs who had signed these treaties had limited control over their lodges, many of which ignored any restrictions. The treaty process suffered further as Washington's promised goods and supplies fell into the hands of corrupt regional officials, who sold them to traders rather than delivering them to the intended tribes. The goods might eventually end up in an Indian lodge, but it would be in exchange for buffalo robes.

Frustration with the Fort Laramie treaty came to a head within three years over a single calf rustled by a Lakota warrior. Although the warrior's chief, Conquering Bear, offered restitution —as the treaty called for—a zealous cavalry troop confronted the encampment, and the ensuing battle led to heavy losses on both sides. The army responded with a stronger force that killed 86 warriors and removed most of the women and children from the camp. The Lakota would never trust the Whites again.

When it came to rerouting supplies meant for the Aboriginals, the same skullduggery was at work in Fort Benton many years later. In 1867 the aforementioned Indian agent, George Wright, proudly boasted of his actions to a local citizen who had watched Wright pocket $800 in exchange for 400 agency blankets. When Wright's practices gained further notoriety and he came under investigation, the same citizen's deposition stated that he saw Wright "furnish [traders] with what I judged to be 2500 dollars worth of Indian annuity goods which were taken to the Blackfoot camp and traded for robes ... about 100 robes were counted out to Mr. Wright who told me they were his share ... Mr. Wright told me that he sold those robes and got money for them."[7] Wright was soon replaced.

Corruption alone may have been controllable, but the flood of humanity was unstoppable. By then an additional 4 million immigrants had made their way across the Atlantic. Those who had disembarked only to be conscripted into the Union army were now war-weary veterans heading west. If they made Fort Benton with a wagon and a load of whiskey, they could get rich in a hurry. Having already overcome so much, many men were willing to take their chances in Blackfoot country.

So in 1868, with the influx of settlers and the growing number of roaming whiskey traders, the government chose not only to ignore its treaty promises, but also to expand further onto the reservation. Rejecting Mountain Chief's pleas to restrict all White men from his reservation, the federal agent licensed two traders to set up forts on the Teton and Marias rivers. The lone condition of the approval was assurance that they would not trade whiskey. Relatively honourable men, John Riplinger of the Northwest Fur Company and Isaac

Isaac Baker & Co.'s success was largely due to the Conrad brothers, who came to Fort Benton in 1868. Charles, 18, and older brother William (right) were Confederate Army veterans from Virginia. Seven years later, the athletic and fearless Charles assumed the lucrative NWMP account as his own.

Baker's delegate, William Conrad, became first-hand witnesses to a chaotic winter while stationed at their outposts.

Riplinger complained that whiskey traders constantly intercepted Blackfoot tribesmen headed his way, filling them with rotgut and garnering their robes. Yet trade flourished at the Baker fort, and William Conrad's efforts yielded a $40,000 profit before spring—even though many wagon traders positioned themselves strategically along Blackfoot travel routes to ply their whiskey and intercept the bounty of robes.

Firmly ensconced that winter amid the growing chaos, at his camp of eight lodges on the Marias River, Jerry Potts also witnessed the deterioration first-hand. Once-proud Piegan hunters who had relinquished their robes only to later awaken from a drunken stupor now floundered under a burden of guilt while their families starved. Whiskey and remorse seemed to flow as relentlessly as the Marias itself.

In Fort Benton, the Montana Territory's Indian Affairs superintendent, W.J. Cullen, took steps to regain control by replacing his tainted agent, Wright, with Nathaniel Pope. "The whiskey trade is carried on at Benton ... to a fearful extent," wrote Pope in his first report to Cullen.[8] The superintendent himself would tell Washington legislators, "There is hardly an Indian camp in that part of the country that is not now being reached by these whiskey Traders." Cullen added, referring to fort operators Riplinger and Conrad, both of whom had $5,000 bonds posted to ensure they would not trade whiskey from their licensed forts, "Traders in their territory who refuse to furnish them with whiskey are threatened with violence. This bad state of affairs ... is believed to be entirely owing to the introduction of poisonous whiskey by bad men who ... rob them of all means of support for their families."[9]

Enough malice had been generated over the years that every new *Fort Benton Record* editorial attacking some Blackfoot action fuelled local animosity toward all tribes. As the antagonism grew and the U.S. Army established a stronger presence in Montana, and as the region's buffalo disappeared, a new trading plan unfolded. Go north! Not only were all the buffalo and the Blackfoot hunters to the north; beyond the border there were no laws.

The exact sequence of events that led Jerry Potts to the notorious Fort Whoop-up in late December 1869 is a matter of conjecture, but five relevant facts are known. Potts had chosen to send his wife back to her Crow people along with his son, possibly to remove them from the deteriorating conditions on the Marias while he was absent. The army and responsible Indian agents like Cullen and Pope were hell-bent on confining the whiskey trade in Montana. There was a new sheriff in town named William Wheeler, and he was beholden to nobody. With the upheaval as it was in Montana Territory, the Blood and Siksika hunters were staying north of the border, doing most of their trading with the HBC in a peaceful climate. Finally, there was no doubt that any expedition heading toward the traditional homeland of the Blood people would benefit from having a hunter, interpreter, and respected sub-chief of Jerry Potts' stature on its side.

Chapter 8

Fort Whoop-up

In the autumn of 1869, Jerry Potts signed on to cross the Medicine Line and help feed the builders of what would become Fort Whoop-up. Money to build the new fort—to be called Fort Hamilton—came from the coffers of Tom Power, a man with grand ambitions, dubious scruples, and a warehouse full of whiskey. The two builders he agreed to bankroll were partners of convenience with contrasting backgrounds. Alfred Hamilton was a nephew of Power's main competitor, Isaac Baker, and a member of the Montana legislature. He had many friends among the Piegan people through his marriage to a chief's daughter and had been trading with various Blackfoot tribes since 1865.

His 29-year-old senior partner, John Healy, had come west to do a brief stint with the army before leaving to chase gold in Washington, Idaho, and as far north as Fort Edmonton, where his Irish soul nurtured his strong dislike of the Hudson's Bay Company and anything British. Healy then managed a farm along the route from Benton to Helena before he and brother Joe started their own store on the Sun River. There he quickly learned the benefits of whiskey as a commodity.

The Healy brothers, gold ever upon their minds, were by this time convinced that a motherlode lay somewhere near the headwaters of the Saskatchewan River or elsewhere in the Rockies and they were intent on finding it. The fact that John and Joe called their company the Saskatchewan Mining, Prospecting &

Trading Outfit suggests that they were planning to hit pay dirt in one form or another. After pulling a few strings among government friends, the Healys gained permission to cross the Blackfoot reservation with their trade goods and headed for the British territories to the north. This was a land in limbo, claimed by the representatives of Queen Victoria as part of her empire but without either law or enforcement.

John J. Healy was a feisty Fenian who never forgave the NWMP for ending the lucrative whiskey trade. A man of many sides, he adopted a mixed-blood orphan after his parents were killed on Healy's Sun River ranch. The boy went on to become a respected chief of the Blood nation.

Healy and Hamilton acknowledged their debt to Tom Power by signing a series of notes. They then used most of the money to buy the tools, supplies, and trade goods they would need from Power's warehouse to start their fort. To shore up their respectability, Hamilton managed to gain a mandate from government officials to investigate a rumour that stolen U.S. horses and mules were being traded to the HBC by a party of Bloods who found great sport in relieving Montana of some of its finest stock.

As the Healy brothers, Hamilton, and some business associates (John Largent, Martin Donavan, Pat Haney, and Bob Mills) turned their wagons north, two mixed-bloods rode with them—Jerry Potts and George Star had been hired on as hunters to keep the new fort in fresh meat through the winter.

The three-week trip covered 160 miles and took them to the mouth of the St. Mary's River where it joined the Belly River (south of modern-day Lethbridge, Alberta). In bitterly cold conditions, and travelling with some Blood hunters they had met en route, the expedition leaders sought out the influential Blood chief Many Spotted Horses, who was known to winter near the Belly. John Healy not only brought the chief gifts and fair payment to gather wood, but he also secured from Many Spotted Horses' lodge a "winter wife," thought to be a daughter of the chief. When all was said and done, Healy also gained permission to build a trading fort.

In the next week, a semicircle of crude log huts linked by a series of flimsy picket fences formed the beginnings of the fort. The trading room was little more than the tailgate of a wagon. As Healy's workforce plugged away, word came to them through their new Blood friends of two new horrors south of the Medicine Line.

Rumours of Blackfoot treachery, fuelled by the editorial rhetoric of the *Fort Benton Record* and *Helena Daily Herald* newspapers, were running rampant in Montana, some even claiming that the Healy party had been ambushed by Piegans. Mountain Chief, the leader who had pleaded with Indian agents to keep traders out of his camp, continued to be painted as a notorious villain. In August 1869, his son, Owl Child, who had been publicly whipped after a dispute with rancher Malcolm Clarke, set out to exact revenge. Clarke was killed at his ranch and his son, Horace, was seriously wounded. Across Montana there was an outcry for military action.

At this time the U.S. Army was in its fourth year on the western plains under the command of General Philip H. Sheridan. In the past two years, despite War Department promises to leave a substantial chunk of Dakota for the exclusive use of the Sioux, the general had watched an endless tide of White farmers stream onto the land. While over two-thirds of the estimated 36,000 Sioux west of the Missouri remained on reservations, the other third, largely the powerful Teton Sioux, led by Sitting Bull and Black Moon, had moved west into Montana, intent on escaping the white influx. For Sheridan there was no telling how the Sioux and Blackfoot tribes would respond to the diminishment of their lands.

Sheridan's ultimate solution was to bring peace to the West with a simple, deadly philosophy: Eradication was his common answer and his orders were succinct. Kill or hang all warriors, he instructed George Custer while issuing orders to attack one Cheyenne camp. At the beginning of 1870, it was the Piegans on the Marias River who had earned Sheridan's wrath, and mercy was the farthest thing from his mind when he telegraphed Fort Shaw on January 15: "If the lives and property of the citizens of Montana can best be protected by striking Mountain Chief's band, I want them struck. Tell Baker to strike them hard."[1]

Colonel Eugene Baker headed north, blood in his eye. He attacked the first Piegan camp he came to, only to discover later that it was the home of the friendly chief Heavy Runner. His troops were merciless, killing almost 200 women and children and even the unarmed chief himself. They burned the village and confiscated 300 of the tribe's horses to take back to Fort Shaw. In the middle of winter, orphaned children and injured, starving, and sick women and elders were left to fend for themselves. Alexander Culbertson, who was by then in his declining years but still trading in the area, bore witness to the after-effects of what became known as the Baker or Marias Massacre.[2] As they tried to escape further horror and head north, Culbertson noted that "a very large number of squaws and children died on the way, from the severe cold weather, and from Small Pox which they had at the time."[3]

The dreaded smallpox had returned and it was purportedly due to "the malevolence of a single white man. An American trader named Evans and his partner had trouble with the Blackfoot in 1868, the partner being slain and all their horses stolen."[4] Swearing revenge, Evans went to St. Louis and purchased "several bales of blankets infected with smallpox, he set them out on the banks of the Missouri, and the plague swept through the tribes like wildfire. The Blackfoot tribe alone lost nearly 1400 men, women and children in five months—truly, a life for a life, with a vengeance."[5]

The disease that had wiped out two-thirds of the Blackfoot Confederacy in 1837 had been effectively turned into a weapon of germ warfare by a single killer. Since that time, Alexander Culbertson, who had played a less villainous but equally deadly role in the earlier epidemic, had enjoyed a lengthy and successful career as a frontier diplomat and chief trader of the American Fur Company, "the company's most important man when McKenzie retired."[6] Less fulfillment came from a retirement to Peoria, Illinois, where bad business decisions had pushed him into bankruptcy. The setback forced him and his wife of almost 30 years back to Montana.

Culbertson had won wide respect from many of the Plains tribes and at least one Jesuit priest, Father Pierre Jean de Smet, who described him as "a distinguished man, endowed with a mild, benevolent, and charitable temper, though if need be, intrepid and courageous."[7] His marriage to the daughter of Blood chief Two Suns, Nayoyistsiksina' (Holy Snake) or Natawista as she was more widely known, had placed the couple at the forefront of many efforts to forge peace with various tribes across the Plains. Natawista's dedication to easing the Blackfoot plight and her influence on federal officials who were trying to bring lasting peace to her people had earned her great respect across the West. Historically, Smithsonian anthropologist John Ewers ranks her with Lewis and Clark's Shoshone guide Sacagawea as a significant female contributor to the furthering of relations between two disparate cultures.

Whether it was due to the frustrations of fighting a hopeless battle against the demise of the Aboriginals, or his dark secret of long ago—insisting that Alexander Harvey bring his disease-ridden goods into Fort McKenzie more than three decades earlier—Culbertson's return to Montana had not been easy. That he was working for John Riplinger in a small fort near the border suggests that the Culbertsons had fallen upon hard times in the winter of 1869. They would get harder still; he was drinking heavily and about to lose Natawista.

Natawista had witnessed and endorsed the Fort Laramie treaty of 1851, and seeing the atrocities committed against the Blackfoot and other nations since then could not help but disillusion her. Conquering Bear and 85 Lakota followers from his village were gunned down because of a dead calf. A decade later, word spread to Montana that a Colonel Kit Carson had overrun the Navajo in the southwest and herded 8,000 people across New Mexico to an arid reservation on the Pecos River. That same year, Chief Black Kettle's Cheyenne encampment near their Sand Creek reservation in Colorado was attacked at dawn by the vigilante force of the "Fighting Parson," John M. Chivington. Two hundred men, women, and children were killed, many still in their beds.

Then General Philip Sheridan entered the fray and a new round of unworkable treaties established more reservations and new restrictions against the nomadic traditions so integral to tribal life. Constant frustrations on both sides led to endless clashes as the U.S. Army, with superior firepower, continued to take over the West. In 1868, Sheridan sent an ambitious underling with flowing golden locks and a burgeoning ego against the Cheyenne in present-day Oklahoma. Black Kettle, who had moved his remaining people farther south after Chivington's attack, would not survive a second strike. Responding to Sheridan's directive, Colonel George Armstrong Custer had the Washita River running red with Cheyenne blood, killing Black Kettle and at least 100 more, both young and old.

For Natawista and Alexander Culbertson, the Baker Massacre, latest in a series of tragedies, was the death knell for all they had cherished and more than the marriage could withstand.

The couple's biographer, Lesley Wischmann, describes the result. "Their youngest child, Joe, called Natawista's departure 'the downfall of my dear old dad.' He tried for several years to get her to come back but she wouldn't. I think her heart was broken and she couldn't live in the White man's world anymore."[8]

By the time of Baker's vicious attack, Natawista had been back in Montana for more than two years, and the onslaught of wagons bearing poisonous firewater must have dispelled any fond memories of earlier days. "She was, after all, the founding mother of Fort Benton," Wischmann reminds us. "She had been queen there since the mid-1840s. But when they came back in 1867, Fort Benton was a rough-and-tumble town. Indian scalps were legal tender in the bars, Natawista's cousin was shot down by other Piegans because he was too friendly with the Whites, one of their friends came to visit and was shot down in the street by Whites, another was killed and thrown into a well ... and then the Marias Massacre."[9]

Culbertson, the lifelong diplomat, had apparently tried to stave off the Baker attack, but was ignored—a final affront to a man whose opinion had once been highly respected. He crawled farther into the bottle and Natawista made her own escape, finding in John Riplinger a conduit north. Son Joe ruefully reminisced 50 years after the schism, "After my father had done everything in the world for my mother, ... she went off with a man by the name of John Riplinger."[10]

Wischmann concludes, "I came to understand why she went back to the Bloods; I was less able to understand why he didn't go with her. I think he couldn't face life in the Indian camps permanently. He stayed on the Upper Missouri and worked as interpreter and general fount of wisdom … until shortly after the Battle of Little Big Horn when he went down to his daughter's where he died in 1879."[11]

Natawista became a respected elder who found her way to the lodges of her nephew, the great Blood chief Red Crow. She was back in the same culture where Jerry Potts' mother, Crooked Back, also resided. While Natawista would live until 1894, the fate of Crooked Back was more immediate and tied to the dreaded flow of firewater; it would change the ways of her son forever.

Early in its history, the makeshift Fort Hamilton was burned by its unhappy Blackfoot customers. Undeterred, Healy and Hamilton used the profits of their first winter season to retain respected carpenter William Gladstone to rebuild a more substantial structure in 1870 that would soon become known as Fort Whoop-up.

With a crew of 40, kept well fed through the hunting exploits of Potts and George Star, Gladstone turned a glade of cottonwoods into a 130-by-140-foot stockade. The new fort was built of heavy rectangular logs, with two bastions on opposite corners covered with earth roofs, each armed with a brass cannon. The walls were set with loopholes for guns, and one had a heavy wooden gate. To the right of the gate were three barred wickets through which trading was done. The interior was designed with spacious rooms and high fireplaces and had a blacksmith shop, cookhouse, storehouses, and living quarters.

A steady influx of Blood and Peigan hunters, their travois laden with buffalo hides, came to the fort and shoved the robes through the wickets. In exchange the Blackfoot received tobacco, salt, sugar, flour, tea, axes, knives, blankets, calico, and trinkets such as wire, beads, and silver ornaments. They also received repeating rifles and whiskey. These last two were to prove a deadly combination.

Although Potts had a taste for firewater himself, at Fort Whoop-up he was exposed to the full extent of the devastation it was causing his people. It was also clear that for a trader to stay in business, he had to trade whiskey: when trading for food and provisions, the Blackfoot were hard bargainers, but when whiskey was available, they would offer a pile of hides for just one bottle.

The concoction was a foul and often fatal brew that the traders passed off as whiskey. The staple recipe called for a quart of watered whiskey, a pound of chewing tobacco, a handful of red pepper, a bottle of Jamaica ginger, and a quart of either blackstrap molasses or red ink to give the desired colour for either rum or whiskey.

Not all families were cursed by the craving for whiskey, but even those chiefs who were able to control many of their braves could face problems. It took only a few rowdies to trigger chaos. Drunken quarrels and savage fights would break out in the camps, often ending in death. At other times, whole camps would erupt into drunken orgies of violence, with friends and brothers turning on one another. Men would sell their wives and sisters for a cupful of the fiery brew. Those driven out of their senses by it would try to scale the walls of the fort, only to be pushed off by long poles that

Here Fort Whoop-up's cannon is secure inside the palisade, aimed at the front gate should any unwelcome intruder choose to enter. John Healy's quarters plus a blacksmith, two stores, and five other dwellings were crammed inside the walls.

were kept close at hand for just that purpose. Even the chimney had to be secured after one attempt by a thirsty drunk to get inside the fort by sliding down it.

For the Bloods who lingered near Fort Whoop-up during its first season, it was whiskey that defined their year. The Kainai practice, called the winter count, was to name each year based on its most significant event. An oral tradition, the count was also recorded in pictographs drawn on treasured pieces of rawhide. The record of Blood chief Manistokos, or Father of Many Children, depicts that 1869 was known as *Keayyetapissiw otsitsetoworpi,* or "Joining the Bear, being drunk, rushes through the camp and kills many." The following year would mark a second wave of tragedy. The year 1870 was simply *Apinosin,* or "smallpox."[12]

In the fall of 1869, a Piegan from the south brought the dreaded smallpox to the Blackfoot camps of the Canadian Plains. As they began to fall sick, the old ones among the tribe recognized the terrible plague that had wiped out almost two-thirds of the Blackfoot Confederacy in 1837. They knew the tribe was just as helpless then as it had been 30 years before. By winter, as the epidemic peaked, many leaders panicked and tried to flee the scourge as if it were an evil spirit borne on the wind.

Whole bands caught on the open plains perished in savage blizzards. In the camps, relatives watched loved ones swell up until their features were totally distorted, the stench of their sickness filling the tipis. Others looked on as the victims became disfigured or passed into a raving delirium from which there was no recovery. Young braves killed themselves rather than face disfigurement. Fathers killed their wives and children, then themselves, in order to avoid the agony of the disease.

Sometimes whole camps went mad, recklessly attacking their enemies in a form of mass suicide. Others attacked Fort Whoop-up and tried to give the plague back to the Whites, whom they believed had caused it, by rubbing their sores on the gates, doors, and window bars. They even stacked their dead to the windward of the fort, hoping the air would carry the disease to the Whites barricaded inside. The traders were not immune to the disease but the mortality rate was very low compared to the Indians.

THE WINTER COUNT

Plains Indians kept track of the passing years by means of the winter count. The Blackfoot tribes would usually identify the single most memorable event of the year, and it would forever more be known as such. Both historian Hugh Dempsey (in "A Blackfoot Winter Count") and long-time clergyman S.H. Middleton (in *Indian Chiefs: Ancient and Modern*) concluded that the most complete of the winter counts was maintained by a Blood chief known first to the Whites as Father of Many Children (Manistokos) and later as Bad Head (Pakap-otokan). A superb winter count hide of the Peigan people is displayed near their current reserve in southern Alberta, at the Head-Smashed-In interpretive centre.

This Blood leader of the Buffalo Followers band of about 40 lodges recorded his winter count on a tanned hide, and translations of his descriptive terms later found their way to various institutions, including the Oblate archives in Edmonton and RCMP archives in Ottawa, based on the respective efforts of Father Emile Légal and retired Mountie R.N. Wilson to preserve them.

Their relevance to this story starts about 1830, a year known as *Itsenipitsop* or "when we were freezing"—a very cold winter. The years 1831 and 1832 in the Blood winter count confirm their awareness of the encroachment of the Whites on the Upper Missouri. Fort Piegan's construction was described as "Kipp/when he lived there/where the rivers meet." The following year described David Mitchell's Fort McKenzie with "when he was camped there/Big Knife/where he wintered."

The most telling of all winter counts was in 1837 and was simply called *Apixosin* (Dempsey's spelling) or "smallpox." Another winter count, *Itsosiw*, means "when it ended." This was the epidemic delivered to the Plains via the AFC's *St. Peter's* and is estimated to have killed about 6,000 Blackfoot people between June 1837 and the following spring.

Fort McKenzie was again prominent in the winter count in the year Jerry Potts was most likely born. The fort bourgeois, Alexander Culbertson, is known to have killed a Blood chief in 1838, and that year is translated in Dempsey as "Calf Chief/when he was killed." The atrocities committed in January 1844 by the White man at Fort McKenzie known as Running Wolf (either Alexander Harvey or Francis Chardon) were also to be remembered forever through the winter count.

The following list summarizes years from the Middleton translation of the same Blood winter count. Interestingly, neither the signing of Treaty Seven in 1877 nor the establishment of new Blood reserve boundaries in 1883 merited recognition.

1831: *Kipp otsitsitapipi etotoartay*—A White man, Kipp, establishes a post at the confluence of Bear River and the Missouri.

1837: *Apinosin*—Smallpox.

1844: *Sorkoyenamay sixikay iteskimarpi napekwax*—A White man named Makoyomarkan (Running Wolf) at Benton fired the cannon at a party of Blackfoot and killed 13 of them. (Note: This event would have actually occurred at the original Fort McKenzie, and Running Wolf would most likely refer to the notorious Alexander Harvey, Jerry Potts' stepfather.)

1855: *Itaomitaohoyop*—The Indians are starving and eat their dogs.

1865: *Sikapinosin*—Black smallpox.

1870: *Apinosin*—Smallpox.

1872: *Spitsi napekwax etawpiyaw*—Some White men settle on High River.

1875: *Ennahen otsitotorpi akapioyis*—The police are at Macleod.

1876: *Itsenowatorpi napiorki*—Whiskey trading is stopped.

1877: *Itakainiskoy*—Plenty buffaloes.

1880: *Itsistsitsisawenimiopi*—The buffaloes are no more.

1881: *Itorkoneopatotsop*—All the Indians of the Blackfoot Tribe leave the territories of the States and come to this side of the boundary.

1883: *Mikahestow itsikamapi*—The Crees steal the horses of Red Crow.

1884: *Istsienakas otsitotorpi*—The railroad is built across the country.

1887: *Otsntsennapi-krisahoy ninnan*—The chiefs of the Blackfoot are taken down on a visit to Ottawa.

1889: *Itsaskinapastsimesop*—Epidemic of influenza.

By spring the plague had run its course and the survivors regrouped to count their losses. The Piegans alone had lost 1,000, while the Bloods and Blackfoot had each lost about 600. The Crees, Assiniboines, and Gros Ventres experienced similar losses. The Blackfoot Confederacy, although not completely destroyed, was decimated. What the White man's guns and whiskey had failed to complete in seven years, disease had done in seven months.

The traders, however, suffered subsidiary effects of the disease. In Washington the War Department banned the shipment of all pelts and robes from Fort Benton, so the warehouses stayed full and the cash flow ended abruptly. It was August before the merchant princes Isaac Baker and Tom Power were able to grease the skids and get inventory flowing again. But in the long run, the setback was minor and the Bentonites prepared for another season of prosperity.

With his new storage bins well stocked, John Healy took charge of Fort Whoop-up after Hamilton returned to Sun River, Montana, before winter set in. Healy was a strapping, six-foot Irishman, known as an opportunist deft at the art of exploitation. He lived up to his reputation during his time on the lawless Canadian prairie, ruling with a short fuse and a large reservoir of rotgut. Vociferously anti-British, he flew his own homespun version of the Stars and Stripes above his frontier fortress. Construction continued for another year on the inner buildings, which Healy had designed to form an interior square accessible only through the main portal.

The following summer, when Healy made the 55-mile journey from his Sun River base to visit Benton, he strutted into the main-street bars with a new sense of wealth and smugness in his step, readily accepting any toast to his new-found affluence. While he was prepared for the praise, he was ill-prepared for the copycat crowd that his success would draw. In November, when he returned to Whoop-up, he found that a phalanx of independent whiskey traders had converged on what was fast becoming a debauched hellhole, where the waters of the St. Mary's and Belly rivers merged with an endless flow of rotgut whiskey.

In his documentation of the terrible impact that firewater had on the Blackfoot, Hugh Dempsey cited Jean L'Heureux, a man who lived with the Blackfoot during the first two years of the Whoop-up trade.[13] The compelling report estimated that 12,000 gallons of whiskey netted 24,000 robes worth $50,000. Firewater had caused the damage and L'Heureux had come to dread the drunken sprees. "More than 112 persons have perished in these orgies and horrors. Mothers forgot their maternal instinct under the influence of drunkenness and let their infants fall from their breasts for starved dogs to devour under the dulled eyes of the unfortunates."[14]

If Jerry Potts bore witness to the carnage and shared L'Heureux's thoughts, there is no record of it. He too was attracted to whiskey in whatever rank form it was delivered. Like those he rode with, he simply believed in the survival of the fittest.

However, even the fit were about to be severely tested.

MOUNTAIN CHIEF

Mountain Chief, a Piegan head chief who traditionally wintered on the Marias River, where Jerry Potts kept his lodges, signed the 1855 Blackfoot treaty that confirmed his desire for whiskey to be banned from Piegan villages and made the Missouri River the southern boundary of their reserve land. After independent whiskey traders ignored the treaty and infiltrated Piegan villages in the mid-60s, Mountain Chief told Indian Peace Commissioner Malcolm Clarke: "We do not wish these pale faces to come to our villages. If we desire to trade, we will go into their forts, dispose of our robes and leave. There is nothing in common between us."[12]

Personally held accountable for every theft or assault committed by Piegan braves, he was often a proponent of peace but was painted regularly by the newspapers of Fort Benton and Helena as a calculating murderer. It was Mountain Chief who was the intended target of the Baker Massacre in January 1870, an event that was triggered after a son of Mountain Chief killed the retired Malcolm Clarke in a domestic dispute. While news of Baker's atrocity outraged eastern politicians, the propaganda against Mountain Chief continued in Montana. On February 1, Helena's *Rocky Mountain Gazette* reported on rumours circulating in Fort Benton, claiming, untruly, that the Piegans were about to descend from Milk River country and attack the town because Mountain Chief had "declared war and vengeance against the whites." The Piegan chief reacted to news of the slaughter and death of Heavy Runner by staying north of the border near Fort Whoop-up, where his trusted friend Bear Child was working for the White traders. In March, finally the battlefield proved inescapable. The last great Indian battle of the Canadian Plains saw Mountain Chief and his warriors, along with Jerry Potts, come to the aid of a small Blood encampment under siege. The enemy was routed and in total disarray. "They would have been annihilated except that Mountain Chief said there had been enough killing and it was time to go home."[13] The next year the chief led his people into a peace treaty with the mountain tribes that came to Fort Whoop-up to trade and into the Cypress Hills to hunt. Facilitating the powwow and smoking of pipes were none other than fort proprietors Healy and Hamilton. Anxious to begin trading with the Piegans and avert any intertribal incidents after the ritual tobacco had been shared, Healy insisted that the mountain tribes retreat to the opposite side of the river while the Piegans handed over their robes and indulged in their drunken revelry. Mountain Chief would survive another three decades and as a respected elder his image was captured forever by the lens of Edward S. Curtis.

Chapter 9

The Last Great Battle

Throughout the summer of 1870, Jerry Potts observed the continued devastation that firewater was bringing to the Blackfoot. As dangerous as the country was for most traders, Potts still moved among the Blackfoot camps in safety. His allegiance was never in doubt, and the more responsible Native leaders knew that their half-brother bore no direct role in the debauchery the whiskey traders were spreading among their tribe. His reputation was firmly established among the Blackfoot as a warrior and chief, and any doubts about his willingness to fight on their side were dispelled in mid-autumn of 1870.

The traditional enemies of the Blackfoot—the Assiniboines and Crees—had taken solace in the rumours that the Blackfoot tribes had suffered greater losses than they had in the smallpox epidemic that had marked the winter count. Believing that their enemies were no longer strong enough to defend their hunting territory, the two northeasterly tribes moved southwest from the Qu'Appelle valley for the fall buffalo hunt. Led by Cree chiefs Piapot, Little Pine, and Big Bear, and Assiniboine chief Little Mountain, a hunting party of about 800 braves crossed the South Saskatchewan River in October and moved deep into Blackfoot country.

Four years earlier, the Cree and Blackfoot had fought a savage engagement on the Battle River far to the north, in which the outnumbered Blackfoot had routed the Cree. More recently, the Cree had lost another battle to the Piegans, who reportedly lost one

Artist John Mix Stanley was one of the first to venture near the Canadian border and portray the buffalo hunt in the Sweetgrass Hills in 1853.

warrior to the Crees' 70. Still smarting from these defeats, Piapot and Big Bear were craving their revenge as they and their Assiniboine allies gathered their forces along the South Saskatchewan River in October 1870. As they moved in the direction of the Little Bow River, they sent scouts toward the nearby Oldman River above Fort Whoop-up, seeking Blood or Peigan camps that were vulnerable to surprise and incapable of resistance—easy pickings to restore their honour.

When they finally did descend on a cluster of 11 Blood tipis, it was during the pre-dawn hours of November 1. The sound of rifle fire rang loud across the silent prairie but in their ardour for revenge, the Cree and Assiniboine chiefs had failed to scout beyond the hilltops. Blackfoot warriors, mainly Blood families, had scattered their hunting lodges in small clusters along the Oldman River for the winter ahead. Steadily they appeared on the horizon, their numbers ever growing.

As the fighting broke out, at least one messenger reached the South Piegans, who were camped only three miles distant near Fort Whoop-up. Mountain Chief and his people had lingered north of the Medicine Line, reluctant to return to their traditional homes along the Marias River, the killing grounds of Colonel Eugene Baker. Potts was settled there, closer to his mother's people, in his own lodge with his two Piegan wives.

Various accounts of the ensuing battle report that White men were present. The Fort Benton papers later suggested that as many as 20 joined the fight on the side of the Bloods and Piegans. Witnesses confirmed that Jerry Potts was one of the first to respond to the enemy attack. As the Piegans appeared en masse from the south, enthusiasm evident in their war cries, courage waned among the Cree and Assiniboine and they soon retreated across four miles of flatland at the head of a big bend in the river.

Some portrayers of the ensuing fight put Potts' friend George Star at his side. Trader Howell Harris claimed to have accompanied the party as an observer and left an eyewitness account of the last great battle to be fought among the Natives on the Canadian Plains. The fleeing Cree and Assiniboine, forced northeast toward the banks of the Oldman, desperately took refuge in a coulee.

> Potts led the Piegans into another coulee that ran parallel to that occupied by the Crees and Assiniboines. The two forces were completely hidden from one another ... [They] crawled up the sides of the ridge to snipe at one another with rifles and arrows and to hurl rocks down on each other.
>
> This stalemate continued for a couple of hours when Potts ... spotted a small butte to the rear of the Cree-Assiniboine lines which gave a commanding view of their position. Picking the best rifle shots, he sent them to the butte to pour a withering fire down into the enemy ranks. From their secure position the small party of Piegan riflemen began to take a heavy toll of the Crees and Assiniboines. Realizing that they had little chance if they stayed where they were, Piapot and Big Bear gave the order to run.[1]

And so, for one last time, Bear Child could be found at the forefront of the battle, a brave warrior leading the charge. At one point during the melee, Bear Child and a few followers, scalp knives close at hand, gained ground on a pair of retreating Cree. One assailant suddenly wheeled, levelled his rifle at Bear Child's face, and fired almost point-blank. At the last instant the invincible Métis threw himself to one side as the sound of the gun roared in his ear. Hitting the ground, he lay stunned for a minute, then jumped to his feet and rejoined a fight that was almost over, at least on his side of the river.[2]

Across the Oldman the killing continued as the original invaders scattered over the plains. One group of 50 Cree tried to make a stand in a clump of trees. They were wiped out to a man. Scores more were killed before Mountain Chief ordered the Piegans to break off the attack. Over one-third of the 800 Crees and Assiniboines who invaded Blackfoot territory did not leave. Wounded but alive, Piapot led his people homeward with a bullet in his leg. For the rest of his life, he walked with a limp.

Back on the banks of the Oldman, Bear Child and the Piegans took stock of their wounds and casualties. The Blackfoot tribes shared losses totalling 40 men and women, with dozens more wounded. The left side of Bear Child's face and ear had severe powder burns from the rifle shot that had almost blown his head off. His Piegan brothers attributed Potts' survival to their leader's strong medicine. The incident only served to deepen their belief that he had supernatural powers and could not be touched by a bullet.

Jerry Potts would long remember the event itself. Twenty years later, no longer Bear Child but an old warrior with battlefield memories, Jerry recalled this day of killing as a near-massacre. With characteristic brevity, he summed it up: "You could shoot with your eyes shut and kill a Cree."[3]

Potts had already earned wide respect among the Native people along the Marias, but witnesses on this battlefield included enough Whites that his feats became part of the lore of both cultures. In the words of one biographer, "The most important thing he won that day was imperishable fame as a warrior and war chief. His able and decisive leadership had carried the day, and the respect and honour he won would stand him in good stead again and again in the years to come."[4]

Chapter 10

The Tragedy of Crooked Back

When the *Helena Daily Herald* announced in mid-June of 1870 that, during their first season, Healy and Hamilton had netted $50,000' worth of buffalo robes and assorted pelts, the stampede to Whoop-up country began. It was further encouraged when the embargo on Fort Benton robes, imposed after the smallpox outbreak, was lifted in September. The influence of Isaac Baker in Washington rekindled the flow of robes down the Missouri and things were soon back to normal—whiskey flowing upriver, furs heading toward New York and Europe.

In Jerry Potts' immediate world, the victims of the whiskey trade were easy to identify—the large number of Blackfoot adults who came to embrace firewater as their greatest addiction, and the children who suffered as a result. The villains, on the other hand, were harder to measure. Eastern newspapers fuelled the righteous indignation of their readers, and politicians responded with legislation aimed at curbing the whiskey trade, but in reality the frontier was a free-enterprise marketplace full of Civil War survivors with little sympathy for anybody, White or Aboriginal, who couldn't fend for themselves. The only rule of the whiskey trade was *caveat emptor*, and if the "buyer beware" warning was ignored by consumers of rotgut, the whiskey trader did not lose any sleep over it.

The most callous even took pride in their work. Dempsey records these words of engineer Frank Wilkeson after listening to Fort Whoop-up whiskey traders in 1871. "Far from being an injury to the United States they said they were a great benefit to the United States as they keep the Indians poor, and kill directly or indirectly more Indians of the most warlike tribe on the continent every year, at no cost to the United States government, than the more regular army did in ten years!"[1] According to Dempsey, the traders went on to extol the freedom of "British subjects ... to pay big prices for poor whiskey and get immensely drunk on the Saskatchewan plains."[2]

The winter of 1871 saw Healy and Hamilton make Whoop-up the hub of the whiskey trade, with a population of over 100. The following summer, new fort-builders and free traders came north from Montana in droves.

Where the Belly and Waterton rivers meet, about 30 miles west of Fort Whoop-up, Joe Kipp erected what became known as Fort Standoff. Not happy with its location, he sold it the next year and built Fort Kipp closer to Whoop-up. Isaac Baker, who seemed to have a genuine aversion to selling whiskey to his Blackfoot customers, set his reluctance aside in the interest of meeting and beating the competition at their own game. He sent his partner, Charles Conrad, to build a fort on the Belly, three miles below Kipp's new enterprise. Like Healy, they encouraged free traders to use Fort Conrad as a base to replenish trade goods and go out into the Blood villages to trade for robes. In the first four winters of whiskey-trader activity above the Medicine Line, an estimated 130,000 buffalo robes were delivered south to Fort Benton warehouses.

As different forts were built, there was usually some connection with either the Tom Power enterprise or the growing business of Isaac Baker and the Conrad brothers, Charles and William. Sometimes they would even co-operate in establishing a fort that could act as the base of operations for their trading wagons. Such was the case at High River, where the Spitzee Post (also called Fort Spitzee) was opened in 1872, with one of Conrad's managers, Howell Harris, in charge. Whereas the Blood winter count of the previous year had honoured their great victory over the Cree, 1872 was "*spitsi napekwax etawpiyaw*" or "some White men settle on High River."[3]

The Spitzee fort was a collaboration of colourful scoundrels. Nine wagons laden with whiskey and other trade goods were hauled by teams of oxen north to a camp near High River and modern-day Calgary. Jerry Potts, who had moved to the Fort Kipp area and remained on good terms with both the Baker and Power operations, joined the Spitzee crew as a hired rifle to help provide food for the fort.

Once the fort was completed, manager Howell Harris opted to winter there rather than at Fort Conrad, six miles to the south. In March 1872, an event occurred that both Harris and his hired rifle, Potts, would later wish had been handled differently.

A quick-tempered Blood youth, well on his way to making his share of enemies, attempted to shoot Harris, and Potts came to his aid. "Jerry Potts would have shot Star Child on the spot, but Harris prevented him from doing so," wrote Whoop-up historian Gerald Berry.[4] Given his life, Star Child would play a role in a murder seven years later that made Potts regret not pulling the trigger. "Harris always averred that he could have averted the tragedy seven years before it happened, and Potts always blamed him for his lack of foresight."[5]

Potts had remained camped near the Belly River, distant from the U.S. Cavalry, or "long knives," and closer to his mother's people. When he was near the lodges of the Many Fat Horses band led by the respected chief Many Spotted Horses (in the Blackfoot tradition, he was later known as Heavy Shield), Potts would visit his mother. Crooked Back now lived in the lodges of Jerry's half-brother, No Chief. There Potts would sometimes witness first-hand the fighting and tragedy that came with excess drinking. It was an omen of things to come.

The leader of the Mules, or Many Children, band was Not Afraid of the Gros Ventres, a prolific man with 10 wives and enough offspring to establish their own band name. It seems that Not Afraid had gained substantial personal wealth simply by selling off his many daughters to Blood braves. No Chief, Jerry Potts' half-brother, was married to one of these daughters, and the patriarch expected his son-in-law to attend the many drinking parties that the family seemed to live for.

The Mules were whiskey-driven hellraisers who seemed to be at the centre of most of the fights and drunken orgies that were fast destroying the Blood nation. Many Spotted Horses, the band chief before Not Afraid, isolated the family under his sole leadership, tended to keep his lodges separate from the Mules, and encouraged his followers, including No Chief and his mother, to stay out of harm's way by living in the main lodge group at a distance from the young man's in-laws. No Chief, his wife, and family, including Crooked Back, thus lived separate lives from the rowdy Mules.

No Chief's isolation from his in-laws was taken as an insult by some of his brothers-in-law. One day when the Many Children's camp sent word that they had a keg of whiskey set aside for No Chief, it was an invitation he could not resist. When he reached the Mule lodges, however, the situation deteriorated quickly into a whiskey-fuelled free-for-all. While his father-in-law, Not Afraid, ignored the rising tension, insults grew into heated argument. Fearing death at the hands of an irate sot, Hairy Face, No Chief fired a lethal shot at this brother-in-law and was immediately surrounded by angry family members. When confronted by his drunken father-in-law, No Chief panicked and drew his knife. "As the crowd closed in, he made a vicious thrust and sliced the chief's stomach open so cleanly from hip to hip that his intestines fell out."[6] His defence was fruitless but No Chief managed one final coup as his knife found the shoulder of another attacker, Big Snake. As he again thrashed his knife in vain, No Chief was shot dead by Good Young Man, another son of Not Afraid. Grieving the loss of their father and brother, the Mules refused to bury No Chief, dragging him outside and exposing his body to their dogs.

Word came to Crooked Back of the shooting and her son's demise. By then a stoic elder, she prepared a travois and mounted her horse to retrieve No Chief's corpse. The Mules' drunken rage had not abated, and the grieving mother was met by a still-hostile Good Young Man. Ignoring his defiance, she stooped to gather her son and positioned him atop the travois. When she calmly turned to lead her mount away, she too was shot and left to rot in the sun.

As a young woman, 35 years earlier, Crooked Back had withstood the devastation of smallpox, survived the vicious killing of her Scottish husband, and escaped the clutches of the volatile Alexander Harvey. During her life the population of her people living in the watershed of the Upper Missouri River and across the Canadian prairie had been cut in half by the importation of disease and whiskey. Now she, too, could be counted among the victims of firewater.

At least one White observer, Donald Graham, documented the dramatic decline of the Mules that followed this event. On previous visits he had numbered the Mules at 28 lodges, but by 1873 "the Mule family had been reduced to two lodges and the survivors had taken refuge in the South Piegan camp in order to avoid complete extinction."[7]

Two months passed before Jerry Potts, working to the west, near Fort Kipp, responded to the tragedy. In Blackfoot tradition, this was an atrocity he vowed to avenge.

It was only a matter of time before Potts and Good Young Man crossed paths. When Good Young Man came to Fort Kipp and was warned that Jerry Potts would kill him on sight, the Mule warrior mounted the back of a horse ridden by his friend Morning Writing and tried to escape back to his camp. Potts, working in a field nearby, sighted the pair and took after them. Gaining ground rapidly, he pulled up his mount as the two Mules struggled to climb a rise. Potts took aim and fired. The bullet found its mark and he watched Good Young Man tumble into the prairie dust, his spine shattered and his body still. An eye for an eye.

Shortly after this incident, Potts quit the whiskey forts and returned to Montana. He never worked for them again.

In the 1870s it was a curious sighting for White traders whey they came across Blood gravesites, erected, according to their customs and beliefs, above ground. Such a sighting inspired the Sydney Hall rendering below.

Chapter 11

A Defining Year

By 1873 the human forces at work in the Upper Missouri country, and the overspill that had adopted the lawless Canadian frontier to the north, had ensured that new cultural clashes were close at hand.

Over the previous decade, one group of men who had earned the wrath of the Blackfoot tribes and their Native enemies alike, despised even more than whiskey traders, were the wolfers. They travelled in gangs, set up camp where they wanted, made the wolf their prey, and used poisoned buffalo meat as bait. Strychnine was their weapon of choice. At the beginning of the year, few in the big eastern cities had any idea of their existence. By mid-summer they would be infamous in both Washington and Ottawa for their deeds and misdeeds in the border country.

The border itself was attracting another group of men—astronomers and engineers on more honourable missions. These were men moving west as close to the 49th parallel as nature and topography would allow. They worked for two governments and they were charged with marking the invisible line between Canada and the United States.

While this border was of paramount importance to both nations, its relevance was more immediate on the American side than it was among Canadian bureaucrats. For one thing, Canada had no government presence at all in its North-West Territories, while Montana and the Dakotas were teeming with military men and

U.S. government officials. And even within this White community, friction was at hand when it came to Indian policy.

The U.S. military, on one hand, seemed intent on using its superior weaponry to overcome any Native resistance to its directives. The Commissioner of Indian Affairs, Francis Walker, on the other, clung to his last hopes for those Amerindians who sought freedom on the western plain. In his 1872 annual report he looked back at the previous five years. "Had the settlements of the United States not been extended beyond the frontier of 1867, all the Indians of the continent to the end of time would have found upon the Plains an inexhaustible supply of food and clothing." Walker feared that within another five years he would "see the Indians of Dakota and Montana ... reduced to a habitual condition of suffering from want of food."[1]

Meanwhile, with a growing White population to protect, General Philip Sheridan, commander of the Military Division of the Missouri, steadily increased his garrison strength at Fort Buford. Sheridan had watched the steady infiltration of settlers into what had been "barren desert ... only a year or two since in the possession of the Indians." By 1872 it was "a grazing ground for stock consumed by the population of our eastern cities."[2] Sheridan's perspective of his responsibility was far different from that of Francis Walker. With settlers and advance survey parties for the railroad in constant fear of attack from the Sioux, the general described the calling of those in his command as "in fact to do everything within our power to forward the advancing wave of civilization on our frontiers."[3]

Railroad survey parties were an omen of the future and would soon have a profile on both sides of the boundary. It was the locomotive more than anything else that was a catalyst for the border-marking project. By the spring of 1873, fledgling Canada was experiencing a new level of interest in what was perceived by many easterners as a vast wasteland. The curiosity was kindled by Prime Minister Sir John A. Macdonald's latest dream, and it meant that another form of infringement on Indian lands was in the works. Manitoba and British Columbia had recently joined the dominion, the latter induced by promises of a transcontinental railway. If Macdonald had his way, iron rails would soon stretch from Ontario to the Rocky Mountains and beyond to the Pacific coast. Unlike the American situation, however, there was no flow of settlement onto the prairie. With the exception of a few missionaries and wagons of westbound Overlanders who quickly disappeared into the mountain passes, the only other intruders were the Indians' half-brothers, the Métis, who made camps on the Saskatchewan River.

While Macdonald and the Canadians seemed prepared to spend money on a boundary commission, the most blatant omission in their management of the North-West Territories was the absence of any administration of law and order. A gang of Cypress Hills wolfers would inspire an end to all procrastination on that front.

In the late spring of 1873 two vastly different groups of men camped on both sides of the imaginary line that separated the Canadian and American frontiers. But in a sense, these disparate neighbours were linked by the inevitable process that would bring a new level of law and justice to the west. The more refined assembly represented a formal agreement by two civilized governments to define their relationship through co-operation and dialogue; the second, a fragmented band of social misfits and independent adventurers, exemplified the hard-drinking life and Wild West justice they adhered to. The former carried telescopes and sextants in their saddlebags; the latter opted for strychnine and bullets.

The International Boundary Commission had started its methodical marking of the 49th parallel the previous year at the Red River, close to where a single post had first marked the northern perimeter of the United States. The commission consisted of two groups of astronomers, engineers, and bureaucrats sent by their individual governments to define a border that had been negotiated almost 50 years earlier. The American camp, led by Commissioner Archibald Campbell and Chief Astronomer Colonel F.M. Farqueher, consisted of a dozen officials and their attendants. The Canadian contingent, under the direction of British Commissioner Colonel Albany Fetherstonhaugh, added another dozen, plus a veterinary doctor to tend the animals.

To the Blackfoot, the whiskey traders, and the large Métis community that had roamed these lands for decades, the actions of this cavalcade must have seemed mysterious—moving camp every day, carefully aiming their instruments at the evening sky, measuring and remeasuring, then driving a stake into the ground to mark their agreed-upon spot. Then, as the measurers moved ever westward, a party of workers used pickaxes and shovels to build an earthen mound or rock cairn that was easily discernible on the flat prairie.

The line established no barrier to entry in either direction, but it was a physical statement that both the youthful Canada and the Civil War-scarred United States were intent on identifying their jurisdictions and needs to govern the West.

Concurrent with the Boundary Commission's orderly move along the border, a clash of Native horse thieves and murderous thugs erupted in mid-June, just above the 49th parallel. The fallout from their showdown would change the West forever and ultimately shape the destiny of Jerry Potts.

The incident involved the notorious wolfers, ruthless hunters who in 1872 had established their own fortress, Spitzee Post, south of the Bow River. An incident would occur late that summer, more than 200 miles southeast in the Cypress Hills, that would actually stimulate the wolfers to form an elected quasi-government. Consisting of a few pragmatic hunters and an assortment of ex-Civil War misfits, they would later call themselves the Spitzee Cavalry and set out to enforce rules that suited themselves.

Wolfers had come to the Plains about the same time as the whiskey traders. Their weapon of choice was not the rifle, but poison: unmarked wolf pelts were worth much more than those scarred by bullet holes. The technique was straightforward: kill a buffalo, freeze chunks of meat after lacing them with strychnine, retire for the night, and the next morning retrieve the carcasses of wolves that had expired after trying to gnaw their way into the poisoned bait. The freezing was deemed very clever, as the difficulty of gorging on frozen meat meant that more animals would feed off the same slab of meat. One spiked, ice-hard animal could garner twice as many victims as would warm feed.

The scope and significance of the wolf trade on the Plains has largely been overlooked in depictions of the West. Artists of the day and, later on, Hollywood filmmakers were far more captivated by the spectacle of stampeding buffalo than by the evasive wolf packs that roamed the grasslands.

But as buffalo diminished through the early 1870s, wolf pelts became an increasingly important commodity to Fort Benton merchants. Wolf fur itself was gradually gaining favour in the fashion world. Two wolf pelts would equal a buffalo robe in value, and a wagon full of the smaller animal's fur could generate much more cash than if it carried hides of the larger beast.

In the south, as more settlers with more cattle appeared in Montana, the wolfers finally found friends in the ranchers, who had no use whatsoever for a hungry wolf. But north of the Medicine Line the animosity intensified. Refining their techniques, camps of three or four wolfers would kill and prepare up to a dozen buffalo carcasses. A mile or two out of camp, they would spread the pieces around in a circle, making it easier to gather up their prey. The following morning they would collect the dead wolves, skin them then and there if they were not frozen, then reluctantly shoot any that had eaten only enough poison to become agitated. To the Indians, the wolfers were interlopers taking pelts from their land without compensation. They made a habit of trying to outwit the wolfers and steal as many of their poisoned prey as they could find. If a Blood managed to get to a dead wolf first, he did not hesitate to skin it and take the pelt to Fort Whoop-up himself. As far as the wolfers were concerned, they would just as soon shoot a Blood pelt thief as they would a maddened wolf. In fact, some of them preferred it: the pelt was worth more to the shooter if the bullet was in the Blackfoot.

By 1872, enough small groups of wolfers had been chased from their camps by Native war parties that they started to seek strength in numbers. At least two dozen fell under the leadership of an ex-Confederate soldier, Thomas Hardwick, a man known to be ruthless and trigger-happy.

Shortly after settling near the slopes of the Sweetgrass Hills, Hardwick's followers were approached by about 20 Assiniboine horsemen. When they ignored Hardwick's signals to stay back, he fired into them. The Assiniboine quickly retreated but returned hours later, their numbers doubled, their formation signalling a desire to trade. Their approach was met with bullets, and when the dust had cleared, at least four Assiniboine corpses were on the ground. As he had done before, Hardwick claimed a scalp to mark another victory over the enemy.

For many prairie tribesmen, there was no greater sport than stealing horses, and the wolfers were prime targets. At the same time, there were few men on that land more determined than Tom Hardwick and John Evans, so when a party of Sioux rustled some of their horses later that summer, the rustlers had no idea they would be pursued for 150 miles by the victims. Hardwick and Evans recovered their animals and then returned to the Bow River for a successful winter of wolfing. The following April they headed back south with a wagon train loaded with pelts. They waited until the spring freshet had receded and the wagons could safely ford the Oldman, Belly, St. Mary's, Milk, and Marias rivers. In mid-May they were camped near the Teton River, just one day out of Fort Benton, when all hell broke loose. Back in the relatively safe haven of Montana, the wolfers' guard was no doubt down when a party of Piegan warriors attacked and ran off most of their horses. The wolfers had no choice but to spend the next three days on foot, helping the few animals they had left lug their cargo to Benton. Given his reputation, Hardwick gained little sympathy from the authorities, a reaction that simply fuelled his anger.

Within days, word had spread from Benton to Helena that Hardwick and Evans were forming their own posse and going after their animals. On June 11 the *Helena Daily Herald* reported Hardwick's vow that "they would recover their property even if they had to go to Saskatchewan for it."[4] Armed with Henry rifles and revolvers, the avengers, a dozen horsemen and their pack animals, set out to settle a score. By the time Helenites were aware of the wolfers' mission, the "massacre" had already happened.

If there was a single turning point in western Canadian history, it was the Cypress Hills Massacre. (The term "massacre" is a misnomer, since the battle, however one-sided and senseless, was fought between armed combatants.) Its aftermath created much uproar in Ottawa and Washington, as well as political tension on both sides of the Medicine Line. The legal issues took years to play out. However, its strongest claim to fame was its catalytic impact on the formation of the North West Mounted Police.

Near the end of May 1873, the wolfers' posse picked up tracks and followed them north toward the Cypress Hills. Hardwick and "Chief" Evans rode at the head of a dozen hardened plainsmen, whose brushes with the Blackfoot had engendered nothing but bad memories.

After rain removed any trace of the trail, they crossed the border and gradually made their way to Battle Creek, where two seasoned traders, Abe Farwell and Moses Solomon, were known to have competing trading posts on opposite sides of the river ford. Nearby, a band of Assiniboines was camped with their chief, Little Soldier. Evans went to Farwell's post and asked the trader if any Natives had

This reconstruction of Abe Farwell's trading post remains today a barren monument to the senseless slaughter of innocent Assiniboine lodges when a dozen drunk, frustrated wolfers and neighbouring Métis opened fire after ignoring Farwell's plea for peace. The post was about one mile from where Fort Walsh would be constructed two years after the massacre occurred.

This northern Assiniboine grouping would be similar to the vulnerable lodges of the family units in the camp of Chief Little Soldier that was attacked in the Cypress Hills by vengeful wolfers in 1873. The event acted as a catalyst to the formation of the North West Mounted Police.

come in with new horses lately. Farwell told the wolfer that Little Soldier had only a half-dozen in his whole camp.

The culprits, he suggested, were probably a band of northern Assiniboines who had passed through the area days before and stolen two horses belonging to former ally George Hammond, who was now a trader in the Cypress Hills. Although he was later lumped in with his American allies, this Canadian hothead had a history of confrontation. And even though Little Soldier's lodge had apparently saved a third Hammond horse from theft and been rewarded with a jug of rotgut by Farwell, in this trader's mind the Assiniboines now camped at Battle Creek were no better than the ones who had taken his horses.

The Assiniboines had observed the arrival of the wolfers and had become a little unsettled as the White men made their camp and nursed their frustrations with a breakfast dominated by copious quantities of alcohol at Farwell's fort. Meanwhile the Little Soldier lodges, enjoying their own rare occasion to drink firewater, grew more vulnerable with each passing hour.

Farwell had a long and friendly history with these Assiniboines, but Solomon would later testify that in recent months, Little Soldier's warriors had been acting in a surly manner and had threatened to kill both Farwell and himself and destroy their posts.[5] Only two days before the wolfers arrived, a Native from Little Soldier's camp had told a group of Métis that they intended to take everything the traders had and drive them out of the hills. If the traders resisted, the Assiniboine said they would kill them.

As the supply of rotgut was depleted at Farwell's, the wolfers moved on to Solomon's post along with a small group of Métis who had been hired to cart the trader's fur stocks to Fort Benton, the season being at its end. Hammond was all the more irate when he found that the horse Little Soldier had retrieved was missing again. Tempers and whiskey would prove to be a deadly combination. While Abe Farwell was frantically trying to mediate the situation, both George Hammond and Tom Hardwick were ready for battle.

Grabbing his rifle, Hammond asked the wolfers to accompany him to the Assiniboine camp to get his horse back. Determined to recover somebody's horse, Evans, Hardwick, and their wolfers agreed to help him. Farwell pleaded for time and went with them to the Assiniboine camp, where he questioned the drunken Little Soldier about the missing horse.

The chief assured Farwell that the horse was not in the camp. As Little Soldier spoke, women and children were sent scurrying into the brush behind the camp and the warriors began stripping as if preparing for battle. In seconds, the wolfers, who had relied heavily on intimidation, felt their mood change to apprehension. They retreated into a coulee about 50 yards away, where Hardwick shouted for Farwell to get out of the way so that he could get a clear shot. Farwell begged the wolfers to go back to the fort, for he was sure he could regain the missing horses.

As the Assiniboine scattered, a sudden decision was made: Hammond fired into the camp and his comrades followed suit. From the protection of the coulee, the wolfers poured a withering fire into the exposed Assiniboines. Incensed and driven to recklessness by whiskey, the warriors charged the wolfers' position three times before retreating into the trees behind their camp to continue the battle from cover.

Evans and Hardwick made their way to a small hill overlooking the Assiniboine position and began an effective flanking action. Little Soldier's men responded with their own circling action, and at one point it looked to the wolfers as if the "Chief" and Hardwick were in serious danger. Several of the wolfers, led by Canadian Ed LeGrace, rode to their aid. LeGrace was first to the rescue, but ended up being the only wolfer killed in the fight.

Seeing one of their own brought down, the wolfers ceased their fire and withdrew to Solomon's fort, where they had a commanding view of the Assiniboine camp. Sipping whiskey, they fired into it all afternoon. Unable to return to their lodges, the Assiniboine men, women, and children scattered into the hills, leaving their camp open to pillage.

Hardwick led a search of the tipis for Little Soldier. When he was found, a French Canadian named Vincent killed the chief, cut off his head, and stuck it on a pole as a trophy, while the wife and mother-in-law of the dead man stood by. The assault continued. In retribution for the killing of Ed LeGrace, the wolfers turned to slaughtering the wounded. While many of the tribe made for the hills, a few women who were left behind were raped repeatedly by some of the men, then killed while clinging to their children.

The next morning the wolfers burned the Assiniboine camp, including all the slain bodies. Evans later told a Montana newspaper that they had "made piles of their lodges and other trash and set them on fire."[6] The traders had headed south, so the wolfers buried LeGrace under the floor of Solomon's store and then burned it to the ground to keep the Indians from mutilating the body.

The wolfers never did find their stolen horses, and eventually they returned to Benton empty-handed. One of the first officials to report on the incident to his U.S. government superiors was the Milk River Indian agent, A.J. Simmons. He understood there to be at least 16 killed and wrote that the Cypress Hills victims "were almost entirely defenseless. [The wolfers] mutilated their bodies in a most outrageous and disgusting manner ... [with] no provocation for this cowardly assault."[7]

It was two years before any of them were brought to trial for murder and when they were, all were acquitted. None of the dead or injured were ever atoned for, the only reasons for their deaths being hatred, whiskey, and a dispute over a horse.

Although it later became a trading fort, the original Spitzee camp was not built for that purpose. Instead, it was the field headquarters for a company of men who rejected trade with the Blackfoot tribes, and if there was any contact, it was usually hostile. Along with wolves, dogs from the Blackfoot camps ate the poisoned meat. Hundreds of these dogs died, and resentment gave way to revenge. Soon wolfers started to become targets for the warriors' Winchesters. The Blackfoot only had good rifles because of the traders, so over time the wolfers came to resent any legitimate trader who supplied guns or ammunition.

The wolfers were led by a pair of rough-and-ready opportunists, John "Chief" Evans and Harry "Kamoose" Taylor. It was this pair that protested to John Healy's Fort Whoop-up traders about their selling weapons to the Blackfoot. The traders had come to despise the wolfers almost as much as the Blackfoot did, and the best way to make their feelings known was simply to trade more rifles. Eventually Evans and Taylor decided to confront Healy directly.

Gathering up their motley Spitzee Cavalry, they headed south, intent on destroying Fort Whoop-up. Jerry Potts was hunting nearby that early summer day of 1873 when a large group of heavily armed wolfers was seen in the distance. Soon they reached the stockade, where the unflappable Healy alerted his men to be ready for trouble. As they gathered around outside his headquarters, Healy sat beside an open keg of gunpowder, ready to receive his uninvited guests.

Taylor and the rest of the cavalry crowded menacingly around the traders while Evans demanded that Healy stop trading guns to the Blackfoot. He warned them to stick to trading whiskey and then threatened to take every trading post in Whoop-up country apart piece by piece. Healy simply grinned, leaned forward, and, taking the lighted stub of a cigar from his mouth, held it over the gunpowder, inviting Evans to get the hell out of his post. He offered only one alternative: to blow the fort to bits, along with everyone in it. Knowing the Irishman's death-wish reputation, Evans retreated as gracefully as possible. The Spitzee Cavalry did not stop until it had reached Fort Benton. There were plenty of lesser men who might cower at their threats; the wolfers never bothered Healy or his trading posts again.

News of the Cypress Hills Massacre, as it came to be called, caused a great furor when it reached Ottawa in July. All opposition to the appointment of a law-enforcement agency in the northwest quickly vanished. Spurred on by inflammatory headlines and editorials, Prime Minister Sir John A. Macdonald hurriedly pushed through the bill he had introduced earlier calling for the formation of the North West Mounted Police (NWMP). By October 1873, amid public outcries that ignored the fact that some of the Cypress Hills culprits were Canadians, Parliament enacted the bill that defined the makeup of the NWMP. It authorized formation of a force of 300 red-coated, pillbox-hatted, mounted soldiers to ride west and quell the abuses being heaped upon the Native peoples by foreign intruders. Newspapers described the hellish habits of Fort Whoop-up and speculated that it would take some doing to drive the gun-slinging Americans out of Canada's newly acquired North-West Territories.

Making his first mistake of the campaign, Macdonald appointed George Arthur French as the NWMP's first commissioner on October 16. Little did either man know that in a matter of mere months, Jerry Potts, a hard-drinking, laconic Métis who cherished his medicine bag and the Blackfoot way of life, would be doing everything in his considerable power to salvage their reputations and save their police force from starvation and almost certain death.

Chapter 12

French's Folly

On July 8, 1874, near the banks of the Red River south of Winnipeg, an assembly of almost 300 men, resplendent in scarlet Norfolk jackets, started a journey that would irrevocably change the life of Jerry Potts.

Given the majestic scope of the undertaking, the original march of the North West Mounted Police across the Canadian prairie has long been portrayed as a grand achievement. It was all of that and more. At two critical points in the journey, however, the march dissolved into three separate columns: two that advanced toward the Rockies and one that headed back to Manitoba. That latter group was under the command of the Force's commissioner, George Arthur French, who abandoned his westward quest little more than two months after his great march began. Historians generally have been tolerant of French's failings, but in his brief command he established only one certainty: he was the wrong man in the wrong place with the wrong horses.

Colonel French had begun losing the respect of his constabulary almost from the first day he arrived at Fort Dufferin, just above the international boundary, where the march began. By September 8, in the wake of a torrential downpour and mired in muck, mutiny was at hand. Ten dead horses lay abandoned in a creek bed when French, determined and unwilling to acknowledge any weakness in his strategy, again ordered his charges to break camp. Grudgingly, the column formed as French's officers responded to his call and stirred their men into action.

French's fall from grace was not caused by his ambitious second-in-command, Colonel James Farquharson Macleod, but the contrasting styles and personalities of the two men magnified French's inadequacies. The only good reviews he received on the Canadian Plains were those he wrote in his personal reports to Ottawa. The original plan had been to follow the Boundary Commission's trail west, its markers being iron pillars or cairns built every one to three miles along the 49th parallel. The commission's campsite choices and field observations were available to French, but he opted mostly to ignore them. It was French's style to blame those around him for all the problems the march would encounter, even though he was the man in charge. He never did publicly admit responsibility for leading a force of 300 into unknown lands without canteens and with uninformed guides, inadequate supplies, and a mix of livestock doomed to breed chaos.

The trek got off to a bad start when two popular officers, Inspector Theodore Richer of "F" Division and Inspector Charles Young of "B" Division, resigned within hours of beginning. Their protests were based mainly on French's insistence that his showcase steeds, handpicked and transported from Ontario, were ideal for the journey that lay ahead. He refused to buy the trained cart horses readily available and recommended by Young and Richer, both seasoned horsemen. French charged ahead, organizing six separate divisions, "A" to "F", of 45 to 50 riders, each with its own colour-matched stock. A self-congratulatory French admired his choices in the next report he sent to Ottawa: "The column of route presented a very fine appearance," he wrote. "First came 'A' Division with their splendid dark bays and wagons, then 'B' with their dark browns. Next 'C' came with bright chestnuts drawing the guns and small-arm ammunition. Next were 'D' with their greys, 'E' with their black horses, the rear being brought up by 'F' with their light bays."[1]

The march made only two miles its first day. Over 70 wagons and dozens of noisy Red River carts straggled into camp well past midnight. The campsite, with no wood, water, or food that first night, was an omen of things to come. Although they made only 14 miles over the next two days, the horses were already showing signs of fatigue. With the exception of a fine duck dinner four days out of Dufferin, there were few good memories of their first weeks on the trail. Plagued by insects, artist Henri Julien wrote in his diary that the Mounties "all agreed that nowhere had they seen anything equal to the mosquitoes of the prairie ... [they] rise in columns out of the spongy soil under our feet and do regular battle with us."[2]

Thunderstorms, typhoid, and a biblical-scale plague of locusts rounded out the first week of the march. The rate of progress was determined by the ox-cart drivers. Mindful of their animals and the obstacles that lay ahead, the 30 Métis at the reins refused to make the pace Colonel French wanted. Every night they would trail into camp too late for food to be dispensed. The next morning they refused to answer reveille, dallied over breakfast, and again set a pace far behind the main column. Holding back his troop for a day and putting the carts at the front of the parade would have solved the problem, but French would not buckle to his surly mercenaries. Instead he reduced his own men to taking on the menial task of walking with stick in hand beside the hired hands. Men who enlisted at 75 cents per day for the righteousness of the cause trudged beside Métis in their carts earning three times that much. Former schoolteacher and new sub-constable Jean D'Artigue wrote in his diary, " ... had we not been a long distance from any settlement, the colonel would have had to make the expedition alone."[3]

Less than 200 miles into the journey, enough horses were dead to turn the mounted force into foot soldiers. The remaining animals were walked half the time, and the men's riding boots soon housed bloodied feet. One feast of fresh meat triggered an epidemic of "prairie cholera," intense diarrhea that kept the men crouched on their haunches for days.

By the time the stragglers reached Roche Percée on the banks of the Souris River, even the stubborn Colonel French had to recognize their plight. Still blaming everyone but himself, he unveiled a new plan. "It was proposed by a sort of triangular distribution of the 300 Police, to cover the whole North-Western territory, and in that way give visibility to authority in all localities."[4]

French first announced that 30 members of "A" Division would branch northwest under Inspector William Jarvis on the unlikely

Henri Julien depicts spent animals and dismounted police struggling to haul their heavy cannons over uneven terrain while their commanding officer looks on.

chance they could reach Fort Edmonton before winter. Before they started, the sheer exhaustion of both men and beasts demanded a week of recovery at the Roche Percée camp.

D'Artigue later called their trek "the most unreasonable and incredible plan that had ever originated in one man's brain."[5] Fort Edmonton, via Fort Ellice, was 850 miles distant. "Sam Steele was sergeant-major with this troop which took with it 55 of the weakest horses, 24 wagons, 54 carts, 62 oxen and 50 cows and calves."[6] Just before the trip started, a surprised D'Artigue found himself transferred from "B" Division to Jarvis's command. French, it seems, had decided that he never wanted to see the judgemental Parisian's face again.

The colonel had commandeered all of "A" Division's healthy horses, had conscripted the best of the wagons and livestock, and had hand-selected the Métis he detested most, along with D'Artigue and a few other enlisted men, to leave with Jarvis.

The mandate given Inspector Jarvis by a leader who had failed so badly seems almost inhuman. Jarvis not only discharged the sick at Fort Ellice, but also reached Fort Edmonton with support officer Sévère Gagnon, Sergeant-Major Sam Steele, and his troop intact—a feat that ranks as one of the great achievements of the Mounties' western march.

While at Roche Percée, the first satchel of incoming mail was brought into camp by their assistant surgeon, Dr. Richard Barrington Nevitt, who had taken sick men back to Fort Dufferin. Nevitt's return helped raise spirits. Enough coal was found near the camp to fire the forge and repair the wagons. Horses were reshod and some extra coal stored in the wagons before the main column again moved west.

French's reports to Ottawa said little of the plight of his men, preferring to extol his own brilliance: "I surveyed our route as well as I could. It entailed on me a very large amount of extra work. I had to be on the alert to take the altitude of the sun and find our latitude ... at night I had to wait up until 1 or 2 a.m. to obtain the magnetic variation of the pole star ... But I was well rewarded for my trouble a month later when, without guides, I was enabled with a certain amount of confidence to strike out for the forks of the Bow and Belly rivers by compass and find the place."[7]

Even though his last camp was known as Wood End, French failed to foresee the need for fuel on the treeless plain that lay ahead. They followed the Boundary Commission's trail until it petered out and orders were given to head farther north.

On August 4, almost a month into the journey and tired of pemmican as a diet mainstay, three of the column's sub-inspectors went hunting. All was well until one of the men, sub-inspector Cecil "Texas Jack" Denny, charged ahead of his companions toward a herd of antelope only to spook the animals and end any chance of fresh meat for dinner. Denny's reputation sank even further the next day when he headed out of camp on his own in an attempt to make amends for the previous day's failures. The march almost lost Texas Jack to quicksand; only the instincts of Colonel Macleod saved the lives of both Denny and his horse.

Later Denny wrote, "Utterly without experience of prairie peculiarities, I rode straight into what looked to me like a perfectly solid patch of ground. It was alkali, and my horse went down until his head only appeared above the surface. I managed to scramble to a firm footing as he sank, and was deeply chagrined."[8] Macleod, travelling with a second horse, found Denny wandering and distraught. Together they located the trapped horse and Macleod, using rope and the pulling power of his own mount, dislodged him. "For weeks he was unfit for work, but at length recovered, and I subsequently used him on many a hard expedition."[9]

French's insistence that two nine-pound artillery guns accompany the trek had severely tested the horses from the first day. Beyond Roche Percée the "horse-killers" became even more of a drag when they encountered over five miles of incline rising more than 1,000 feet in the Dirt Hills. A day of marching seemed to demand a day of recovery as French resolutely pushed his troops forward.

Briefings before the march started made French aware that the Boundary Commission camp, that summer, was at Wood Mountain to their southwest. While intent on maintaining his northerly course, he sent Colonel Macleod in search of the surveyors in a desperate attempt to get much-needed supplies. Macleod started his journey with 10 men guiding empty carts into unknown country. Six days later he caught up to the main camp at Old Wives' Lakes. He returned, to a round of cheers, with enough pemmican, dry meat, and grain to avoid starvation, as well as "several cartloads of oats, which were much needed for horses dying daily for the want of them."[10] Knowing that the supply remained inadequate, Macleod made another foraging trip while French again headed west.

Until this point in the journey, 500 miles from Dufferin, they had yet to encounter any of the Native tribes they had heard so much about. On August 12, they saw their first cluster of Assiniboine tipis. Unimpressed, Cecil Denny would describe them, in retrospect, as "not an imposing lot or a good type of the plains aboriginal."[11] Here, Colonel French again rid his ranks of the weakened, establishing what he called Cripple Camp. Denny recalled that "the grass and water were good, 14 wagons, 28 of the poorest horses, and seven men were left with a half-breed and some footsore cattle."[12]

Macleod's second supplies mission left oats and food at Cripple Camp and caught the main column on August 15. He then took a longer train of carts on a final journey to the border to a second camp known as White Mud River.

Artist Henri Julien documented the bad days, as in Dead Horse Valley *above, and the few good days of Colonel George French (inset) as he struggled onward. Below, in* The Sweet Grass Hills in Sight, *he portrays the weary column making its way to an oasis of grass and spring water that would be its salvation.*

Denny recorded a meeting with a caravan of Métis hunters. Laden with buffalo robes and pemmican, it had already travelled to the Cypress Hills, filled its carts with bounty, and was headed back to Winnipeg. The hunters warned that there was no grass ahead for French's animals due to fire and a massive herd of grazing buffalo. The only water was alkaline or had been soiled by the buffalo herds. French pressed onward until the green slopes of the Cypress Hills beckoned. On September 1 they killed their first buffalo and made camp near a clear stream, where hay and antelope were close at hand.

The next few days were idyllic compared to what the men had been through. They ate buffalo, drank good water, and rested—but it was a brief respite. The sixth of September introduced a new enemy: a thin crust of ice in the water buckets. Possibly struck by a new sense of urgency, French argued with his scouts, challenged their directions, and finally set his own course. In his diary he wrote of his most recently hired scout: "He is the greatest liar I have ever met. He is suspected of being a spy of the Whoop-up villains ... I will do the guiding myself tomorrow. If I could have relied on Palliser's map I would have taken this duty sooner."[13]

The morning of September 8 started with the usual 3 a.m. reveille and no hot breakfast due to rain. They marched from five until after dark, dampness and cold always their companion. With no scouts in his plans, French had no idea what lay ahead. Finally a ridge and a river below stopped them in their tracks. Exposed, woodless, and exhausted, the men circled their wagons as the storm raged relentlessly.

The next morning would effectively be the beginning of the end for George French. The morning mood had started badly and it continued to deteriorate as an ill-timed authoritarian tantrum set the tone for the rest of the day. As dawn broke over their camp, and men who had worn through their boots again wrapped damp burlap around their blistered, decaying feet, George French lashed out at his night sentries, accusing them of stealing biscuits during their watch. Unwilling to listen to reason, he ordered them into irons, only to face resistance from his assistant commissioner, Colonel James Macleod. Citing his knowledge of law, Macleod refused the order, all the while trying to extract his boss from the dicey situation he had created. French persisted until Macleod was forced to outright disobey. "I'm sorry, sir," he said. "I cannot allow this to happen."[14] It would take many months to make it official, but from that time forward the NWMP had a new leader.

A week later, French had made it to his destination: the confluence of the Belly and Bow rivers, where a map from the earlier Palliser Expedition suggested they would find Fort Whoop-up. It was a dismal disappointment.

He sent scouting parties up both rivers, but to no avail. With no shelter other than the remnants of three small cabins, no grass, no river ford, and no wood, French was in trouble. He sent officers along the rivers seeking pasture, shelter, wood—anything that might ease the situation. Instead he got rain.

Within 60 days, one in every six of their animals was dead. Their carcasses, food for vultures and wolves, stretched from near Fort Dufferin to the ridge above the valley of the South Saskatchewan River, which was where the men made camp that September night. The state of the remaining horses was such that only one-third could be ridden that day, and 13 miles was all they could cover, rain pelting on their soggy backs the whole way. The camp they had abandoned that morning would be forever known as Dead Horse Camp. In many ways, the day would also ring the final death knell for the command of the commissioner.

French's vision for the march had been that the force of 300 would congregate in Fort Dufferin and then set out. All the necessary supplies were to be moved by 30 Métis drivers and teams of four oxen for each of the 30 Red River carts in a column. The alternative, and to many the logical choice, would have been to travel lighter and ship the majority of supplies up the Missouri to Fort Benton. Ironically, the whiskey merchants whom they intended to put out of business had already proven that this was the most viable route to get to Whoop-up country. But French was having none of it. They were a Canadian police force that would haul everything they needed over Canadian soil.

Of course that philosophy had been compromised from the beginning. French and the 150 recruits and 300 horses he had brought from Toronto were taken by train across numerous

American states to the railhead at Fargo, North Dakota, then followed the Red River to the Canadian border.

An omen of things to come occurred within days of French's arrival at the Dufferin camp. A severe lightning storm spooked the horses, sending them on a mad tear across the plains. It was then and there that the mettle of some of French's key officers was tested. Officers Walsh, Jarvis, Walker, and Steele logged over 100 miles rounding up and steering the runaways back to camp. Some animals were never recovered.

The troubles that assailed the Mounties in their first weeks on the trail could largely be traced to the fact that nobody, including the inept scouts they had hired, seemed to know where they were going. Injured horses meant slower progress, and lack of drinking water or proper shelter weakened both man and beast.

One mystery of the journey was their failure to use the boundary line itself as the route west. The International Boundary Commission had staked the route over the past two summers, clearly marking it with pillars and mounds every mile of the way. French's camp certainly knew the whereabouts of the cluster of Royal Engineers and astronomers who were marking the line; on one occasion, Colonel Macleod had made his way south to the commission's camp to secure oats when animal feed was getting low.

Finally French ordered a move south to Three Buttes and the Sweetgrass Hills. "Pressing on my mind," he wrote in his report to the government, "[is] that on the 20th of September last year the whole country from the Cypress Hills to the Old Wives' Lakes was covered with a foot of snow, several oxen and horses having been frozen to death."[15] French now recognized how exposed his troop was. Hastily he prepared himself to head south and seek supplies and assistance in Fort Benton, Montana, homeland of the whiskey traders he was commissioned to eliminate.

With Colonel Macleod at his side, he bid adieu to his main force, leaving them to linger and wonder what their next predicament might be.

The small party that descended out of the Sweetgrass Hills rode the best of the remaining horses. In addition to the two commanding officers, Sub-inspector Brisebois, Dr. Nevitt, French's favourite scout, Pierre Léveillé, and five wagons manned by either sub-constables or Métis arrived on the outskirts of Fort Benton after noon on their third day. The town itself had been described as "sagebrush Sodom," a main drag beside the Missouri River made up of saloons, gambling houses, whiskey warehouses, and a few merchants. The mud-rutted streets "were infested with the rough breed of the frontier: wolfers, blacklegs, outlaws, Indians and general, all-around hard cases."[16]

According to his diary, however, Colonel French was confident that he would find salvation amid Benton's dens of debauchery. Though one of the original motivations for their journey was to eliminate the whiskey forts, somewhere in his wilderness travels the commissioner had redefined his focus. Less than two weeks earlier, Fort Whoop-up, a primary target at the start of the march, was given a new description in his diary: "It is principally a trading post of the

Sternwheelers like this one in the foreground made Fort Benton the transportation and freighting hub of Montana until railway construction bypassed it in the 1880s and shifted the regional focus to Helena. The NWMP provided enough business over the years that one of Isaac Baker's steamboats bore the name Colonel Macleod.

firm of Baker & Co. of Benton, highly respected merchants who do not sell whiskey or spirits."[17]

Isaac Baker himself greeted French and Macleod, oozing hospitality from every pore. His partner, Charles Conrad, an astute merchant who would quickly gain the favour of French and Macleod, soon joined Baker. The I.G. Baker company had long worn the cloak of a reluctant whiskey trader, driven to it only by the need to compete with the aggressive business tactics of its main Benton rival, Tom Power. Baker and Conrad thus applauded the arrival of the Canadian police, professing a strong desire to meet their needs, stock their forts, and aid their mission however they might.

Over dinner that evening Baker listened to the trials and tribulations French had encountered. French reeled off a long list of needs, and it was agreed that Conrad would personally manage and transport the caravan of goods by ox cart across the Medicine Line.

Regardless of what might have been going through George French's mind as this small ray of light appeared on the horizon, he made contact with his government via the telegraph and awaited instructions. Conrad, in the meantime, explained that Fort Whoop-up was on the Belly River, but closer to the junction of the St. Mary's River, not the Bow. Aside from the well-built Whoop-up, most of the "forts" that dotted the prairie were little more than log huts, Conrad told French and Macleod. There were no citadels to lay siege to, no great walls to penetrate with their nine-pound cannons.

Conrad listened as French criticized his scouts and described the misfortunes his men had been forced to overcome. He particularly distrusted Moreau, the Métis who had suspiciously appeared in their camp in late August and could easily have been a plant sent by the whiskey traders to steer the Mounties in the wrong direction—a course, Conrad might have concluded, that they seemed perfectly capable of maintaining on their own. Surely there was some honest soul, French lamented, who was not in the pocket of the whiskey traders, someone who could both guide and interpret.

Charles Conrad paused only a moment. He knew just the man. In fact, only the previous day he had paid the mixed-blood from the Marias River $450 for six of the horses he would sell to French at a healthy markup. Provided the man could be sobered up and made presentable, Conrad would arrange for a meeting.

Both French and Macleod would later admit to being unimpressed by the odd, tilted character who appeared for the interview on September 25. While Conrad's description had painted an ideal candidate, this account of their initial reaction suggests they did not share the merchant's enthusiasm. "When Jerry Potts walked into the store they were not so sure. They were not very impressed with the short, bow-legged, slope-shouldered little man who stepped through the door. He looked almost comical as he stood there holding a Winchester '73 rifle that was nearly as long as he was, and the incongruous little bowler hat he wore just did not belong with the greasy buckskins and moccasins. Potts did not offer much conversation to inspire confidence either. Yet the Canadians were in no position to be critical. They graciously, albeit reluctantly, accepted the services of the diminutive guide."[18]

More than any other photo, this picture has come to symbolize Jerry Potts. Potts' trail garb featured his beaded cat-skin amulet, a gun belt complete with extra rounds for his handgun, and his trusted repeater rifle.

The second day, after a fine dinner hosted by Baker and a comfortable night's sleep, French and Macleod set about ordering supplies. Grasping the scope of their plans to build a winter fort in Whoop-up country, a project that would require both a workforce and supplies, Baker quickly realized that Charles Conrad could do more than serve the Canadians: he could get a head start in establishing a company store at the fort to meet the needs of the community that would no doubt grow around this new base.

Telegrams that French received from his political bosses in Ottawa ordered him to return to Manitoba, surely a blessing for the men he would leave behind. Once he and Macleod finalized supply arrangements with Baker and Conrad in Benton, French was anxious to get on his way east. Of the 15 horses he had selected from the I.G. Baker corral, the commissioner assigned one horse to Colonel Macleod and kept the other 14 for his own troop, yet another action on his part that displayed a predictable bias toward his own self-interest.

At noon on September 26, Macleod watched his commanding officer turn his back on the West, leaving Brisebois and himself to sort out their needs. French took with him his scout Léveillé, his wagons, and two sub-constables. Macleod didn't know it then, but the North West Mounted Police had just made the finest person-nel exchange in its history. It was the last time he would ever see Colonel French and it was the beginning of his relationship with the man he would come to call the greatest scout in the history of the West: Jerry Potts.

Over the next couple of days Macleod made inquiries regarding the culprits in the Cypress Hills Massacre, while Conrad organized a wagon train of supplies for the as-yet undetermined site where the Canadian police force would spend the winter. Macleod sent word to the Sweetgrass Hills for his officers to move their three divisions west. "On September 29," wrote Cecil Denny, "word came from Colonel Macleod at Benton that we were only 40 miles from Fort Whoop-up. We were instructed to move camp 15 miles west, [to] a well-beaten trail leading to that notorious rendezvous with Benton."[19]

As Macleod and his men set off on the last, most crucial part of their journey with their new guide leading the way, a new sense of optimism was born. French's blundering shadow was lost in their dust while the trail ahead seemed blessed by a soft westerly breeze and a fresh new air of expectancy and adventure.

Chapter 13

Crossing Over

By 1874, the Fort Benton that Jerry Potts left behind as he rode north with Colonel Macleod had declined substantially from its glory days. The crisp white adobe fort that had made Alexander Culbertson proud, and figured so prominently in the Benton of his youth with Andrew Dawson, had been reduced to a decrepit freight station recently abandoned by the U.S. Army.

Potts could recall the *Chippewa* and the *Key West No. 2*, the first two steamboats ever to get that far up the Missouri. The year was 1862 and the 300 soldiers who disembarked on July 2 celebrated Independence Day before heading west to Oregon. A decade had passed since May 1864, when the American government created the Territory of Montana, only eight months after Jerry's last great ride with the resolute Dawson.

Under Dawson's management, the AFC had shipped an average of 20,000 buffalo robes per year to Fort Union. It was only after the influx of independent traders and White buffalo hunters that the wholesale slaughter began in earnest. Between 1866 and 1870, four steamship companies made 150 trips. I.G. Baker's *Red Cloud*, *Helena*, and *Rosebud* were joined by a dozen other steamboats. Once gold was discovered, it was a transportation heyday with full cargo holds going in both directions. Buffalo robes and wolf pelts went downriver while 10,000 self-proclaimed miners and much-in-demand supplies used the boats to get to Montana. Gerald Berry records that "the total freight and passenger charges in 1867 amounted to approximately $3,000,000. One pilot ... received $7500 for making one round trip from St. Louis." Money flowed fast and loose along the Missouri. The pilot made it downriver, but his money did not last long. "He lost every cent of it in one evening's gambling in St. Louis. He flipped his last dime to decide [between] a drink or a sandwich and coffee. The dime rolled down a crack in the floor."[1]

As the population mounted, so did demands for protection, leading the U.S. Army to establish Fort Shaw between Helena and Fort Benton.

Whether it was the hordes of Whites or the evil act of a single wolfer that had brought back the deadly smallpox remained unclear. Potts and his Piegan brothers had no doubts, however, that Fort Shaw had given the people of the Marias River the murderous Major Eugene Baker.

Potts, by this time, could have likely taken some solace regarding his old friend Joe Cobell. Cobell had led the Baker assassins to a death camp full of starving, smallpox-infested men, women, and children. The trader, who had ridden with Potts and the Dawson party on their downriver retrieval of trade goods in 1863, was said to have fired the first shot on the Marias. Cobell may not have been the heartless killer that history has painted. The scout knew that Baker's assembled killing squad was told to forget about taking prisoners; the targeted camp was doomed.

If Potts were in Cobell's fix, how would he have reacted? Cobell had steered Baker to a den of doom, where a warrior's last hope was that a proud death could come in battle, a final gift of the gods. Did Cobell know that Baker's real quarry, Mountain Chief and his followers, were farther north? Had he duped a bloodthirsty soldier into claiming victory out of nothing more than a mercy killing? Potts would have known one thing for sure. Baker had no knowledge that Joe Cobell's wife, the mother of his children, was the sister of Mountain Chief.[2]

Three winters had passed since that terrible January and now Potts was himself aligned with a new influx of soldiers. Barroom talk suggested that the Canadians in their odd little hats would only last months before retreating back home. The redcoats said they had been sent to protect Indians from the whiskey traders, but it was hard to believe that this inept band of tattered soldiers could protect anyone when they were only days from either starving or freezing to death.

Indian scouts who had watched the pathetic march of these newcomers into their hunting lands could only judge them as harmless. Their horses were half dead, and their train stretched so far apart they could never defend themselves against attack. It was said that the Great White Mother, the powerful leader that the men of Fort Edmonton in the north referred to as "the Queen," sent them. The HBC men would mutter her name before they drank the fine whiskey Potts had once tasted when he had led a black robe to that fort.

Charles Conrad was one of two Virginian brothers who had come west at the end of a civil war that had torn his community to shreds. He was part of the first census ever taken in Fort Benton, in 1870, when his was one of 115 families occupying most of the 145 dwellings.[3] Now the astute partner of Isaac Baker, he was anxious to drum up new business. Conrad had risen to merchant prince status during the past five years, but when the gold rush petered out, so did the business outlook in Fort Benton; he had seen his town's waterfront traffic reduced to a trickle after the miners had stopped coming.

After years of moral compromise, his mercantile enthusiasms fed primarily by the ugly whiskey trade, Conrad saw, in the arrival of the Canadians, a unique business opportunity. He also knew that when it came to whiskey he should be on his best behaviour. At least with Potts he could feel comfortable that the scout would be discreet about any past misdeeds. Potts was a man of few words who knew the game and how it worked; nothing would be said by the wily mixed-blood to link Charles Conrad to the whiskey trade.

While there was some talk of Macleod's troops wintering in the Sweetgrass Hills near the Milk River, it was Conrad who suggested "that they not stay on the Milk River, which lacked adequate timber, but proceed north to the center of the whiskey trade on the Belly and Oldman Rivers."[4]

Conrad could have led Macleod there himself—with his eyes closed. He knew every foot of the trail north and could maintain that he had always found the whiskey trade vulgar and shameful, a necessary evil to survive. His economic tide had suddenly turned as he now headed north with a full year's contract to supply Macleod's planned Canadian fort. His mixed-blood ally could also take comfort in the regular monthly salary that he would earn through the coming winter. As they headed north, Conrad and Potts had to be mildly curious about the British-trained officers and the rumoured chaos that lay ahead. On the surface, Colonel Macleod seemed anything but incompetent. How could he have so misjudged his troops' needs?

Along the trail to the border, things did not start well when Macleod sought their insights on what misfits Fort Whoop-up would yield. Did they expect resistance? How rampant was the trade? First Potts and then Conrad dispelled Macleod's illusions. Potts was confident that they would find no whiskey at this time of year, and the police would find few, if any, traders. Conrad dismissed any notion that they were headed toward a landscape of fortified trading posts. Certainly Whoop-up was more substantial than the rest, Conrad acknowledged, but it was probably in the hands of a lonely caretaker.

If Macleod was growing frustrated, he didn't show it. Before they left Dufferin, Commissioner French had made Fort Whoop-up the march's destination. Then, out in the middle of nowhere, he had dismissed its significance, even calling it legitimate and the property of Isaac Baker. Baker had denied ownership, but Conrad's actions and knowledge of the terrain suggested he knew more about whiskey forts than would a desk-bound wholesaler. Potts was Conrad's recommendation. Was he like the last guide to ride into their camp, another "bought man" Colonel French was sure had steered them away from their quarry? The answers would come along the rutted trail to Fort Whoop-up.

When Jerry Potts signed on with the Canadians, it meant returning to the scene of both the tragedy of his mother's death and his greatest moments as a Blackfoot warrior. After avenging Crooked Back's death he had turned away from the Blood Nation, especially the Mules who had killed his mother and the Many Fat Horses band who had failed to protect her. As for the battle where he and the Piegan leader, Mountain Chief, had led the assault on the hated Cree, driving them once and for all out of the hunting ground, it was an event he would fondly recollect for the rest of his life.

Macleod's patrol followed the Whoop-up Trail to the Milk River, where he planned to meet up with his allotted force and the man he had left in charge, Inspector William Winder. Neither of the newcomers, Potts nor Conrad, could have had any sense of the level of animosity that had developed among the redcoat recruits toward their leadership. Macleod certainly had to be aware of it; he was also well aware of the men's resilience. By the time he reached the camp, Macleod would find not lingering bitterness, but a mood of renewed enthusiasm among the three divisions that were now under his sole direct command. The reason for the optimism was obvious, summed up by one diarist's entry, written the day Colonel French left camp: "He left here with the best wishes of the men—that he may never come back."[5]

Inspector Winder had received Macleod's orders and moved the men west in order to intersect the Whoop-up Trail by October 1. The next day they followed the trail until they reached the Milk River. Two days later the place erupted in cheers as their official commanding officer entered camp.

Jerry Potts could have no way of knowing that the reason for the apparent joy among this tattered army, bootless in some cases, with shredded gunnysacks wrapped around their feet, was Macleod himself.

James Macleod had come to Canada from the Isle of Skye as a child and earned his law degree at Toronto by age 28. He had first ventured west 10 years later as part of the Red River expedition that helped stabilize the soon-to-be province of Manitoba. He knew and respected the law, and every man in camp knew he had used his knowledge of the law to protect them from the irrationalities of Commissioner French. Macleod was the type of leader who generated loyalty rather than demanding it. It was a style that could quickly appeal to a man with a keen eye. By this point in his life, Jerry Potts had proven himself a good judge of horseflesh and a better judge of men. It seems quite likely that he knew before he crossed the Milk River that he had signed on with a "great chief."

Potts and Conrad were introduced to Macleod's officers. Inspector James Walsh, by this time, had fully recovered from one of French's last desperate decisions. Only 42 hours before Macleod had headed to Benton with his boss, Walsh had re-entered the Three Buttes camp with his small patrol after being recalled from what would almost certainly have been a death march. Fortunately, a rider had reached the resolute Walsh with word that French had rescinded one of his impulsive orders

Walsh's journey into the unknown had been initiated by French, who had already sent an advance scouting party headed by Sub-inspector Denny north to assess the plausibility of a trail to Fort Edmonton and to gauge the water supply along the way. Impatient when Denny did not return the next day, and personally anxious to head south to more comfortable climes, French had then ordered Walsh, with 70 men and 58 horses, to march north and join Inspector Jarvis, on the assumption that his division had made it to Fort Edmonton. The risks to Walsh's party were magnified when a second scouting party returned from farther west to report that massive buffalo herds were encountered moving north to south as far as the eye could see. Their path ensured that fouled drinking water was all that existed to the north. Ignoring the consequences to his men, French stood by his order; unwilling to wait even for morning light, he had directed Walsh to organize the river swim late on September 13 and start his march at dawn.

Whether Macleod sensed real trouble ahead or simply felt compelled to stay away from French and his questionable decisions is a moot point; he forded the Saskatchewan in the wake of Walsh's entourage. Following the riverbank, Macleod rode all night, intent on finding the original scouting party that was long overdue. With all trace of Denny's trail obscured by buffalo tracks, he persisted. Finally at dawn, he spotted the amiable sub-inspector and his three Métis scouts. Denny told him that, after some nervous moments when challenged by a band of Assiniboines 50 miles into their journey, they then had travelled at night, ultimately halting their trek 90 miles from its starting point. He had nothing good to say about their findings.[6]

Macleod and Denny rode hard through that day, both no doubt concerned about Walsh's situation. It was late afternoon when they crossed the last river ford and found a lone constable posted at the now-abandoned campsite. He led the riders south, where they finally joined the main camp, to the relief of all.

French chose to ignore Denny's personal assessment of the terrain, adding insult to the latter's fatigued body. French made it clear that any judgement he made would be based on input, not from his own officer, but from the scout, Pierre Léveillé. Still angered by the slight three decades later as he wrote his memoirs, Denny would diplomatically revert to French's own formal report of the event to describe the commissioner's actions: "Denny's party ... gave a dreadful account of the country; neither wood nor grass ... Mr. Levaille [sic] was with Mr. Denny and placing great reliance on his judgement I asked him if the party could get through to Edmonton." Told by both Denny and the scout that it was next to impossible, French concluded in his report, "With much reluctance I had to counter-order the Edmonton party, and instructed Major Walsh to follow the main party south to the Three Buttes."[7]

On the 18th· the camp was dusted with snow as reveille sounded at 6 a.m. and the men anxiously readied for their final leg. After six miles they stood near the U.S. border, on the ridge of the Milk River, agape at the sea of buffalo on the prairies around them. In camp, Macleod, Denny, and his fellow officers were again feeling concern for one of their own. Walsh was nowhere to be seen.

Finally on the 20th, Walsh straggled in. He reported that he had tried to keep as many men, oxen, and horses alive as possible. Six horses had already succumbed from sheer exhaustion, and one despondent sub-constable named Elliot Thornton had wandered off to hunt and had never returned. Distraught at this discovery, Walsh had searched and then waited as long as was reasonable. Finally he had led his troop south to the Three Buttes.

On the 21st the glum Walsh was given some relief when a half-dead Thornton staggered into camp. Reporting that his horse had died after they had lost their way, Elliot Thornton had walked south, covering 80 miles in five days.[8]

Commissioner French assessed Thornton's explanation of events and, neither impressed by his perseverance nor sympathetic to his plight, issued one final reprimand. Before allowing the constable some rest, he fined him five months' pay for losing his horse.

On that sour note, Walsh, Denny, Thornton, and the three troops destined for duty farther west watched the back of George French as he left camp on September 22. Now, 12 days later, they celebrated the return of their true leader with a feast of buffalo, shared by men and officers and the odd little man Macleod had brought with him, Jerry Potts.

Over the next few evenings of campfire chatter, Potts and Conrad no doubt heard enough of what had transpired in recent weeks to feel thankful they were riding with Colonel Macleod and not the commissioner himself.

On the morning of October 7 Potts and Macleod broke camp and started along the trail to Fort Whoop-up, leaving Cecil Denny behind with a small detail. Denny recorded: "I watched as Charles Conrad, Jerry Potts and three troops moved away ... I was left at the camp with my troop horse, many wagons, the nine-pound guns and loads of ammunition ... I had besides, several sick men, a corporal, and a few others—about 20 in all. My instructions were to await the arrival of the bull teams, attach wagons and guns to the train wagons, and have accommodation made for the sick men."[9]

Denny and his underlings waited a week for the arrival of the bull trains, but in the meantime an enterprising independent trader from Benton reached them first. Denny wrote, "John Glenn passed on his way to locate wherever the Force determined to make their headquarters ... the men in my party, clubbing together, bought a sack of flour [$20], a barrel of syrup [$3] and much canned fruit ... these unusual luxuries were quickly disposed of; cooking went on continuously until they were gone."[10]

Once underway, Denny's "men who were well had to walk [and] were three days in reaching the St. Mary's River where [they] camped not far from Fort Whoop-up."[11] Days later Denny caught up to Macleod's final camp beside the Oldman River, well beyond Fort Whoop-up. Denny soon heard that in his short reign at the head of their column, Jerry Potts had made an indelible impression and firmly entrenched himself as indispensable.

Sam Steele later wrote that Potts "won the confidence of the ranks the first day out, and when morning came he rode boldly in front of the advance guard. It was noon when the party reached Milk River, and found him there sitting near a fat buffalo cow he had killed and dressed for the use of the force."[12] Macleod must have been equally impressed because he later recounted to Steele "That evening he turned towards the Milk River ridge, selected a campground, then led [us] to some fine springs containing the best water tasted for many a long day."[13]

There was more to come on the following day, a mass congregation of sorts that could have easily ended in disaster. "At dawn, the men awoke from a fitful sleep, disturbed by an incessant rumble, to find themselves surrounded by a sea of buffalo."[14] It was a sensation that no man there would ever forget. "As far as the eye could see there was a black mass moving eastward." Fearing that "guns might stampede the herd," not a shot was fired and on "Jerry's advice ... the wagon train and guns were closed up to one yard distance, the men marching quietly alongside the train and thus all day they thrust their way through the immense herd."[15]

By the time Macleod and his officers looked down on Fort Whoop-up, one simple description summed up their opinion of their new scout: "He appeared to know everything."[16] Although he did not reveal his personal way of handling sinners nor the bad memories conjured up in his own mind, Jerry Potts did offer an opinion on the fort itself: "Bad medicine, many ghosts," he muttered.[17]

Macleod had come too far not to judge the situation for himself. After assigning an officer to make camp near the river, he rode with Potts down the hill. The fort's sturdy palisade and strategic bastions would be nearly impregnable if they had to fight their way in. He might have to wait for Denny to arrive with the cannons, but one way or another the tattered Stars and Stripes that fluttered from a flagpole within was going to be dealt with.

The fort consisted of "palisades of sturdy cottonwood, bastions of squared timber at the north-west and south-east corners, all windows faced inward to a square decorated by two ancient muzzle-loading cannons that had been dragged from Fort Benton but looked of dubious value. After one successful foray by a thirsty Peigan warrior, metal bars had been installed in all chimneys to keep unwanted visitors from the hearths. A lone brass bell was strategically mounted to sound the approach of new arrivals, friendly or ótherwise. Two large gates swung outward to the south providing an uninterrupted view of all comers."[18]

When Macleod pounded on the gate, a single unimposing figure, Dave Akers, opened it. Congenial and with no sense of trepidation, he invited Macleod in and offered water from his well and vegetables from his garden to accompany a feast of buffalo. They would have to forego any whiskey, he said, for at Fort Whoop-up there was none to be had.

A first-hand version of events from another perspective was recorded soon after by freighter Charles Schafft, one of the few present for Macleod's arrival. "The Major, some other officers and a squad of men paid us an official visit. They acted with courtesy toward everyone," he wrote. After they asked for whiskey and were told it was a rare commodity, Schafft watched them start their hunt. "Several details under command of proper officers were soon engaged in trying to find the 'critter.' They searched up stairs and down ... [to] no avail and they left for other fields."[19]

Schafft also made it clear that Akers and his comrades had received regular reports on the progress of the police as they stumbled their way west. The traders had no idea to "what extent the red-coats would interfere in business matters," and as they neared, "those who had contraband in stock cached it; everything was quiet and trade nearly at a stand still."[20]

Before he left Dufferin, Macleod had read many reports sent east, some official, others from anxious men of the cloth, both Catholic and Methodist, about the hundreds of bootleggers trading whiskey at this very site. Conrad had denied ownership, and in fact that was true. It had been the fervent John Healy who had used Tom Power' money and his own gall to hoist the American flag in Canadian territory. Aware that the Canadian police were coming his way, Healy had tried to sell Fort Whoop-up the previous September by placing newspaper ads in Montana, but there were no takers. When Macleod arrived at Whoop-up, Healy was back in Montana and Akers was in the employ of T.C. Power, reputedly also managing nearby Fort Kipp. Whether Akers knew that Charles Conrad was riding with the Mounties before his arrival was a moot point. Macleod, much in need of a winter shelter, offered to purchase the fort for $10,000 in the name of the Canadian government but found the counter-offer of $25,000 unacceptable. Was this inflated price a ploy? Was it Dave Akers, Tom Power, or John Healy and his partner Alfred Hamilton who were making the call? Not one of them would be happy about the fort's occupants going to the aid of their main competitor, Charles Conrad. And without this shelter, maybe the Mounties would make a run for home. But they were wrong. The owners "would have been wise to have accepted the offer, for the coming of the Police marked the end of the whiskey trade, and the post fell into disuse except as a ranch headquarters for Dave Akers."[21]

Two inspectors were assigned to search the

This 1878 contrived re-enactment photo of Fort Whoop-up manages to include Blood families soon to be victimized by the whiskey trade. A man and his cannon are strangely positioned where no armament would reside, an apparent lookout sits atop the block house, and fluttering in the breeze is an American trader's banner or possibly his version of the Stars and Stripes that he liked to flaunt before British eyes.

entire fort. With no whiskey to be found and winter closing in, James Macleod asked Potts to identify the best place for them to winter. Jerry Potts did not hesitate. The next morning, after fording the St. Mary's River at Whoop-up and the Belly at a rundown trading post that Potts called Slideout, he led the column along the Old North Trail to the lush valley of the Oldman River, where "the Rocky Mountains ... seemed like a great wall to the west. Chief Mountain, like a huge square block, reared its remarkable head through the clouds."[22]

Potts' choice of location for his newfound masters in itself spoke of the respect he now had for the redcoats. He had brought them to the land of the magical spirit, Napi, the Old Man, and to the river that legend said flowed mysteriously out the side of a mountain. It was the site where, as a boy, he had heard the stories of the Sun Creator and experienced the rituals of the Sun Dance. It was a place of prominence that he now opted to share.

When James Macleod headed toward Whoop-up, his was one of four distinct directives to commanding officers of the Force during that second winter of its existence. Men like Walsh under Macleod's command, and Sam Steele under Jarvis farther north, had suffered severe conditions at the Stone Fort near Winnipeg the previous winter, but this year looked to be even harsher for most of them. Those men who had retreated east with Colonel French would at least be closer to their own world, divided between the spartan shelter at Fort Pelly and the relative comforts that the commissioner would enjoy back beside the Red River at Dufferin. To the north, Jarvis, Steele, and their followers would endure the most treacherous trail, but at least at HBC's Fort Edmonton there was a shelter on their horizon. As historian R.G. MacBeth observed, "Colonel Macleod had the most difficult and dangerous situation of all. [He] was out in the open with the winter coming on and no shelter from the blizzards ... He was hundreds of miles away from any possibility of help in men or substance from Canadian sources, and he had only three troops of fifty men each in the midst of a turbulent gang of outlaw whiskey-peddlers and horse-thieves. He was completely surrounded by thousands of the most warlike of western Indians, with thousands still more warlike just over the line ... he and his men knew that they had 'burned their ship behind them' and that they must hold their ground or perish."[23]

Potts' choice for a building site sat well with everybody who saw it. When Cecil Denny finally reached the camp, he noted: "Our tired horses and oxen, freed at last from the wearing drag, grazed unworried; the many white tents of the Force gleamed white among the trees." Men were already felling cottonwoods, readying a perimeter for construction of what would be named Fort Macleod. "We arrived the fourth day from the Sweetgrass Hills," Denny wrote. "We had a hearty welcome, glad to be at our journey's end. The location chosen looked beautiful to us after the long and weary march ... the lofty barrier of snow-draped peaks to the west, the timbered range of the Porcupines to the north, and the Old Man valley as far as the eyes might reach, lined with sheltering woods. Buffalo in bands dotted the prairie to the south."[24]

By the time Denny arrived, Macleod had already decided that Potts and Inspector Walsh would be charged with rounding up the weakest of their horses and livestock and driving them south into Montana, where Potts said there was enough feed in the Sun River valley that they might have a chance of survival. Potts had watched the unhesitant Walsh volunteer for the mission and knew that he would be in good company. Despite their profoundly different backgrounds, they would become soulmates in the years that followed. But before their journey south could begin, Potts would have to spend some time dealing with whiskey peddlers.

On October 29, as Potts and Walsh were preparing to take 64 horses, 20 oxen, and 10 head of cattle on the 200-mile journey south, a lone Blackfoot horseman bearing the markings of a chief rode into camp. Potts quickly ascertained that the man was Three Bulls, who had surrendered two of his finest horses to a Black trader named William Bond at Pine Coulee, 50 miles north. For the horses, he had received two containers of bad whiskey.

Macleod appointed Lief Crozier, a former major in the 15th Argyle Light Infantry and a no-nonsense disciplinarian, to deal with the situation. With Jerry Potts leading the way, Crozier and 10 of his men headed north. Two days later they returned with five prisoners in tow, including the accused, William Bond. Crozier had confiscated two wagons full of whiskey, which he brought back as evidence, plus the men's rifles and revolvers, 16 horses, and more than 100 buffalo robes.

Potts, and no doubt some of the enlisted men, must have thought there was a better use for the gallons of liquor that Macleod poured on the ground. But Macleod was all business as he declared his role as magistrate and quickly found the five men guilty of selling contraband in defiance of the law. Three hirelings were fined $50 each, but Bond and his apparent partner, Harry "Kamoose" Taylor, the former Spitzee Cavalry leader, were fined $200 each for their first offence.

Before Potts and Walsh left for the journey south, a friend of the five prisoners conveniently showed up. After hearing the amount of the fines, John D. "Waxy" Weatherwax, professing to be a little short on cash, offered goods to cover the fines for the four White men, leaving William Bond to his own devices. The fines were a pittance compared to Waxy's summer profits and a deal was struck: 326 pounds of bacon, 5 gallons of syrup, a pitchfork, some axe handles, and 105 buffalo robes.[25] Before mounting his horse for the ride south, Potts assured Macleod that Waxy and Kamoose would probably be repeat offenders.

Macleod's satisfaction with Jerry Potts could not have been greater by this point. He had led them to a place where they might actually survive and he had helped them nab their first whiskey traders. Walsh also earned his praise. "Walsh was anxious to be sent and he deserves great credit for the way in which he is performing this service," Macleod wrote in a field report.[26]

Potts and Walsh made it to their destination in Montana before parting company. Walsh wasted little time getting his men back to Canada, but Potts headed east. He had found men he could trust and respect in Macleod and Walsh; he would return to the "land of many ghosts" and he would take his family with him.

Potts went on to Benton, where he quenched his thirst, got the lay of the land, and then headed to his lodges on the Marias River. There he gathered up Panther Woman, Spotted Killer, his extended family, and his own horse herd and led the procession of travois north to the slopes near the island where Fort Macleod was taking

Inspector James Walsh of "B" Division (left, and originally in charge of "D" Division) and his counterpart for "F" Division, Lief Crozier, were the two men that James Macleod would rely on most often when there was an extraordinary circumstance to overcome. Both would earn accolades for their bravery and dedication on the NWMP front lines throughout their careers before retiring with ambitions unfulfilled.

shape. Macleod must have wondered at the scope of his recruitment when he saw Jerry Potts supervising the placement and erection of his lodges. Wives, children, elders, a healthy herd of horses, dogs—when Jerry set out to move, he didn't travel light.

Leaving the camp-making to his wives, Potts undoubtedly sought out Colonel Macleod to fill him in on news from Benton, where the smart money was betting that the Blackfoot war chiefs had been stirred up enough that they would have all of the redcoat scalps by spring.

Chapter 14

A Trusted Voice

When Jerry Potts parted company with Inspector Walsh at the Sun River ranch and headed east toward his lodges on the Marias, it must have seemed only natural to make a small detour to Fort Benton's main street and a saloon where he could quench the powerful thirst he had built up since leaving Montana. It was hard on a man of Jerry's persuasions to see good whiskey dumped in a snowbank.

The bars of Benton were full of wolfers and whiskey traders bragging about stories they had spread among the Blackfoot before heading south to avoid the Canadian police. The Mounties, they had told the Bloods, Peigans, and Siksikas, were no different than the blue-coated long knives who had massacred the South Piegans on the Marias and were now hell-bent on ridding the country of the Sioux. The Blackfoot, they hoped, would step up and do the dirty work, either making war on the Mounties or chasing them back to where they came from. When it was all over, the traders, of course, would bring whiskey north to celebrate. It was to the Blackfoot chiefs' credit that they reserved judgement; most of them were able to discern that it was the traders and their firewater that posed the greater threat.

Farther north, Macleod had little idea as to how much the redcoats were respected among the Blackfoot. After all, the traders had fled even before the Great Mother's policemen had arrived—at least all traders not in the employ of Waxy Weatherwax. Potts had warned Macleod that Waxy would be back, and Macleod had no reason to doubt him.

Bitter cold motivated the workforce as the officers supervised the construction of barracks, for the men first and the officers later. It was this kind of priority that entrenched loyalty deep in the ranks, but loyalty only went so far.

That Jerry Potts was paid an amount slightly more than Macleod's inspectors were, and nearly three times the salary of the sub-corporals in their tattered uniforms, was widely accepted. He was worth it, whatever he was paid. However, one harsh fact was breeding dissension. The paltry wage the enlistees had signed on for was bad enough; now, here they were, almost five months into their stint and they had yet to receive a paycheque. Macleod's sole means of helping his men was to take the robes he had seized from Bond and Taylor and, with the aid of Native women like Potts' two wives, have them turned into coats, hats, and blankets for his men.

The successful arrest and detention of William Bond and his cohorts and the seizure of robes and contraband served notice to the Blackfoot community that the Mounties meant business. But there had been no follow-up visits and, in fact, the Siksika and Blood tribes had been conspicuously absent from the Oldman valley. Anxious to speak with their most influential leaders before the harsh winter set in, Macleod asked Potts to ride into their camps and assure the chiefs that they had nothing to fear in coming to the fort. He was also to find out whether there was any substance to the stories of the whiskey traders' caches. In mid-November, with brisk hints of winter in the morning air, Potts disappeared into his other world.

He travelled to the scattered camps of the Bloods, Peigans, and Siksika and was always welcomed. Here he was Bear Child and never failed to respect the chiefs and the rituals that had to be followed when entering their presence. While Potts was terse in the White world, Bear Child always honoured the smoking of the pipe and other elaborate formalities that were part of entering a chief's lodge. At each sitting he explained the presence of the NWMP and gained assurances from the tribal leaders that they would deal with the police in peace. At the end of the month, when he returned to Macleod's quarters, he was confident the chiefs would accept the Mounties' invitation in their own time.

Macleod's officers, greatly relieved that their trek to nowhere was behind them, rallied the troops throughout November and had them sheltered in a barracks by the time Potts returned from his mission. Charles Conrad had delivered more workers and his bull train of provisions after overcoming a raging blizzard along the trail, a storm fierce enough to cost him 30 oxen. But even with all their efforts, the living space was cramped, and with a single location, Macleod's force was too concentrated to discover the rumoured caches of whiskey.

Macleod's horses were in terrible shape, so he went to Fort Kipp to requisition the 10 tons of hay known to be stored there. After examining the fort and discussing with his host, John Kerler, his need for more living space, he proposed to turn Fort Kipp into a boarding house. The fort was conveniently situated near the confluence of the Belly and Oldman rivers, halfway to Fort Whoop-up. At the time it was being managed by Kerler, an experienced Canadian whiskey trader employed by T.C. Power.

Macleod's desire was that Inspector Brisebois and 10 members of his division take up residence there for the winter. When he got wind of this turn of events, Tom Power was not amused. He may have sought out these red-coated intruders as paying customers for hay or whiskey, but he had no desire to be their landlord. Only five months earlier Power had agreed to assume control of Fort Kipp from his business ally, John Healy, and had hired Kerler to run the trading post while Dave Akers watched over his other property at Fort Whoop-up. Power, who had arranged the harvesting of the hay crop, knew that feed would be a valued commodity for anybody trying to survive a winter on the Canadian prairie. He had every intention of carrying on business while adjusting to the new law enforcers. The first step was to eliminate the obvious. Knowing that the hated wolfers and the so-called Cypress Hills Massacre had triggered outrage in Canada, he cautioned Kerler, "If you have any strychnine take it off the invoices ... If officers of the police or boundary survey call you, treat them well."[1]

Power wanted all whiskey kept well away from the fort. Of course the redcoats were potentially good customers and should be courted as such, yet Tom Power was of a different mind. Notified by Kerler of the 10 new boarders, Power wrote Kerler to reject the proposed $1,000 fee and get rid of the redcoats. "We can not suffer to have them in the Fort and lose our winter's trade," he protested.[2] Kerler knew that was easier said than done and ignored Power, confident that the Mounties would attract more trade than they would scare away.

While Power was penning his instructions to Kerler, there were signs that Jerry Potts' invitations to tribes to visit Fort Macleod were beginning to pay off. When a small group of Bloods and Peigans entered the fort, Macleod received them with all the pomp he could muster. Potts was summoned to listen to the Native spokesman's extended oratory while Macleod waited for an interpretation. Unfamiliar with the dramatic gestures and expressions before him, the colonel could only hope that the demands were not unreasonable.

Finally the speech ended and Macleod turned to Potts. For one of the first but not the last times, he got a succinct Potts translation: "Dey damn glad you're here."[3]

Although he probably was not aware of it, when Macleod had taken up the cause of the complainant Three Bulls only two months earlier, he was getting closer to the great chief Crowfoot. Three Bulls, as it turned out, was half-brother to Crowfoot, and Macleod's response to this minor chief's initial visit had no doubt impressed the Blackfoot leader. In late November, a lone messenger representing his chief told Potts that Chief Crowfoot wanted to meet. Would the redcoat chief assure his safety if he came in peace? Potts knew then that his diplomacy had worked. He explained to Macleod that Crowfoot, or Isapo-muxika, head chief of the Siksika, was widely respected for his wisdom and was the most influential of all the Blackfoot chiefs. Macleod's challenging future would benefit greatly from his ability to win the trust of Crowfoot.

Potts held Crowfoot in high regard, both as a leader and as a warrior. On many occasions the chief had shown not only sound judgement but also courage and fierceness in battle. Both wise and perceptive, Crowfoot had seen enough to know that the redcoats might be the best allies he could find as the world changed around him. He had seen the ruthless bluecoats at work below the Milk River and could only hope that not all White men were bent on war. He hoped that these new arrivals, sons of the Great Mother, were as just and respectful of his nation as they seemed to be.

Crowfoot's father, a Blood warrior, had been killed in a battle with the Crows when the boy was only two. His mother married a Siksika man, who took his new wife and son to live with his relatives. He named the boy Bear Ghost, but after the son joined other warriors on raids against their traditional enemies to the south, he earned the name Isapo-muxika, meaning Crow Indian's Big Foot. It was Jerry Potts who shortened the translation to Crowfoot.

The great warrior was about eight years older than Potts. Crowfoot had been about seven years old when the great smallpox epidemic first hit Fort McKenzie and was carried north across the prairies by unknowing tribesmen trying to escape the plague. By the time a young mixed-blood boy had come north from the trading forts and was being christened Bear Child by his mother's people, around 1850, Crowfoot was already a 20-year-old war chief. Reputedly, Crowfoot was wounded at least six times during his many raids.

As he rose in stature among all of the Blackfoot tribes, Crowfoot kept his people isolated from the White invasion. Certainly there was trade with the Hudson's Bay Company, a practice that had gone on for generations. Then came the American Fur Company and its white adobe fort below the great falls on the Missouri River, the place they called Fort Benton. He had learned that, like most tribes, the AFC was a mix of good and bad men, but the Americans offered better guns than the British, and they traded freely for whiskey.

Crowfoot's Siksika villages in the valley of the Bow River were, of all Blackfoot settlements, the most removed from the trading forts. They were buffered from White migration by their enemies to the east, the Crees and Assiniboines, and their allies to the south, the Bloods and Peigans. After the best White leaders—old Hudson's Bay factors and American Fur Company bourgeois—gradually retired, the independent traders came to the Siksika, and with them came better killing weapons, more violence, more disease, and much more whiskey.

In 1865, when widely respected Siksika elder chief Three Suns died, many of his tribe rejected their old chief's son as not being strong enough to lead them. Instead they turned to Crowfoot, who had won new status after a Cree war party attacked a Blackfoot encampment near what became known as the Battle River. There, a savage fight was in its second day when a messenger reached Crowfoot's camp; the chief roused his warriors and charged several miles to the aid of his besieged brethren. After turning the tide of battle against the more numerous Crees and causing them to retreat, Crowfoot became the undisputed leader of the Siksika people.

But poisonous firewater that ruthless traders brought across the Medicine Line was a greater enemy than the Cree. It turned father against son, friend against friend, celebration into chaos. While there is no record of them sharing the same battlefield, Crowfoot probably had heard of the mixed-blood warrior named Bear Child. It was he who had led their Peigan brothers in the last great victory against the Crees and in recent years avenged his own mother's tragic, whiskey-driven death. If Bear Child spoke well of the redcoats, then that was who Crowfoot would go to for aid.

It was December 1, 1874, only six weeks after they had started to construct their fort, when Macleod first heard the impassioned speech of Crowfoot —several minutes of extravagant eloquence that Potts reduced to a few monosyllables. Macleod would have noted that his brief response also took much longer for Potts to translate to the Siksika chief. The ways of the Blackfoot, he was quickly learning, involved much ado.

The success of the first meeting was proven when Crowfoot returned to Fort Macleod a few days later with Red Crow of the Bloods and Bull Head of the Peigans to hold a

Crowfoot was perceived by the NWMP as the most influential leader among the Blackfoot chiefs, and he and James Macleod developed a strong respect for each other's integrity early in their relationship.

grand council. Potts, who had been instrumental in setting up the meeting, knew that such a gesture by the chiefs was rare, and he carefully instructed Macleod in the proper procedure for receiving the three most prominent Native leaders of the Confederacy. He explained to Macleod and his officers that all ceremony had meaning and must be observed, including prayer and smoking the pipe.

The three chiefs entered Macleod's quarters while hundreds of armed braves watched from the perimeter. Macleod extended a hand of greeting to the trio and then Crowfoot thanked the Great Spirit and the distant Great Mother for sending the redcoats to save them from the firewater traders. Red Crow, who had killed men himself in a drunken stupor and seen his own family decimated by drink, endorsed Crowfoot's words. Bull Head nodded assent.

Bull Head was a man who less than a decade earlier had led a war party south to the Sun and Dearborn rivers, burning farms, killing cattle, and scalping three innocent Whites to avenge the murder of four Peigans by drunken miners.[4] Red Crow was also a feared warrior, renowned for his bravery and, in recent years, for his own drunken sprees. "Just as he had thrown caution to the winds when he went to war, so did he cast aside all restraints when he drank," wrote Dempsey in his biography of the "warrior chief."[5] Of the three chiefs, Red Crow had the most reason to have respect for the White man. His highly regarded aunt, Natawista, had been married to the trader-diplomat Alexander Culbertson, who had brought the Bloods closer to treaty tables than anyone else.[6]

Macleod then told the chiefs that the Great Mother had sent the police to apply the same law to the Blackfoot people and Whites alike. He was there to uphold the law—to *maintiens le droit*," as the badge on his red coat stated. If the great chiefs of the Whites far to the east wished to do something in the land of the Blackfoot, Macleod promised to hold a council beforehand.

One Mountie who listened to Potts' translation wrote, "After [Jerry] had interpreted from the Blackfoot into the English language, you weren't very much farther ahead, for his English was weird." Working in the other direction was the opposite. "When he translated from English to Blackfoot his eyes gleamed as if his soul were in it, and as if showing that he felt that every word of it was good for the Indians."[7]

The council proved to be a momentous one. As an intermediary, Jerry Potts had become a trusted voice. In the years of hardship that were to follow, the Blackfoot Confederacy never caused the Mounties serious trouble. Neither Macleod nor Crowfoot ever abandoned the commitments interpreted by Jerry Potts in that first historic meeting of Blackfoot chiefs and Canadian authorities.

As one chief said, "Before you came the Indian crept along, now he is not afraid to walk erect."[8] After listening to Potts' translation and the passion he evoked on behalf of Macleod, Bull Head was so impressed that he gave the Mountie his own name, Stamix-oto-kan. After the Blackfoot chiefs left the council, James Macleod must once again have been impressed by and appreciative of his little bowlegged scout. Without Potts, it was unlikely that such a council could have happened.

The day after the council, Macleod received chilling news. Prisoner William Bond had escaped into the night while being escorted to the latrine. A guard thought he had wounded the escapee as he fired at his back. Macleod was furious. Having detailed three men to be with the prisoner at all times, he discovered that only one had been present on this occasion. All three spent some time in the cell where the fugitive should have been.

Bond, as it turned out, had earned the same animosity among the Canadian tribes that Alexander Harvey, Potts' "second father," had earned along the Missouri among Natives who traded there. Known to the Bloods as Estapomau, or Money, for his greed and cheating,[9] Bond was said to have raped and killed many women, regardless of his victims' ages. Over the winter, it was also determined that Bond was wanted in Ontario on suspicion of killing a family in Chatham. Though little is known of his origins, he was half-American Black, half-Mexican, and it is most likely that he escaped the south via the underground railway that brought many Blacks to Ontario prior to the Civil War. Most Mounties and Blackfoot alike hoped the wound he had suffered was a bad one, but the next morning a search party turned up nothing. Bond was gone.

It was obvious that Macleod, with the help of Jerry Potts, had made substantial progress with the Blackfoot chiefs. Then, as a follow-up to the council with Crowfoot, Macleod had a second opportunity to prove his sincerity.

The Blackfoot chiefs sent word that they wanted to honour the Mounties' arrival with a feast of their own. It was an invitation that could not be refused if the Mounties were to gain Crowfoot's trust. Potts prepared the officers in Blackfoot protocol and stressed how they should behave when the chiefs beckoned. With Potts and the colonel leading the way, the red-coated party rode into the Blackfoot camp.

After the smoking of pipes, the festivities began. The feast was grand and the dancing grew frenzied. Whiskey, of course, was taboo, so drink took the form of strong tea laced with black tobacco—a stimulant strong enough to provoke tragedy. According to one account, a jealous older husband, tired of watching his young wife dance with a man her age, got his gun. "Cutting a slit in the teepee from the outside he poked his rifle through and shot his young wife dead. The woman fell across the fire right in front of where the Mounties were sitting."[10] The evening had not been what Macleod or Crowfoot had in mind.

The killing not only resulted in instant chaos, but also left two opposing families challenging one another. Macleod seized the moment to demonstrate how justice would prevail under the new law. Speaking through Jerry Potts and summoning all his diplomatic prowess, he persuaded Crowfoot and his council to put the killer before the Great Mother's justice system. Eventually the old man was sent to Winnipeg for trial, found guilty of the savagery, and sentenced to a prison term at the Stony Mountain penitentiary. As Macleod kept the Blackfoot chiefs informed of the process through Potts, they were satisfied that they could trust the redcoats to keep their word.

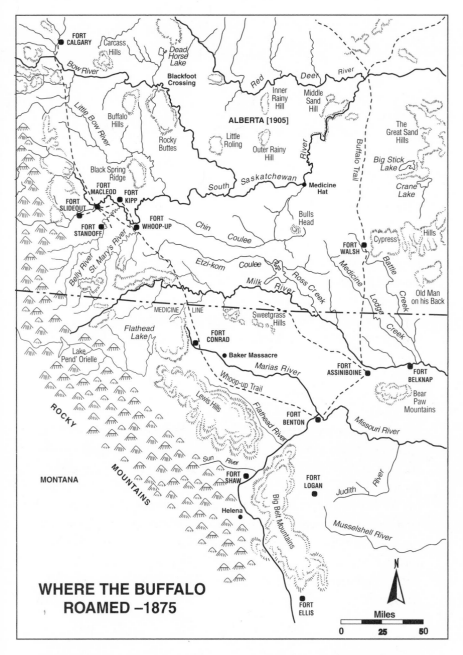

WHERE THE BUFFALO ROAMED −1875

The world of Jerry Potts after 1874 was focussed largely on the Benton-Macleod-Walsh triangle of forts, but his travels also extended south to Helena, north to Calgary and beyond, and east past the Cypress Hills.

Chapter 15

The Winter of 1875

One event that cast an air of melancholy over the men as they built Fort Macleod in mid-autumn 1874 was the death of Constable Godfrey Parks. In the annals of the march west he would always be known as *primus moriri,* the first to die. Parks was one of many who had drunk contaminated water during the arduous journey, and although he reached their final destination, he survived only a few days before becoming the only victim of the march.

For the most part the commanding officer and his men were a compatible group. If there was one of his officers who Macleod clashed with, it was Ephrem Brisebois, a man of awkward personality who had seen fit to resist some of Macleod's wishes during construction of their new fort. Brisebois' obstinacy eventually shattered Macleod's patience and as an early Christmas present to himself, the assistant commissioner had happened upon a convenient way to exile the surly French-Canadian officer and about a dozen of his men to Tom Power's fort, a good winter day's ride southeast of Fort Macleod. Jerry Potts responded to Macleod's wishes by leading Brisebois down the Oldman and presenting him to Fort Kipp's manager, John Kerler. Potts took with them enough of the horses to consume the 10 tons of hay that Macleod had already requisitioned from Kerler.

Potts soon returned to Fort Macleod, where Charles Conrad's manager, D.W. Davis, had his store up and running. Another resourceful trader was building a billiard hall, guaranteed to be a favourite haunt of the fort dwellers during their off-duty hours, and two discharged Mounties had set up shop as barber and cobbler. And then there was whiskey. As one scribe put it, "Booze, although unlawful, was not unknown in the backwoods burg and some of the most fervent users of the 'bottled devil' were the NWMP themselves. Even Macleod was not unknown to spend some of his free time enjoying a toddy or two. Stories of his two-fisted drinking bouts are a matter of record and a regular companion on these excursions of diversion was his gruff little scout, Jerry Potts."[1]

Potts knew both the lay of the land and the whiskey traders pretty well, and he brought Macleod information that a fur fort run by Dick Berry and financed by Waxy Weatherwax was still operating in the north, beside the Bow River. Waxy was also calling the shots from his own fort, which, unfortunately for him, was close enough to Fort Macleod that Potts or other patrols could keep a ready eye out for any traders' wagons that might head Waxy's way. Sure enough, in late January two wagons from the north, laden with robes, reached the Weatherwax fort. After he had dealt with the situation, Macleod wrote this account of it to Commissioner French: "I at once made up my mind to act on information received ... so I issued a Summons against Weatherwax and sent Inspector Winder with a party of men to seize the robes."[2]

Macleod seized over 450 robes and faced Weatherwax as a magistrate on February 1. The policeman/judge had already confirmed through the men who had delivered the robes that they had come from Berry's Bow River fort. He had also determined through the testimony of other witnesses that there had been whiskey there. Macleod, always respectful of the law, still found the evidence circumstantial and, as a result, stayed the case and sent Jerry Potts north with Inspector Lief Crozier to arrest Berry and gather more evidence.

Weatherwax remained in custody while Potts, Crozier, Sergeant W.D. Antrobus, and nine men headed out. Antrobus, who wrote an account of the journey, described Potts' uncanny ability to keep his bearings, even in a blinding blizzard. But he also noted his more human vulnerability, commenting that the first night, "[even] Jerry Potts, although he remained rolled up in his blankets, did not sleep at all."[3]

It took four days to reach shelter at a place Potts called Pine Coulee. Crozier had no idea how Potts located the pine structure, which Antrobus compared favourably with Fort Macleod. Potts probably failed to mention that he had been there with Kamoose Taylor in the Spitzee Cavalry days. For the dozen half-frozen men, warmth was the main goal, and when they achieved it they turned their attention to the lone Weatherwax employee stationed there and guarding a wagonload of robes.

To this point Potts had guided them over 60 miles, but they were still well short of their destination. Eventually reaching two separate outposts, Crozier interviewed additional witnesses, confiscated two more wagonloads of robes, and arrested another Weatherwax associate, Edward Smith. Among those interviewed was the head Siksika chief, Old Sun, who told Potts that he did not know what to expect from the policemen and was hesitant to meet with them. Sergeant Antrobus, listening to the exchange, concluded: "[The Blackfoot] know the traders are afraid of us, so that in their eyes we are no common men."[4]

Weather continued to delay their return trip, but the wait netted Crozier even more robes. If there was still whiskey cached somewhere, he never found it. Finally a break in the weather allowed Potts to lead the convoy of sleighs south, only to run into another savage snowstorm. "We could not be guided by the wind," Antrobus reported, "because it did not blow five minutes at a time from the same direction."[5] As the storm worsened, the party became separated, with Antrobus and some of his men stranded at the back of the column. Antrobus was lost and knew it, but he also knew he could rely on Potts, recalling: "Some of the boys became greatly alarmed ... one of them wanted us to try and get back to [the fort] about eight miles. I refused saying that Jerry would return for us."[6] And so he did. Potts found them and reunited the group. Antrobus would later conclude his assessment of their ordeal thus: "This Jerry Potts is justly called the best guide in the country ... I do not believe there is another man who could have guided us through that storm as he did."[7]

When Crozier recounted this ordeal later at Fort Macleod, those listening marvelled at how Potts could have accomplished such a feat, and in his years with the Force the stories of his durability and sense of direction became legendary. Sam Steele, with whom Potts worked closely for many years, wrote in his memoirs: "He possessed an uncanny sense of locality and direction. Others could guide travelers through country they had visited before, but this man could take a party from place to place by the quickest route, through country altogether unknown to him, without compass and without sight of the stars. Unlike other guides, he never talked with others when he was at work. He would ride on ahead by himself, keeping his mind fixed on the mysterious business of finding the way. He was never able to give any clear explanation of his method. Some mysterious power, perhaps a heritage from his Indian ancestors, was at work."[8]

Assistant Commissioner Macleod was happy, no doubt, to have both his new prisoners and his own men safely back at Fort Macleod. He also had more confiscated robes and new evidence to further the case against Weatherwax.

In his quarters Macleod listened as Crozier tried to make sense of Potts' uncanny abilities. At a loss for words, the thankful officer finally concluded that to appreciate their scout's skills, anyone who doubted him would simply have to suffer a similar experience first-hand. The hero of the moment had abandoned the accolades being heaped upon him, preferring the warmth and comforts provided by wives Panther Woman and Spotted Killer in his own nearby lodges.

Much to his dismay, Waxy Weatherwax was sentenced to six months in prison and a $300 fine when Macleod was through with him. Edward Smith was given a lesser sentence because he co-operated with the investigation; Macleod exiled him from his domain for at least a year. That left Smith the unenviable job of heading for Benton, where he became a messenger boy. The whiskey trade above the Medicine Line was no longer an option for those who wanted to get rich.

It was February before Colonel Macleod and his men received a second mail dispatch from the east. While it did not include any pay packets for the men, it did contain instructions for Macleod to make a 300-mile journey to Helena, Montana, to meet the newly appointed NWMP officer, Acheson Gosford Irvine, a soldier whom Macleod knew from their shared experiences as part of the Red River expedition of 1870.[9] Irvine had most recently served as commander of the Provisional Battalion of Rifles in Manitoba, but his new mandate was connected to the event that had triggered the formation of the Mounties. Irvine was to initiate extradition hearings for the alleged killers who had participated in the Cypress Hills Massacre. Displaying the lack of forethought evident in so many of his prior decisions, Commissioner French instructed Macleod to make this arduous journey, giving little consideration to the fact that March weather on the prairie could be perilous at best.

It was a foregone conclusion that Potts would lead the way, and Macleod picked Sub-inspector Cecil Denny, Sergeant Dave Cochrane, and Sub-constable Charles Ryan to set out "with saddle and packhorses, blankets, tea, bacon and hard biscuits but no tent."[10] They bypassed Brisebois at Fort Kipp and made 30 miles to Fort Whoop-up the first night out. There Macleod and his men again enjoyed the hospitality of the resident manager, Dave Akers, a man who had seen enough of the prairie to recognize its omens. "As we were leaving the next morning," wrote Denny, "Akers pointed out two rainbow-like halos around the sun that he called sun dogs. He predicted a blizzard within 24 hours."[11] The party planned to make camp at Rocky Springs on the Milk River that night.

Denny described the event in great detail in his memoirs. The five men were in good spirits as they rode out into the frigid morning air, taking rare comfort in knowing what lay ahead at their next destination, a campsite Potts had first introduced them to on their original trip west. All but Denny, who had trailed behind on the main column's trek north the previous fall, knew that they could look forward to good shelter, wood, and grass at day's end.

The prairie vista seemed to stretch forever as Potts led them southeast. Dense herds of buffalo ebbed and flowed like a great muddy brown sea while snow-white, gentle slopes surrounded them. The sun dogs stared down on all. Macleod, perhaps moved by the majesty of the moment, lit out after an old buffalo bull, not with the intent to kill, but for the pure sport of it. Potts, Denny, and the others turned their mounts to watch the chase. Macleod appeared to have gained the upper hand after about a mile but, as Denny would later record, he was in for a surprise. "As he drew alongside, the bull suddenly swung his massive head in a vicious lunge at the horse. The sharp horn caught the stirrup leather, ripping it clear away from the saddle."[12] Macleod fell back from the beast, a new lesson learned, fortunate that his horse had not been disembowelled.

As he rode up to the four amused observers, Macleod did not get a chance to speak. Potts, a little twinkle in his coal-black eyes, grinned at the others and then at his leader. "Colonel," he said, "I guess you leave dem ol' buffalo bull alone after dis, hey?"[13]

Macleod's stirrup was repaired while Potts dug buffalo chips from the snow for a fire. As they finished lunch, a grey mist rolled in, obscuring the ominous sun dogs and stirring in Denny a sense of foreboding. Macleod's horse was hurriedly resaddled and Potts upped the pace, intent on making the steep slopes of the Milk River before they stopped again.

A harsh north wind cut across their path, and all five men hunched their shoulders to ward off the bitter cold. Snow fell hard and then fell harder as the sudden blizzard obliterated any sense of trail. Potts rode on, finally making the north shore of the Milk River. Grass and wood were no longer on the bill of fare; shelter itself was in question. Denny writes that Potts took charge in the crisis: "On the advice of our guide we unsaddled and stowed our packs under a snowbank."[14] Potts pulled out his hunting knife and started cutting his way into the frozen bank, and the others followed suit, gradually creating a cave large enough for five. As the men huddled together, Potts offered no comfort—only the sense that he had probably survived worse. The swirling wind quickly covered them in a thick blanket of snow. How long before it would pass, someone wondered. Potts told them that late-winter storms could last for days. Denny writes, "We afterwards learned that a temperature of -65°F had been recorded during this blizzard, the worst seen in Montana in many years."[15]

As the storm worsened, an endless stream of buffalo moved into the river valley, gradually becoming so dense that the men feared for their horses. At two-hour intervals they took turns protecting their mounts from the crowding bison. Both horses and buffalo seemed to instinctively close ranks in their own efforts to conserve body heat. For sustenance the men gnawed on raw, near-frozen bacon.

After a second miserable, sleepless night, Macleod and his mates stared, willing the storm to abate. The horses would not last another day standing still, without food. Their best chance for survival lay 25 miles south of the border at a place called Rocky Coulee. Getting the horses saddled was a monumental chore in itself, after beating 36 hours' worth of caked ice and snow from their tough hides. Potts told the four Mounties that all were to walk their horses at first, each man stretching his own joints, stirring some warmth. He led the way, followed by Macleod. The other three were close behind, using sounds more than vision to follow the scout. Sub-constable

Sir Cecil Denny became known to the Blackfoot as Beaver Coat and was widely respected in their camps. He rode often with Jerry Potts and was the beneficiary of the scout's trail instincts during at least two serious blizzards. In 1922, the same year he became Alberta's chief archivist, Denny inherited his family estate and became the sixth baronet of Tralee Castle, Ireland. He never returned to his ancestral home and in his will bequeathed half of his estate to the RCMP Veterans' Association.

Ryan was the first to succumb. When Denny realized he was no longer bringing up the rear, the party halted. They backtracked, always staying within hailing distance, until Denny found the young trooper sitting in the snow, spent. Ryan's pants were frozen so solid he could not mount his horse, and he had walked as far as he could. Denny and Cochrane helped lift the lad into his saddle and the journey continued.

"We plodded on without resting. Our guide was a marvel," Denny would write later. "He rode steadily ahead with short stops at intervals when he seemed almost to smell out the trail, for nothing was to be seen in any direction."[16] As darkness loomed again, Potts led them down into Rocky Coulee; somehow he had stayed on course. Ahead lay another freezing, fireless night, but the shelter was better than it had been at the Milk River. Potts told them they were only a few hours from the Marias River and that once they got there, they would be fine. The snow continued; Sergeant Cochrane slept with the horses while the others again huddled under a buffalo robe.

With the storm nearing its end and stomachs growling, Potts lost no time breaking camp. The heavy snowdrifts made for slow going, but the party reached a cluster of log buildings, perched above the Marias, by mid-afternoon. As Potts had suspected, a U.S. Cavalry unit occupied the outpost, and once the Americans determined that their bedraggled guests were not whiskey traders but frozen policemen, they were most hospitable. The commanding officer, Captain Williams, invited the sorry-looking Mounties into the warmth of his cabin. While they shed their frozen clothing and sought comfort near the fire, Williams had the cook prepare plates of medium-rare buffalo steaks and cups of steaming tea. It was a feast that none of the four Mounties nor Potts would ever forget.

While the men proved resilient, their horses were completely done—three would die within days—so they were provided with fresh mounts and a sleigh escort to Fort Shaw on the Sun River. With 400 soldiers, Shaw was the largest cavalry concentration in western Montana, and there Macleod allowed his men a full two days of hard-earned rest. Sub-inspector Denny had fallen victim to a severe case of snow blindness, and Potts admitted that he also had been blinded on their approach to Rocky Coulee, leaving the four men he had saved from freezing to death all the more amazed as to how he had ever found it at all. If Colonel Macleod had been unable to fully appreciate the blizzard exploits of Jerry Potts that had been described by Inspector Crozier only a month earlier, doubtless he would never again question the abilities of his tight-lipped scout.

Colonel John Gibbon, Macleod's host at Fort Shaw, offered a room in his home for Denny to recover in and sent the rest of the Canadians toward Helena with an escort. Without incident they made their way through Prickly Pear Canyon, over the summit of the Rockies, and down into the old mining town that had quickly grown into a settlement of 3,000 people.

At Helena, the Mounties found that Irvine had not yet arrived, so they sent notice east of their arrival. Taking advantage of this brief respite and still waiting for Cecil Denny to rejoin their ranks, Macleod enjoyed some of the hospitality offered up by local army officers and other dignitaries. Both Potts and Denny eventually got in on some of the fun. "The surveyor-general of the territory, Mr. Smyth, showed us the sights," wrote Denny, "not forgetting Chinatown and the dance and gambling houses."[17]

Only 16 months after hosting James Macleod and his men, Colonel Gibbon would lead the western column of the Seventh Cavalry out of Fort Ellis to the south, where he planned to meet up with General George Custer in the pursuit of Sitting Bull.

During the wait for Inspector Irvine, one unexpected group sought out Colonel Macleod. Arriving with hats in hand, more than a dozen ex-Mounties who had abandoned Fort Macleod for the Montana goldfields approached their old commander. "The majority of them called shamefacedly on Colonel Macleod and begged to be taken back in the Force. A few of the best were re-engaged."[18]

Growing impatient with the lack of news from Irvine, Macleod bought horses and supplies and, taking advantage of a break in the weather, sent Potts and the three Mounties back to Fort Macleod. He outfitted those he had re-engaged, then headed north with them a week later, after finally receiving word of Irvine's whereabouts.

The trip had been delayed, and Irvine now had to wait for a riverboat to take him up the Missouri to Fort Benton in June. Macleod and his devoted men had been asked to risk life and limb, but the trip to Helena had been for nothing.

Chapter 16

Into the Cypress Hills

After Inspector James Walsh retrieved the animals that had wintered in Montana and brought them north to the Oldman River, James Macleod announced his latest plan. He would dispatch two of his most valued men, James "Bub" Walsh and Jerry Potts, to build a fort close to the whiskey trade in the Cypress Hills, a rendezvous point for various Indian tribes during their seasonal buffalo hunts. The area was rich with water, wood, fresh game, and pasture. It was a natural place for trade to flourish. Inspector Walsh kept a cool head under pressure, and with Potts at his side he could handle anything that came his way.

Before Walsh and his scout could head for the Cypress Hills, Jerry Potts had one score to settle. While he was away from his lodges on duty, Assiniboine raiders from the south had taken 35 of the Potts family's herd of horses. Potts went to Colonel Macleod, saying he might have to deal with the matter the old-fashioned way, but if Macleod wrote a letter to the U.S. Cavalry requesting their aid, he would try the White methods.

The ink from Macleod's pen was hardly dry when Potts headed to Fort Belknap, where the might of the written word fortunately manifested itself. Potts "took the message to Major Ilges who, anxious to co-operate with the newly-arrived Canadians, personally escorted Potts to the Assiniboine camps. The triumphant guide, sneering at his enemies, rounded up fifteen horses on the first day and had the remainder before the end of the week. He left some infuriated Assiniboines behind and scored one of the best bloodless coups of his career."[1]

While Colonel Macleod had become a lifetime believer in the ways and methods of Jerry Potts after surviving the blizzard near the Medicine Line, it was only when Potts returned to the Oldman valley with his horses that this full trust and respect became reciprocal. The ways of the redcoats worked. Less than a year earlier he would have rounded up his Blackfoot brethren and waged war on the hated Assiniboines to avenge the rustling. This year, not a shot had been fired nor a scalp taken—but he had his horses back.

In early May, Walsh and Potts made preparations to head toward the Cypress Hills.

Like his head scout and interpreter Jerry Potts, Inspector James Walsh preferred buckskins and a brimmed hat when in the saddle and reserved his red tunic for more formal occasions. He rode with Potts many times during the early years of the NWMP and went on to become the most famous of the redcoats with the American press after Sitting Bull sought refuge near his Fort Walsh detachment.

Walsh was now in charge of "B" Division, with sub-inspectors Vernon Welch and Edwin Allen and Sergeant-Major John Henry Bray under his command. In Bray, Jerry Potts saw a seasoned veteran about his own age, a durable fellow who had spent a decade with the 10th Hussars in India before finding new adventure in the Canadian West. Bray organized 30 men and eight wagons, along with the tools to build a fort similar in size to Fort Macleod. In the mind of Cecil Denny, they were headed to "about as lawless a section as could be found in the Territories."[2]

While Walsh and his officers were readying their garrison, Potts had his own family to look after. Tipis, robes, and other belongings were loaded onto travois and Potts' personal herd of horses was organized by his relatives. As the column left the fort, Spotted Killer and Panther Woman took their children in hand and kept them close to the wagon train. The Potts entourage was always a curiosity to many of the young Mounties. One went so far as to ask the man they often referred to as "Old Jerry" about the merits of having two wives. "One wife fights her husband, but two fight each other" was his simple answer.[3]

Three weeks later, after high water delayed the crossing of the St. Mary's River, Potts and his charges made camp six miles southwest of a small Métis settlement on what was now called Battle Creek, a short distance from where the Cypress Hills Massacre had occurred two years earlier. The next day Potts led Walsh and some of his officers over a small hill and looked down on a frontier Eden, where several young women were moving about, performing the morning's chores.

The men eased their way down the slope, and Walsh soon found out that five of the women were the Métis daughters of squatter Edward McKay. McKay treated the Mounties to a fine meal of buffalo, potatoes, onions, and baked bread with fresh butter and raspberry jam. He agreed to share the valley after Walsh explained that it was an ideal site from which to establish order among the area's assorted tribes and settlers.

One reason it was ideal was that the charred remains of Abe Farwell's and Moses Solomon's trading posts were only two miles away, making it easier for the inspector to investigate and report on the heinous crime that had spurred the formation of the NWMP in the first place. Perhaps more important were the smiling faces of calico- and muslin-clad maidens—women had existed only in the men's dreams since the Mounties first rode west. (Sergeant-Major Bray was one of the first Mounties to wed a McKay daughter, and in March 1877 he and his wife had the first baby born to the Force at Fort Macleod.)

Having travelled together to the Sun River grazing grounds the previous November, Walsh and Potts knew each other well by this point, and for anyone who stepped in their way, the two made a formidable pairing. Their pluck was soon tested. Only a few days after the white canvas tents were up, Walsh received his first party of mounted warriors. They rode in from the south, and Potts quickly identified them to Walsh as Teton Sioux, his involuntary sneer raising an alert to possible trouble. Walsh donned his red coat and sat at a table outside his field tent to receive the visitors. Suggesting that the Sioux were probably hostiles chased across the border by the U.S. Cavalry, Potts kept his hands near his weapons, prepared for trouble.

The Sioux leaders were immediately suspicious of the White faces and the uniforms, since some of the policemen were wearing blue jackets, a symbol of the hated long knives. Walsh explained that some of their clothes had been bought from American traders after their own uniforms had worn out.

Walsh asked Potts to explain the Union Jack flag of the Great Mother, but a few of the more aggressive Sioux pressed around Walsh and Potts, threatening to wipe out the camp. Firepower gradually became more even as men who had been out cutting wood returned to camp with their rifles and ammunition belts. Walsh held his adversary's eye as Potts interpreted his words. "If any of you fire a shot," he warned, "more redcoats will come, more redcoats than there are buffalo on the prairie and none of you will be left alive."[4]

At that moment a band of Cree known to be friendly to the police came into view, riding from their camp to the east. Hearing their traditional enemies approach, the Sioux quickly withdrew. It was quite possibly the only time in his life that Potts welcomed the arrival of Cree warriors at his doorstep.

In June and July, while Fort Walsh, as it would be known, took shape, Walsh and Potts wreaked havoc on the whiskey trade. Effectively, Potts performed the same double duty that he had done around Fort Macleod the previous November. First he played the diplomat by making peaceful contact with various tribes in the region and convincing many chiefs that the redcoats were brave and honourable and unlike whiskey traders, wolfers, or even the bluecoats to the south. As Bear Child, he assured all that these were men who could be trusted.

When not practising detente, he turned enforcer. Within a single month, Fort Walsh patrols led by Potts had evicted or arrested so many whiskey traders that Bub Walsh was sure that word of their deeds was now widespread. He called on his scout to arrange a council of all tribes. Walsh and Potts had stared down a rebel party of Teton Sioux only days after arriving at Battle Creek, and now, within the month, they had sent the whiskey traders packing.

All the old chiefs knew the legends of Bear Child and the strong medicine that rode with him, but the redcoat chief, they had concluded, was also brave and powerful. He displayed confidence in his every gesture and rode as if invincible. Potts spread the word that Walsh had called a council for July 1, the eighth birthday of the Great Mother's newest dominion. It was a special day, and when the day arrived, Walsh greeted them in his scarlet finery, the mantle of a young, great chief. It was known that he already had the blessing of Crowfoot and Crowfoot's trusted friend, the redcoat chief Macleod, or Stamix-oto-kan (Bull Head) as he was now known.

At the time of the council, Bub Walsh was still two years away from becoming the most famous Mountie in America. Although they shared many traits, Walsh was cut from a different cloth than his immediate superior, James Macleod. Whereas Macleod had completed law studies in Ontario, Walsh had left school early due to lack of interest and became a much-praised athlete on the lacrosse field and in other sporting endeavours. He grew bored in most jobs he started and ultimately found the military life to his liking. After earning top marks at Kingston School of Cavalry, he left behind a serene family life with a new bride and yielded to his quest for adventure by becoming the first Mountie hired as a recruiting officer. Walsh's own personal passion instilled in others a real eagerness to join the Force.

In the field, Walsh rarely wore his red serge if the day's schedule would allow him to parade about in his buckskins and soft-brimmed hat. He has been described as "one of the most flamboyant and controversial figures ever to ride onto the Canadian plains. His position as a NWMP officer made his actions all the more vexing to his superiors in Ottawa, but Walsh was a man who cared little for bureaucratic authority, and it was this disdain of his unknowing superiors that was to mark his volatile career with confrontation."[5] Unlike Colonel Macleod, Bub Walsh was not a diplomat.

Still, Walsh was Macleod's logical choice to take charge of the Cypress Hills. Macleod had watched time and again as Walsh showed the qualities of leadership that the fledgling Force needed. The difficult journey west had sorely tried the obedience of the rank and file, and it was due largely to Walsh's and his fellow officers' adherence to discipline that the march had avoided mutiny of some kind.

On July 1, Peigans, Bloods, Crees, Assiniboines, and Sioux gathered at a site about 20 miles west of the Cypress Hills to listen to the redcoat chief's words. "The major was impressively resplendent in his loose-fitting Norfolk jacket edged with gold braid, his white-striped cord breeches tucked into black top boots with spurs," writes one historian.[6] With a backdrop of mounted scarlet lancers, he laid down the law.

Speaking through Potts, he stated, "Those who obey the law will be protected by me. I will always be on the side of the law-abiding people, whether they are white, red or black. You can only be an enemy by disobeying the law, and that is my sacred charge, one that I will defend even at the expense of my own life."[7]

Law and order meant no horse stealing or warfare. Pipes were smoked to confirm peace pacts between the tribes, and as the council broke up, it appeared that Walsh had replicated Macleod's triumphs in Whoop-up country. The main common denominator in both events had, of course, been Jerry Potts.

Fort Walsh was completed by mid-July and it appeared that in short order, Walsh and his detachment, with the invaluable help of Potts, had stamped out much of the whiskey trading, thieving, and killing that had been a way of life in the hills for years. The perpetual intertribal warfare that was considered normal also seemed to have stopped. As Macleod had done in Blackfoot country, Walsh gained the confidence and trust of the different tribes and convinced them that the law the redcoats enforced applied to all men.

As at Fort Macleod, the Mounties' newest post quickly became the nucleus of another town. I.G. Baker & Company, once again the beneficiary of a NWMP supply contract, established a store. This time, however, Tom Power, Isaac Baker's persistent Fort Benton competitor, also set up shop. Soon a makeshift hotel, a laundry, and a blacksmith shop were part of the landscape.

Among the visitors to Fort Walsh that summer was a man who would play a significant role in the NWMP. The elusive Acheson Gosford Irvine had finally found his riverboat and made it to Fort Benton. Arriving there about the same time that Walsh had started building his fort, Irvine spent much of his time in Benton first arresting the accused Americans and then, in extradition hearings, arguing to have the prisoners sent to Winnipeg to stand trial for the Cypress Hills Massacre. Whether he knew it or not, his chances of winning the extradition case were remote from the outset. The Fenian influence of men like John Healy made Fort Benton an unlikely place for sympathy for British justice. Irvine left Montana empty-handed, but was able to arrest two wanted Canadians north of the Medicine Line, giving him cause to return to Winnipeg.

The I.G. Baker & Co. store was constructed outside the walls of Fort Macleod by Charles Conrad and became the cornerstone of a small main street that took shape over the next five years. Manager D.W. Davis, leaning on post to left, later became a prominent federal politician.

When Irvine arrived at Fort Walsh, he was the Force's most recently appointed inspector. At 39, he was four years older than Walsh and far better connected. His family had a long history in Quebec politics and, like Walsh, Irvine had attended military school at Kingston. He first reached Winnipeg with the Quebec Battalion of Rifles after joining the 1870 Red River expedition. He had stayed in Manitoba overseeing the 20 officers and a force of 244 members of the Manitoba Provisional Battalion of Rifles during a four-year stint. On May 7, 1875, he received his commission as a NWMP inspector charged with bringing to justice the alleged Cypress Hills murderers.

With most of the Blackfoot summer camps leaving the hill country and more of the interaction with different tribes being conducted farther east among the Cree camps, Walsh and Colonel Macleod soon decided that the resourceful Potts could provide better value back at Fort Macleod. Hence, Walsh recruited the previously employed Cree Métis Louis Léveillé to act as his interpreter and ordered Potts to uproot once more.

As he prepared for his family's return to the Oldman River, had he been so inclined, Potts could have looked back on a remarkable year. From September 1874 until a year later when he re-entered the gates of Fort Macleod, he, more than any other man born west of the Red River or Mississippi, had helped secure some sense of order and organized protection for the Blackfoot peoples. He had kept many officers of the NWMP alive under harrowing circumstances; he had been the conduit promoting peace among the various tribes and nations who called the great prairie their hunting ground. Possibly more than can ever be realized or appreciated, he translated the White man's words in his dialogue with chiefs like Crowfoot, Three Bulls, Red Crow, and countless others in a passionate manner that convinced the rightly suspicious Native leaders to place faith in the redcoats. Nobody will ever know what he said, but it had a profound impact on the future settlement of western Canada.

Chapter 17

A Change of Command

The arrival of the redcoats in the Canadian West helped to restore stability to the Blackfoot Confederacy after five years of relentless whiskey trading had almost destroyed its culture. Except for mindless decisions made when they were full of firewater, the Bloods, Siksikas, and Peigans were wily traders and their robes yielded fair returns. Now the followers of Red Crow, Crowfoot, and Bull Head started to recover their wealth by trading robes for horses, ammunition, and food. While this meant costs were much higher for Montanan traders, who continued to spread out across the prairie, the opportunity for profit remained. The flow of robes seemed endless—60,000 made their way down the Missouri in 1876 alone.

Still, all was not well. To the dismay of the Native chiefs, much of the spoils was going to the detested Manitoba Métis, who littered the prairie with carcasses, interested only in quickly skinning their latest kill before resuming the hunt. Always familiar with vast herds of migrating buffalo in their midst, neither Métis nor Indian could imagine living without them. Yet even more than whiskey, it was the overkill of the buffalo that would spell the end of the nomadic Blackfoot culture that had prospered for thousands of years.

South of the Medicine Line, the slaughter was encouraged. Various American army generals under William Sherman— Sheridan, Terry, Miles, Crook, and Custer—all recognized that the fastest route to conquest of the Sioux and the Blackfoot tribes was through the eradication of the buffalo. These were men of battle, steeled by the harsh realities of the Civil War, and the power brokers of Washington backed them up.

In the American West, the elimination of the buffalo was greatly facilitated by well-armed professional hunters and the sheer numbers of settlers who were making their way across the Mississippi and up the Missouri. Although no official policy existed to exterminate the buffalo, the Secretary of the Interior, Columbus Delano, spoke for the government when he reported to Congress, "The buffalo are disappearing rapidly, but not faster than I desire. I regard the destruction of such game ... as facilitating the policy of the Government, of destroying [the Indians'] hunting habits, coercing them on reservations, compelling them ... to adopt the habits of civilization."[1]

General Sheridan wanted medals of gratitude struck for the White buffalo hunters. "These men have done more in the last two years, and will do more in the next year, to settle the vexed Indian question than the regular army has done in the last thirty years." With some satisfaction, he concluded, "They are destroying the Indian's commissary."[2]

An estimated 13 million buffalo roamed the western landscape when the Civil War ended and hordes of disillusioned people discovered the West. Within two decades, the herds would suffer almost complete annihilation. The demise of the buffalo and the nomadic Native tribes that relied on them for life support was irreversible given the political will of men like Delano and the military will of Sherman and his hierarchy of sympathetic generals. Their greatest weapons were the steady flow of immigrants and the commitment of a government to protect them. The population west of the Mississippi would more than quadruple to 8.5 million Americans by 1890. U.S. Army skirmishes with various tribes would total 1,000, leading to almost 6,000 casualties and over 10,000 captives.[3]

To the north, Jerry Potts' chosen homeland was evolving in a completely different way. Certainly there was no intent to destroy the buffalo, nor was there any conscious desire to wage war against the Aboriginal peoples. As Crowfoot, Red Crow, and Bull Head listened to Colonel Macleod the previous autumn and heard their

The circular NWMP tents had much in common with the Blackfoot tipis. Here in 1876, as seen at Fort Walsh, they remained a common bivouac for troops until permanent barracks were completed. The second photo shows the fort 87 years later, after it was rebuilt as a breeding ranch for the RCMP's trademark black horses. Palisades were rebuilt on the original perimeter after 1966, when it became a national historic site in Cypress Hills Interprovincial Park.

respected brother Bear Child translate, they agreed the redcoats were sent by the Great Mother to protect them. The Blackfoot leaders consented to share their land with the Mounties and even accepted a few black robes, missionaries of various faiths who had won their friendship. But within a year of their arrival, the redcoats had attracted a new evil—settlement.

Compared with the flow of people to Montana and the rest of the American West, the number of settlers who ventured beyond the Red River in Canada in 1875 was minuscule. The Cariboo gold rush in British Columbia had attracted some Overlanders onto the prairie. They followed the rutted trails made by Métis carts in the 1860s, but rarely remained in the foothills of the Rockies. After that gold bubble had burst, only those who came back through the mountains in search of the latest motherlode lingered briefly before being lured to Montana. In that sense, the Blackfoot villages in the Rocky Mountain foothills had been left undisturbed for a long time.

When he returned from Fort Walsh to Fort Macleod in the autumn of 1875, Potts was not surprised by the changes. They were similar to those he had witnessed in the Cypress Hills that summer. Clusters of Cree, Assiniboine, or Sioux lodges and a constant flow of Métis and White traders had brought a sense of permanent settlement to Fort Walsh; both Isaac Baker and Tom Power had established stores. In his absence, the periphery of Fort Macleod had also acquired a steadily growing population.

Colonel Macleod briefed Jerry Potts soon after his arrival back at headquarters. There seemed to be renewed restlessness among the nearby Blood and Peigan bands. If there was a problem, the Mounties needed to know what it was, and Potts was the man to find out.

Potts learned that a third NWMP fort was being built on the Bow River. Macleod had assigned "F" Division under Inspector Brisebois and Sub-inspector Denny to head north to the Bow and build this fort before winter. By August they had made camp at the fork of the Bow and Elbow rivers and started construction on a plateau between the rivers.

Construction had barely gotten under way when a number of Métis appeared from the north, drawn simply by the moccasin telegraph and word of a new settlement. A week after Cecil Denny organized the NWMP camp of white tents, a heavily laden I.G. Baker bull train brought winter clothing and much-needed supplies from Fort Benton. Also on the train was a work crew that went up the Elbow and floated down hundreds of pine logs to be used for lumber. Within five weeks, the ever-observant Denny made note of two oddities. "No Indians visited us until we had been a month in camp, but quite a number of half-breeds from Edmonton arrived with their Red River carts and built cabins on both sides of the Elbow. Before winter arrived a little settlement had sprung up."[4]

Blackfoot chiefs from the various tribes did not like what their scouts were telling them; some were concerned enough that they banded together to make a formal complaint to the Great Mother. The council convened with the Bloods represented by Red Crow, Medicine Calf, Father of Many Children, Many Spotted Horses, and three other chiefs; Crowfoot, Old Sun, Eagle, and Low Horn represented the Siksikas; many Peigan and Sarcee chiefs were also present. They showed appreciation to the Mounties in the petition they drew up, but also reminded Macleod of his original pledge that no land would be taken by Whites without a "Council of Her Majesty's Indian Commissioner and the respective Indian Chiefs." The petition went on to accuse Cree and Métis hunters of taking "buffalo summer and winter in the hunting grounds of the Blackfoot nation."[5]

The document required much review by the different chiefs and as a result it would not be delivered to the Indian commissioner's office until spring 1876. Amid the formalities of intertribal talks, Red Crow grew impatient and chose to act on his own. In November, leading a delegation of 10 Blood chiefs, he went to Macleod to express his irritation with the large number of Métis and White hunters now camped along the Belly River and farther north on the route to the new Bow River fort. They had positioned themselves to intercept the traditional winter flow of buffalo into the Blood hunting ground. No laws were being broken, so Macleod could do little but buy some time. He asked Potts to tell the Bloods to let him contact Ottawa and represent their grievance.

Before Christmas, word came down from the Bow that the Mounties' new fort was complete. Macleod also learned that his presumptuous officer, who had overseen construction, had proclaimed the new detachment Fort Brisebois, a name that would never be official. According to Cecil Denny's first-hand account, Macleod dismissed the suggested name and personally declared the new base would be called Fort Calgary—Gaelic for "clear running water"—in honour of a Macleod clan castle on the Isle of Mull. By then the settlement had a billiard hall, numerous log residences, and its first church.

Christmas was a buoyant time as the enlarged contingent of two

Major Irvine would come to rely on Potts to lead the way and interpret Native dialects over the years, whether it be to describe ailments, express grievances, or solicit counsel.

divisions established new friendships over a feast worthy of the occasion. One of the recent arrivals was Sergeant Sam Steele, who reported that "civilian friends, to the number of 20, sat down with us, and our bill of fare consisted of turkeys, wild geese, antelope, other venison, buffalo tongues, boss rib, plum pudding, California fruit, raisins, nuts and milk punch, for which a permit had to be obtained to enable us to pass the Christmas satisfactorily."[6] One can only presume that "milk punch" required unknown ingredients to help it pack a wallop.

In January Colonel James Macleod, along with Major A.G. Irvine, recently arrived from Fort Walsh, scout Jerry Potts, and their medical officer, Dr. Richard Barrington "Barrie" Nevitt, made their way north to the Bow River fort for a first-hand look at the recently completed quarters. Macleod and Irvine soon went on to Edmonton, expecting to return in 10 days. Dr. Nevitt, one of the more prolific letter writers among NWMP officers (he wrote almost daily to his fiancée, Elizabeth Beatty) set out to tend to the ill, be they man or beast.

Many of the early illustrations of Fort Macleod and the surrounding landscape were the work of the NWMP assistant surgeon, R.B. "Barrie" Nevitt. The original forge is portrayed here the spring after the fort was first constructed.

Nevitt pulled teeth, patched egos, and even tended to the poisoned dogs—victims of wolfers' strychnine—belonging to the local missionary. Among the enlisted men, he found the most prevalent malady at Fort Calgary was low morale; some attitudes bordered on the mutinous. Inspector Brisebois was not well liked.

Potts delayed his return trip to Macleod for almost a week due to a stretch of bitterly cold weather. Shortly after he finally left, Reverend John McDougall, the son of the well-regarded Methodist minister George McDougall, came to Fort Calgary and reported that his father was missing from their hunting camp. Early the next morning Cecil Denny and a scout headed out along the Bow River only to return well after dark, Denny's ear and nose partially frozen. He would later recall, "The minister left camp one morning to hunt. A blizzard came up during the day and he never returned ... police searched for several days and picked up the horse, but it was a week before the body was recovered ... this was the first death at Calgary ... and it cast a shadow over the New Year."[7]

A chinook wind put a temporary end to winter, and February seemed to herald the beginning of an early spring. Time passed at

George McDougall and Father Albert Lacombe were the two most prominent missionaries among the Blackfoot tribes in the years of transition for the Blackfoot Confederacy.

Fort Macleod without incident; there were a few minor injuries for Dr. Nevitt to see to, and all the officers had to complete year-end reports. Potts found time to lead Dr. Nevitt and three sub-constables (Kidd, Robinson, and Adams) on a hunting trip. The doctor, a man of good humour who liked to sketch as well as write, decided to commemorate the trip in a drawing, highlighting the fact that their smoky lodge had left the whole party with blackened faces. Nevitt had mentioned Potts and his escapades in his earlier writings, and in one letter to fiancée Lizzie, he enclosed the sketch with a note that stated, "The red coat is Adams. I am next—Jerry Potts is the full faced ugly man & Kidd is the happy man."[8] Nevitt mentioned Potts often in his correspondence, but his most glowing comments revealed his admiration of Colonel Macleod, who he hinted in his letters was a soulmate. Macleod also had a bride-to-be waiting for him in Manitoba.

By mid-month Macleod announced his plan to have Potts lead Nevitt and himself to Fort Shaw and then on to Helena, Montana, to attend to business matters. The trip took eight days, and Macleod's party arrived to some startling news. Sub-inspector Edwin Allen had recently arrived from the Cypress Hills in search of medical help for James Walsh, who wasat death's door. Nevitt was dispatched to Fort Walsh on March 11, while Macleod remained in Helena. Nevitt was back in Helena by the end of the month, when he reported to his Lizzie, "I found Major Walsh just hanging between life and death."[9] He and Allen had first boarded a stage to Fort Shaw, then onward another 65 miles to Fort Benton. From there they struggled on horseback through harsh cold and storms to make the Milk River. On the fourth day they reached a frozen crossing before noon, where a temporary lodge and help arranged by Fort Walsh awaited them. Nevitt was bundled onto a dog sled, and Walsh's trusted scout, Louis Léveillé, made 25 miles before dark, mushing the dogs as fast as they could run.

Nevitt wrote, "The next morning was again stormy with snow and a strong wind dead in our faces. I was buried in the dog sleigh and covered with blankets and robes."[10] Léveillé ran behind, spurring the dogs onward. "I learnt more profanity expressed in bad French than I had ever known before," recalled Nevitt. "[We] travelled on without stopping for 63 miles and arrived at Fort Walsh about 6 o'clock."[11]

Nevitt learned from the ailing inspector that he had lost confidence in his own staff doctor; his own timely arrival was a godsend. Walsh, a strapping fit man otherwise, had a medical history plagued by recurring bouts of erysipelas, a bacterial disease characterized by acute skin inflammation and harsh fever. Nevitt altered the treatment drastically and within five days Walsh had made a substantial recovery. The revitalized major celebrated the next day by holding court and trying several prisoners accused of whiskey trading. Sentences were handed down and Walsh, heeding his new doctor, made plans to accompany him back to Helena. Nevitt, by all accounts a man not inclined to exaggerate, wrote a final assessment of the trip. "I am positive that my coming saved his life and so in the least do not regret my long and dangerous journey."[12] In Helena a grateful Walsh presented Nevitt with "a beautiful cameo ring—a memento of my trip to Cypress and also a token of his appreciation."[13]

Dr. R.B. Nevitt sketched and painted many scenes around Fort Macleod while stationed there. During his first summer there, he completed Half-breed Camp at Fort Macleod, *a watercolour landscape of tipis and the Red River carts made famous by the Métis.*

Colonel Macleod had seen little of Walsh since assigning him to his challenging post in the Cypress Hills and was very happy to see both his trusted inspector and Dr. Nevitt. Walsh's condition was severe enough that he required extended leave in the east to recuperate. Macleod announced that he too needed to return to Ottawa to complete evaluations of all his officers. He took his leave from Nevitt, saying, "Dr. you may be assured that I have nothing but the very highest praise & commendation for you. You have no idea of the amount of good you have done at the Fort."[14]

After saying goodbye to Macleod and Walsh, a homesick Nevitt travelled to Fort Shaw, the first leg back to Fort Macleod. Dozing en route, the sleep-starved doctor dreamt that it would be dear Lizzie who would welcome his arrival when the stagecoach reached its destination; the only greeter was the "ugly" Jerry Potts. With two supply wagons in tow, Nevitt and Potts spent three days crossing swollen rivers and still-frozen countryside before they reached the Milk River. On the fourth day, awakening to chinook conditions and melting snow, they had a difficult time reaching the south fork of the Milk. Potts did not like what he saw. The rapid melt had generated so much runoff that a waist-high current of icy water was now running atop the frozen river. Underneath that ice flowed at least another three feet of freezing water. Somehow Potts found a safe crossing and managed to get both wagons to the far shore. As Nevitt wrote to Lizzie, "We congratulated ourselves on getting across so well—we had dinner here & at two o'clock started again. Jerry had gone on in front and said that if he found a bad place he would wait for us."[15]

Potts again tried to establish a trail that the wagons could handle but there was water and slush everywhere. At one point, Nevitt's wagons caught up with Potts while the scout was testing the ice thickness in a small coulee. One of the wagons accidentally careened in Potts direction, its weight cracking the ice surface. Potts' horse fell through, and the scout was momentarily fighting for two lives, including his own. "Jerry had to jump off to save the horse," wrote Nevitt. "He sank into the cold ice water up to his shoulders. He waded out—turned his pistol upside down—and went to try another place."[16]

Nevitt, by then a believer that Potts' medicine bag held many lives, could not resist asking his scout for his opinion of the crossing. "Damn bad," Potts muttered as he struck out on a new course.[17] The melt continued. After four hours they were only half a mile from the North Milk riverbank where they planned to spend the night. The next morning they bridged the northern arm of the Milk, crossed the boundary, and made their way to the still-frozen St. Mary's River. While Potts built a fire, Nevitt walked along the river and saw three riders approaching the opposite bank. "I got a pair of glasses and recognized Major Irvine," wrote Nevitt. "I gave him his mail and we had a cup of tea—he told me to leave the wagons and come on to Macleod with him ... We got in just at dinner time driving 35 miles in 4½ hours ... I was glad to get back."[18] Potts and the two wagons arrived the next day at noon.

Potts had little time to visit his family and lodges. Two days later, Major Irvine announced that he had new information: whiskey traders were back at Whoop-up. Potts rode out in front of a patrol that was hastily mustered, and after a merry chase two prisoners and their confiscated contraband were trotted into Macleod the following day, a Sunday. Irvine waited only until Monday morning to put on his magistrate's robes and fine each man $200. Nevitt felt they got off easy, but they had sold no whiskey so no real harm had been done. Potts perhaps found a means to confiscate a bottle or two for himself—and possibly a Mountie friend or two to help drink it.

Potts was not a man to drink alone and it was broadly accepted by this time that whiskey was a basic need of any thirsty White man. This included more than a few Mounties. For the officers, Dr. Nevitt was always a ready source, since he had alcohol on hand for medicinal purposes. Jerry Potts would drink just about anything, and he had no problem recruiting an NCO or two who felt it fully acceptable to "investigate" the contraband. One such lad was Sam Steele, who had recently arrived with the commissioner's expanded contingent of troops and was a connoisseur of milk punch.

In his biography, published almost 40 years later, the then highly decorated Steele fondly recalled his relationship with Old Jerry, describing him as "a remarkable scout and interpreter ... one of the most important aids to us in carrying out our duties, both military and civil ... indispensable as a teacher of the mysteries of the plains."[19] There is some evidence in Steele's own words that his recollections may have been garbled by lack of sleep or the excessive amounts of whiskey he and Potts had shared over the years, but his overall assessment was that it "would take a large volume to describe even a small part of the usefulness of this man."[20]

By the end of April, Fort Macleod's officers were again spread out in many directions. Nevitt went north to Fort Calgary (the fort that Brisebois was still insisting should be named after him). Inspector Crozier was sent to Fort Walsh to fill in for the ailing James Walsh. Major Irvine set out for Fort Shaw, as the American post remained the closest link to the telegraph and speedy communication with Ottawa. Inspector William Winder, the official commanding officer of Fort Macleod, was still on leave in Ontario.

Apart from the Blackfoot Confederacy's ongoing grumbling about settlers, there seemed to be a new sense of order amid the isolation at Fort Macleod. Bull trains regularly stocked the fort and the Baker store, and more services were offered along what now amounted to a main street. The settler issue was starting to sort itself out. Some of the more naive ranchers were having second thoughts about their new home. They usually blamed the Indians for missing cattle although buffalo accounted for some of their losses. Many an adult bull wandered onto the open prairie, only to be gored to death by a testy bison counterpart.

Farther east in Manitoba, more than an innocent animal was about to get gored; Canadian politicians were also butting heads over the status of the western police force. Between the time Potts left Helena in early April and the first weeks in June, when Major Irvine reached Fort Walsh, events occurred that would dramatically change both the chain of command and the morale of the North West Mounted Police. First came the resignation of the police force's assistant commissioner. Colonel Macleod announced that while he wished to retain his stipendiary role as magistrate in the North-West Territories, he wanted to spend less time in the saddle maintaining the rigorous travel schedule that the job required. His new priority, he announced to his many friends, was marrying his fiancée, Mary Isabella Drever, at Fort Garry.

But all was not going well for Commissioner George French. From his headquarters beside the Red River at Fort Dufferin, French had taken issue with various fiscal and political decisions in Ottawa, and in the course of events acquired his own share of professional enemies. When an order-in-council notified him that the "conditions of the Force [were] unsatisfactory and reform [was] required in command; [and] services no longer required,"[21] he indignantly appealed the claim. The final wording was amended, and he was allowed to resign in July. With the possible exception of Inspector Brisebois, every redcoat in the west cheered when word came that James Macleod had reconsidered his recent resignation and would return to the NWMP as French's successor.

July was also not a good month for one of Colonel French's peers to the south—General Alfred H. Terry. Terry, the long-established commander of the U.S. Army's Department of Dakota, with headquarters to the south of French in Minnesota, was of a much different disposition than the NWMP commanding officer. As an articulate and well-to-do volunteer general in the Civil War, he had earned such respect among his peers that he was sent west by his political and military leader, President Ulysses S. Grant, with an added star on his uniform. Reporting directly to the U.S. Army's commanding officer, William Sherman, things had gone reasonably well for Terry as he coped with the stubborn resistance of the Teton Sioux and Blackfoot tribes of the Upper Missouri. Then he gained the dubious benefit of one too many ambitious officers.

While eastern Americans were celebrating their hard-earned centennial, word came from the western frontier that Terry's underling, the impetuous General George Custer, along with "half the Seventh Cavalry," had been slaughtered in a battle with the Sioux along the Little Bighorn River in late June. The reference to "half the cavalry" actually covered both the dead and wounded, but it still translated into one of the worst battlefield losses in U.S. history. The culprit who was held to blame for this unacceptable and surprising turn of events was a Sioux spiritual leader called Sitting Bull.

Chapter 18

A Study in Contrast

The NWMP presence on the Canadian frontier was still too new to have earned much scrutiny south of the border. That this small band of undermanned idealists with no experience and little firepower had survived two winters among the Blackfoot tribes defied both the predictions and wishful thinking of the old Fort Benton whiskey traders. Although still anxious to restore their enterprise, they could not help but admire the impact the NWMP had on the Blackfoot chiefs. The few who had ridden with Jerry Potts most likely knew that they could blame him for much of the Mounties' success.

Acceptance of the Mounties could be attributed to the fact that, given their small numbers and pacifist ways, the redcoats posed no threat whatever. If a Blackfoot chief decided to wage war, sheer numbers would assure his warriors of victory.

By early 1876, James Macleod and some of his officers had made enough trips south and spent sufficient time within the palisades of Fort Shaw and other U.S. Army enclaves to understand the challenges facing their bluecoat counterparts. For the most part, they kept their judgements about U.S. government tactics in the West to themselves. But Macleod's men made a simple statement by their actions alone. After 18 months on the prairie, no Mountie had had cause to kill any Blackfoot, Cree, Assiniboine, or Sioux warrior.

Although Macleod was diplomat enough not to criticize the American approach directly, he did give an honest assessment to his political bosses in Ottawa. "I think the principal cause of the difficulties which are continually embroiling the American Government in trouble with the Indians, is the matter in which [they] are treated by the swarms of adventurers who scatter all over the Indian country in search of minerals." Any approaching Indian, friendly or otherwise, was fired upon at will south of the border. "Such a rule is not necessary in dealing with the worst of Indians," he concluded.[1]

His appointment as commissioner thrust Colonel Macleod into the middle of two vastly different situations. To the north lay pending treaty activity with some of the Saskatchewan River basin tribes. In the boundary country of the Cypress Hills, a more volatile issue was bubbling, centred around Sitting Bull and the Sioux Nation. As news of Little Bighorn made its way north, there was no immediate sense of alarm at Fort Walsh or Fort Macleod. War was bound to have its bad days, and if one boy-general had underestimated his enemy, it was not the first time such a thing had happened. At this time, two of the Mounties' most prominent officers were far from their posts. Macleod was in Manitoba, and James Walsh was on sick leave in Hot Springs, Arkansas, nursing his painful and persistent skin disease.

James Macleod had much on his mind during that turbulent July. On the 20th of the month, with news of Sitting Bull's stunning victory still on everybody's lips, he assumed his role as commissioner. Irvine and Crozier were in Fort Walsh, and James Walsh had been ordered back to duty, so Macleod turned his attention to the Cree and Assiniboine. Anxious to complete treaty talks, he immediately set out with a small party on a two-week journey up the Assiniboine River to the Swan River detachment. Sam Steele, one of his original NCOs, welcomed him there.

James Macleod's stamina was by this time legendary. Steele wrote, "They arrived at the Swan River barracks at 6 a.m. on August 6, and gave orders for the headquarters and all but a handful of "D" division to start by 9:30 a.m. for Fort Carlton, where the Indian treaties were to be concluded. It was a march of 1,150 miles and we were to have all that we required to enable us to halt anywhere and spend the winter! ... We pulled out at 9 a.m. with a half hour to spare."[2]

It had only been two summers since the original march west; this one made much quicker progress. Under Macleod's leadership, the column achieved almost 100 miles per day, arriving at the long-time Hudson's Bay trading post Fort Carlton on August 18, 1876, to begin the treaty process with the Cree and Assiniboine tribes of the North and South Saskatchewan River basins. The pomp and ceremony of the following week led to the official treaty signings at Carlton, and Macleod immediately started toward Fort Pitt, the halfway point between Carlton and Edmonton.

By mid-September, the principal Cree chief, Sweet Grass, had signed the treaty at this location, but the war chief, Big Bear, refused to endorse the document. However, Big Bear was there for the leave-taking, his main concern offering ominous undertones. Sam Steele, now a permanent member of Macleod's column, wrote, "On September 13, Sweet Grass and others came to say their good-bye to the commissioners. Big Bear did his utmost to extract a promise that there would be no hanging. He seemed in great fear of the rope, but was given to understand that anyone who took a life must die for his crime."[3]

These treaties completed, Commissioner Macleod announced that the Force's headquarters would be moved from the Manitoba-Saskatchewan border to his permanent home base, Fort Macleod. Not only was Swan River inadequate in its amenities to serve as a headquarters, but its northern locale was also too far from the centre of action. Based on the latest communication from one of his officers, Macleod was aware that new winds of war were blowing north from the land of Sitting Bull.

After two months of peace talks and diplomacy with the Cree, Macleod once again perused the report Cecil Denny had penned in late July. After Macleod's appointment as commissioner and the ensuing resignation of Ephrem Brisebois, Denny had been promoted to inspector and the new CO at Fort Calgary. Macleod was anxious to get first-hand accounts from Denny and scout Jerry Potts regarding the current moods of the Blackfoot chiefs.

James Macleod was not only an able commander and magistrate, but a tight-fisted administrator as well. His payment to I.G. Baker & Co. for work done on the construction of Fort Calgary was based on his terms and expectations, not theirs.

(Copy.)
J. F. McLeod to N.-W. Telegraph Company, Dr.
Dec. 2, 1875. To 22 messages to Bernard, Ottawa, $5 08
" 15, " " 12 " " 3 18
Jan 24, 1876. " 13 " Morris, Fort Garry,........ 5 12
" 24, " " 13 " Bernard, Ottawa, ... 3 37

$16 75
(Gold, $15.23.)
Certified.
JAMES F. McLEOD
Paid by check, 1621; Feby. 24th, 1876.
(Signed)   J. A. B.

Fort McLeod, 31st December, 1876.
North-West Mounted Police: In account with J. G. Baker & Co, Dir
To building barrack at Bow River................. $2,476 00
" extra expense incurred by locating post by Captain
Brisebois further from timber than agreement with
Col. McLeod... 1,000 00

$3,476 00

My returns show only 8,520 feet closed in, which, according to agreement, at 25 cents per foot, reduced amounts to $2,130.00; balance disallowed. Messrs. Baker and I disagree about the extra expense of location Fort more than one mile away from timer. I have made enquiries and do not think that any extra expense was incurred. They reserve the right to make good their claim for the balance.
(Signed)   JAMES. F. McLEOD.

Denny had prepared his official report recounting a chance meeting with several Blackfoot chiefs at Blackfoot Crossing, but he knew that Potts' oral report would definitely be more succinct and possibly more insightful. As did most of the officers, Denny got on well with the straight-shooting scout. Denny, who took a special interest in the trail smarts of Jerry Potts, became an extraordinary scout in his own right and also earned the trust of the principal chiefs.

Denny's report stated: "About a month ago the Sioux had sent a message to the Blackfoot camp, with a piece of tobacco ... sent them to smoke if they were willing to cross the Line and join the Sioux in fighting the Cree ... and also the Americans."[4] He said the Sioux had promised their potential ally many horses, mules, and captured White women if they joined the battle. The Sioux also had offered to come north and help Crowfoot rid his lands of the Whites, assuming that they were as hated above the Medicine Line as they were below it. The Blackfoot leaders had sent word back to the Sioux that they would not smoke the tobacco, as the redcoats were their friends and they would not join the war against them.

When Denny arrived at the camp at Blackfoot Crossing, his interpreter explained Crowfoot's latest dilemma. "Crowfoot, the head chief," Denny reported, "was authorized by the nation, many of whom were present, to ask me whether in case they were attacked by the Sioux, without themselves being the aggressors, and they called upon us, the Mounted Police, to help them, would we do so?" Denny did his commissioner proud, telling them "that if the Sioux crossed the line and attacked without cause we were bound to help them, they being subjects of the country, and having the same right to the same protection as other subjects."[5]

Crowfoot knew that the buffalo were fast disappearing, and he knew what that meant for his people. Still, he chose the redcoats as his allies over the Sioux. When he first met Commissioner Macleod face to face, he was able to reconfirm Denny's recent assurances. Because the police were willing to help them, "[the Blackfoot] would in case of being attacked, send two thousand warriors against the Sioux."[6]

Given this voice of co-operation and the recent successful agreements made with the tribes to the north and east, Macleod knew that his next move had to steer the Confederacy toward the treaty process. With the endorsement and interpreting skills of Jerry Potts, the task seemed possible. Only one dark cloud loomed on the horizon, and as winter deepened, that cloud blew north.

In December 1876 the Sioux threat took on a whole new dimension. Rumours said that an estimated 3,000 tribe members were ready to cross the Medicine Line near the Wood Mountain trading post of Jean-Louis Légaré, 160 miles east of Fort Walsh. The inspector knew they had been headed that way, with thousands more also doing their best to evade the U.S. Army. Along with the frigid temperatures and uncertain food supply, the sheer number of the Sioux refugees concerned him. With a patrol of a dozen men behind him, Walsh spent two days fighting snowdrifts in the Cypress Hills before descending the southeast slopes to open prairie. They fought blizzard conditions as they followed the south bank of the White Mud River on the trail to Wood Mountain to meet with Sioux chiefs Black Moon and White Eagle. It took the patrol a full week to reach the encampment where Walsh laid out the law and the terms of the Sioux stay in Canada: there would be no ongoing skirmishes across the Medicine Line, and protection would not be forthcoming if they ventured south with malice in their hearts. The chiefs gave their assurances and then Walsh did the unthinkable. He authorized Légaré to not only give the Sioux some basic supplies, but to give each family a few bullets for hunting as well—a single act that would endear him to the Sioux forever. The fact that there were buffalo in the region for the first time in years, along with Walsh's sympathetic gesture, saved the encampment from starvation.

By the first spring melt, both Walsh and his commissioner knew they were in for an eventful summer. What would happen when Crowfoot's people made their traditional migration to the Cypress Hills to hunt during early summer? How many more Sioux would cross the Medicine Line?

While all was quiet enough on Commissioner Macleod's western front that he was able to return to Ottawa at the behest of his political bosses, trouble was brewing. With Denny overseeing Fort Calgary, the ever-competent Inspector William Winder administering Fort Macleod, and Jerry Potts acting as the go-between with the Blackfoot chiefs, Macleod's biggest problem was the Cypress Hills and the Sioux issue. Walsh, too, was certain that the quiet would not last. Not a man to procrastinate, he decided to act first.

Mail, newspapers, and the flow of traffic from Fort Benton, along with the reports of his own scouts, kept Walsh aware of what was going on south of the Line. General Terry and his more southerly peer, General George Crook, were having trouble finding Sitting Bull's elusive Sioux to exact revenge. Custer may have been a reckless fool, but his defeat demanded retaliation. Terry's Seventh Cavalry seemed stunned into a state of inertia for months, while Crook's troops, with a few scalps to their credit, had paid a terrible cost. "Crook's sole success had been at Slim Buttes, South Dakota, where he massacred 37 lodges of Sioux. He had also almost starved his own army to death, applying some misguided strategies ... Critics in the U.S. Congress pointed out that the three-month campaign was costing about $1 million per dead Indian."[7] It was dubbed the Horsemeat March, as men subsisted solely on the meat of their dying animals. Most of the poorly armed Sioux escaped into the hills, leaving Crook's army fortunate to suffer only three deaths and 12 wounded soldiers.

With the arrival of autumn, Sitting Bull's main nemesis was General Nelson Miles, one of Terry's looser cannons. Miles was vain, ambitious, and ruthless, but he was also a sound tactician with boundless energy and high spirits, relentless in pursuit of his quarry. "The army contained few top officers so little deterred by obstacles," wrote one military historian.[8] Miles drove Sitting Bull north by establishing a permanent post near the confluence of the Yellowstone and Tongue rivers. He pursued the Indians' northeast trail into mid-October.

Under a flag of truce, which came down on October 21 after two days, Sitting Bull told the Whites they should get out of his country and that he would never be an agency Indian. Miles, standing erect in a full-length bear coat, issued a final ultimatum only to watch the Sioux quickly start their retreat into the evening dusk. Fearing their escape, the general decided "that something more than talk would be required."[9] He attacked the Sioux camp, forcing the Sioux to abandon their stores of food, horses, and equipment. Within days some lesser

While General Alfred Terry (left) commanded his forces from the relative comfort of St. Paul, Minnesota, preferring diplomacy to battle, he was often at odds with his field officer, Nelson Miles (right), who sought a "might is right" solution to the suppression of the Sioux.

Miniconjou and Sans Arc chiefs surrendered to Miles, but Sitting Bull remained both adamant and elusive in his bid to escape. Miles chased him around southern Montana until mid-December before returning to his cantonment on the Yellowstone.

While a frustrated Miles bypassed Terry and asked General Sheridan for more power and a broader command, Sitting Bull awaited news from his brothers in Canada. Black Moon sent word of their talks with Inspector Walsh and his resolute stance that one law applied to all men in Canada. Most impressive, however, was the redcoat chief's willingness to ration them bullets to hunt buffalo and feed their families. On hearing that, Bull assembled his large village of followers beside the Tongue River and told them that he was heading to Canada.

Back at his own fort, Macleod had other things on his mind. While the beginning of autumn had seen treaty matters put to rest farther east with the Cree, the foothills of the Rockies were the home of growing discontent among some of the Blackfoot chiefs. Macleod had a clear understanding of the issues based on a petition brought

WARLORDS OF THE WESTERN PLAIN

Ulysses S. Grant, president and chief commanding officer: "Settlers and emigrants must be protected, even if the extermination of every Indian tribe is necessary to procure such a result."

William T. Sherman, military commander, U.S. Army: "They all have to be killed or maintained as a species of paupers."

Lieut.-General Philip Sheridan, commander, Division of the Missouri, speaking to Custer before attacking a Cheyenne village: "Kill or hang all warriors and bring back all women and children."

In 1840 the U.S. government established a permanent Indian Country on the Great Plains of the American Midwest. The chiefs were assured the land would be forever theirs. This proved a shallow promise as politicians proclaimed their "Manifest Destiny." After January 31, 1876, any Indians still off the reservations in this territory were deemed to be hostiles, in a state of war with the U.S. Army. General Philip Sheridan, with the blessings of the army's overall commander William Tecumseh Sherman, set in action a plan that would use soldiers from various cavalry units to pursue the enemy. In ensuing months, and relentlessly for the next two years, the armies of commanders Sheridan, Alfred Terry, George Crook, John Gibbon, and Nelson Miles would battle the Sioux Nation and its allies. Only one general failed to survive the campaign—George Armstrong Custer.

to Fort Macleod the previous spring by Jean L'Heureux, a White man who lived among the Blackfoot and assisted in writing the document. Commissioner Macleod had his assistant, A.G. Irvine, deliver the formal request of the chiefs to the then lieutenant-governor, Alexander Morris, in Winnipeg. It reiterated the promise made by Macleod that his government would not "take the Indian lands without a Council of Her Majesty's Indian Commissioner and the respective Indian Chiefs."[10] The message expressed a preference for the return of the Hudson's Bay traders to replace the aggressive Americans, and it requested restriction of the Cree and Métis from Blackfoot hunting grounds.

From their grand council that had produced the written petition came a clear message that the Confederacy was ready to talk treaty. On his return to Fort Macleod, knowing of the Sioux victory at Little Bighorn, Macleod's first priority was advancing the treaty process, and mixed messages were coming from the different tribes. By November 1876, it had been a year since the grand council, where a dozen chiefs had voiced their concerns. The L'Heureux handwritten summary of their concerns had not reached the Great Mother's representative for eight months, and Red Crow and the Bloods in particular were no longer in the mood for treaty talks.

The summer hunt had yielded over 60,000 robes along the Belly and Oldman rivers alone. The Bloods sold many of the robes to traders, but they also hoarded and dried the meat for their own use or to sell. The Métis hunters, however, took only the hides and left the carcasses for the wolves, dogs, and hawks to feed on.

Before the arrival of the redcoats, a Blackfoot warrior had protected his hunting grounds simply by warring with any invaders, be they "Crees, Halfbreeds, Sioux, Assiniboines and others," wrote Macleod to the Secretary of State in mid-November. "Now that we have come into his country he finds that from all sides his old enemies, who he dare not attack, are under our protection pressing in on him."[11] The frustration did not end there because the weaponry of these adversaries was now superior and the Métis came "armed with the breech-loader which they procure at Fort Garry ... a better rifle than his."[12]

The Blood grumblings and suspicions were fuelled by the memories of the elder chiefs, Medicine Calf, Many Spotted Horses, and others, who could speak of two treaties with the Americans that had been followed by deceit and dwindling rations. The Bloods didn't want to wait for a treaty; they wanted a solution immediately. Red Crow and Medicine Calf led nine other chiefs into Fort Macleod, where they were received by Macleod and the ever-present Potts. Jerry listened, then explained their grievances to the commissioner, who would again report to Ottawa of "great irritation amongst them ... not to be wondered at ... there is a regular cordon of Half-Breeds and Crees from Belly River [to the Bow] interposing between the buffalo and the part of the country they usually winter in."[13] Potts translated as Medicine Calf spoke, announcing that he had changed his mind about treaty talks and that he would support the process the following spring. Red Crow, too, expressed his willingness to support the process.

For Red Crow in particular it was a matter of trust. Macleod had always been honest with him, and any words that Bear Child had ever uttered on his behalf had proven true. For the Mountie and his interpreter the day had been a small victory to celebrate—perhaps with a good dose of Dr. Nevitt's medicinal whiskey.

R.B. Nevitt's Blackfoot Camp *shows women and their dogs hauling precious wood into their campsite.*

With the Yule season approaching, Fort Macleod was about to take on a whole new air of civility. When Inspector Denny rode down to Macleod a week before Christmas, he found his fellow officers in festive spirits. Since his last visit the wives of Colonel Macleod, Inspector Winder, Sub-inspector Shurtliff, and at least one other local settler had added a welcome dimension to the community. Shurtliff had started a farm for the Mounties near Pincher Creek that fall and was now one of a handful of ranchers raising horses, cattle, and grain in the area—with the NWMP being their primary customer. It was no doubt a joyful reunion for the men and their wives as the New Year's renditions of "Auld Lang Syne" rang out.

Chapter 19

The Pursuit of Lasting Peace

As the first signs of the 1877 spring emerged, Walsh was sure that it was only a matter of time before Sitting Bull showed up near Wood Mountain. He had posted a small patrol to the area, where they used an old Boundary Commission cabin as their primary shelter. Finally, with the ides of March upon them, his scouts reported to Walsh that a large band of Sioux was just south of the border. Walsh went to welcome Four Horns, the Sioux hereditary chief who had adopted Sitting Bull at a young age, and his followers. After exchanging greetings he slept in their camp, demonstrating a trust in their integrity they had never seen below the Line. Next morning the rules were explained again and the Sioux were allowed to join the growing camp at Wood Mountain.

Walsh sent word to Fort Macleod of the unfolding events and the growing likelihood that Sitting Bull would appear soon. Confident that Walsh remained up to the task in spite of his health problems, Macleod left well enough alone. With confirmation from the Secretary of State that the government wanted to push forward with Blackfoot treaty talks, he devoted his own efforts and those of Jerry Potts to that end.

In May, word reached Walsh that Sitting Bull had finally crossed the border and he again headed southeast and was welcomed into the Sioux camp. When Sitting Bull came forward, the two men shook hands and Walsh asked if they could hold council so he could speak to all the chiefs. Bull consented and the redcoat sub-chief again won over his audience. He accepted Bull's offer to eat at his lodge and spend the night in his tipi. "Sitting Bull smiled, seemingly touched that there were white men prepared to eat and sleep among his people."[1]

Sitting Bull's arrival on Canadian soil was significant news on both sides of the border, and the peaceful, if firm, manner in which Bull was accepted created headlines in both Chicago and Ottawa. The latter was not a place where they applauded upstart heroes, but the Montana press and eastern scribes were fascinated. When their own reporters confirmed that Bull's defiance had ebbed and he obeyed the Mounties' orders, "Bub" Walsh became the charismatic "Sitting Bull's Boss" in the *Fort Benton Record*.

While Walsh was enjoying the limelight into which he had been cast, James Macleod, with Potts interpreting, was pursuing the treaty talks he considered critical. While he realized it was impossible to preserve the Aboriginal nomadic way of life, the NWMP commissioner was dedicated to providing the tribes with fair haven and lands where they could maintain as much tradition as possible while learning the ways of the rancher and the farmer. That, and protection under the law, was all he had to offer.

It is the way of traditional Euro-American history to record the words emitted by the English-language orator and presume that this was the message transmitted to the non-English speaker. Yet in the case of Jerry Potts, it is well known that his translations back to English included little of what was actually said. His much-repeated "Dey damn glad you're here" translation of a long-winded speech is one of the better examples. Less known are the names he originated that have become part of Canadian history and geography. His translations shortened "Crow Indian's Big Foot" to Crowfoot and Peigan chief "Many Eagle Tail Feathers" to Eagle Tail. "The-River-the-Old-Man-Played-On" became the Oldman River.[2]

What has largely gone unrecognized, however, is that no record actually exists of what Potts said to Crowfoot, Red Crow, or any other chief he encountered, though whatever he said almost always had the effect that Commissioner Macleod and his officers desired. This could certainly be said of the months leading up to the great Blackfoot summit in the late summer of 1877.

The word "treaty" had first been uttered to a Blackfoot on behalf of Canada when Red Crow, Medicine Calf, and their fellow Blood chiefs visited the commissioner and Potts at Fort Macleod in November of the previous year. The Bloods were by then aware that their arch-enemies, the Cree and Assiniboine, had through their treaty become formal allies of the Great Mother, and fear that the redcoats might abandon the Blackfoot tribes was becoming a real concern, especially for Medicine Calf. Macleod made it clear that he had no instructions from his government, but he "believed it was the intention of the government to treat with them next year."[3]

Based partly on background information provided by Potts, Macleod had great respect for Medicine Calf, describing him as "a very fierce, intelligent fellow."[4] Having participated in two treaty negotiations on U.S. soil, Medicine Calf heaped scorn upon the broken promises his people had suffered at the hands of the bluecoats. "The Americans at first gave large bags of flour, sugar, and many blankets. The next year it was half the quantity and the following years it grew less and less, and now they give only a handful of flour."[5]

When the government of the day announced its intention to pursue Treaty Seven with the Blackfoot people, the site of the negotiation became a stumbling block. While Crowfoot had pledged his support to Macleod and the Mounties when it came to fighting the Sioux or any other usurper who entered their territory, he was adamant that the talks would not be held in one of the White men's forts; they must take place at his beloved winter grounds near Blackfoot Crossing. (In the Siksika language, the name of the chosen location would translate to "the ridge under the water," a natural ford in the Bow River. In his succinct manner, Jerry Potts had called it Blackfoot Crossing. The name stuck.)[6]

James Macleod and the Honourable David Laird, lieutenant-governor of the North-West Territories, were designated as the treaty commissioners. Laird had shown so much faith in the Mounted Police the previous year that he had recommended Macleod's officers pay out the money delivered to Cree and

Assiniboine families as the result of what was officially known as Treaty Six. The chiefs who had signed that treaty not only trusted the police more than any others; they also well knew from the corruption among Indian agents in Montana that eastern-appointed bureaucrats could not be trusted.

As the time approached for the great council at the Bow River site chosen by Crowfoot, Macleod had only one serious concern. Aside from the committed Medicine Calf, other Blood and Peigan chiefs seemed unsettled that they were being asked to travel 80 miles north of Fort Macleod simply because of the whims of Crowfoot. Red Crow in particular considered Fort Macleod a more neutral venue than Crowfoot's camp, and in early September, as the declared September 17 treaty date approached, he remained noncommittal. Other chiefs were scattered near the border, apparently more interested in the fall hunt than treaty talk. Macleod and his emissaries persisted. Red Crow later recalled that the White men encouraged him to attend—through the words of Jerry Potts.

As mid-September approached, mounted forces from Fort Macleod and Fort Calgary made their way to the crossing. Inspector Denny and his column out of Fort Calgary were among the first redcoats to arrive in the three-mile-long valley, and what they saw was majestic. Over 1,000 lodges dotted the riverbanks, where there was plenty of timber for lodge poles and kindling. The ochre cottonwood leaves provided vivid contrast to the outcroppings, and clear mountain water rippled over the gravel ridge crossing. Downriver, to the east, a herd of buffalo grazed peacefully and the bountiful northern and southern slopes ensured that 3,000 horses would not run short of grass. Many of those already camped were in festive mood, preparing themselves to celebrate the actual signing days before it would occur. Denny describes the event: "Dancing, feasting, conjuring, incantations over the sick, prayers for success in the hunt or in war—all went to form a panorama ... seen but once. Never before had such a concourse of Indians assembled on Canada's western plains; never had the tribes appeared so contented and prosperous."[7]

In addition to Crowfoot's lodges, Peigan, Blood, Sarcee, and Stoney lodges stood in clusters. From Fort Edmonton came Chief

Factor Richard Hardisty with his whole family in tow, along with wagons full of Hudson's Bay trading goods. From the south, American horse traders and entrepreneurs with cartloads of wares awaited the moment when treaty payments would be doled out to the tribes and the spending would begin. I.G. Baker and T.C. Power personnel had even erected canvas-roofed stores, each stocked with a bull train's worth of merchandise. The McDougalls, Methodist missionaries, were there to protect their chosen flock, the Stoneys, many of whom had already converted to the Christian faith. John McDougall, being Hardisty's brother-in-law, camped near the factor's white tents, with the Stoney lodges nearby. Oblate missionary Father Lacombe, a trusted advisor, was in Crowfoot's camp.

In all, over 7,000 Natives awaited the arrival of Stamix-oto-kan, or Bull Head, Colonel Macleod, their trusted ally. About 5 p.m. on Saturday, Macleod, Jerry Potts, Inspector Winder, Dr. Nevitt, and a scarlet column of 60 Mounted Police marched in from the south and made camp near Crowfoot. The Honourable David Laird arrived the next day from Fort Macleod, escorted by Major Irvine.

The meetings were to be held where a white council tent was erected to shield Laird and the officers from the midday sun. Despite the magnitude of the gathering, many familiar faces were missing. As the Blackfoot leaders assembled, Potts could see that most of those gathered were followers of Crowfoot. Only a few Blood and Peigan chiefs were present; Red Crow was nowhere to be seen. While the Whites still understood little about the nuances of intertribal relations, it is likely that Potts was able to help Macleod sort out this dilemma. Red Crow had sought to treat separately from Crowfoot at Fort Macleod, near his own home base. This proposal had been rejected by Laird; the Great Mother's representative wanted a single treaty for all Blackfoot tribes. Red Crow would be late but he would appear when it was necessary. Laird consulted with Macleod and then decided on a two-day delay. Their interpreter passed the word that the Great Mother's message would be spoken on Tuesday, September 19.

Sam Steele, one of the Mounties in attendance on the 19th, wrote: "The chiefs ... seated themselves in front of the Council Tent, and about a third of a mile behind them some 4,000 men,

Colonel Macleod and Lieutenant-Governor David Laird are attentive listeners as Crowfoot stands before them at the 1877 Treaty Seven signing.

women and children were on the grass watching the proceedings with interest."[8]

Beckoning for silence, Lieutenant-Governor Laird was the first to speak. He spoke of the Great Spirit and the Great Mother, of evil and good men. "The Great Spirit has made the white man and the red man brothers, and we should take each other by the hand," he stated. Laird spoke of a new law to preserve the buffalo. "To prevent them from being destroyed [the Great Mother's] councillors have made a law to protect them ... it says that calves are not to be killed in winter or spring except by the Indians when they are in need of food." Laird proclaimed that this obviously unenforceable law showed "that the Queen and her councillors wish you well."[9]

When Laird had finished, Macleod turned to Potts, signalling him to convey the White message as he had done so many times before. This time, startlingly, Potts just shrugged. Either he did not understand—or he chose not to lie. The fate of the buffalo was already sealed, and no law was going to change that. Laird's message was confusing. He had a law to save the buffalo, but moments later he said, "In a very few years the buffalo will be destroyed." He said he was there "to help [them] live in the future in some other way. [The

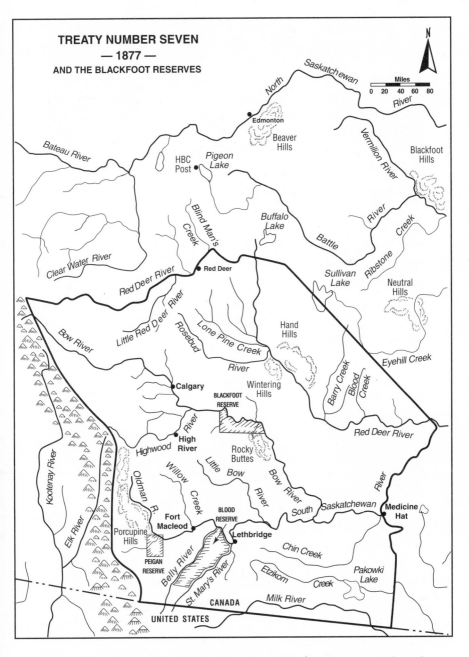

The final boundaries of the Siksika, Blood, and Peigan reserves are indicated above, as set out in Treaty Seven and later amendments to revise the Blood and Peigan reserve locations.

Queen] wishes you to allow her white children to come and live on your land, and raise cattle and grain."[10] Every person present would get money. Chiefs would get more than their followers, plus a new suit of clothes every third year. The details were many; the messages were mixed. Jerry Potts bowed out.

The chiefs stirred as confusion reigned. Hurriedly an alternate translator was rounded up and efforts were made to convey the government's offer to the assembled chiefs.

A few questions were asked before the proceedings closed, and that Tuesday night, much talk occurred among the lodges. Medicine Calf, by then 73 years old, took the stage the following morning. He wanted more annual money if they were to surrender their lands, and compensation for what had already been taken. Anxious to preserve his people's hunting grounds from the Métis, the Crees, and White hunters, Medicine Calf insisted that interlopers be expelled. The request was dismissed out of hand by Laird: "They too are the Queen's children … We have done all we can do in preventing the slaying of the young buffalo and this law will preserve the buffalo for many years."[11]

Various chiefs spoke, some, like Medicine Calf, negotiating for a better deal, others simply extolling the virtues of life before the White man. Laird remained unbending in his offer, and the chiefs left restless. "The evening was a turbulent one in the Blood and Blackfoot lodges. Medicine Calf was angry about the curt refusal of his requests … At one point … some leaders threatened to leave."[12] While the chiefs debated, the independent traders, with their own objectives, went among the tribesmen, assuring them they would receive instant "money" and describing how the new paper money would allow them to trade for goods as soon as the treaty was signed. By Friday night the entire valley was rife with suspense while the chiefs continued their talks. Then, as Macleod and his men enjoyed the grandeur of the evening, a murmur arose. From lodge to lodge word quickly spread. Red Crow was coming! Not only Red Crow, but the respected elder chief Father of Many Children, pulled on a travois so that he could attend the council.

Having swallowed his pride and joined Crowfoot in his home lodge, Red Crow was received with respect. Crowfoot explained the

Queen's offer, described the rebuffs to their counterproposals, and spoke of the impatience and wants of their followers. But Red Crow had not travelled here to reject Stamix-oto-kan. If Macleod said the treaty was good for his people, he would trust his friend.

Crowfoot spoke with dignified eloquence on behalf of all the tribes the following morning about the serious deliberations and their willingness to place their fate in the hands of the Great Mother. He represented many peoples and began slowly.

"While I speak be kind and patient," he asked. "I have to speak for my people, who are numerous, and who rely upon me to follow that course which in the future will tend to their

Despite his history as a great warrior and defender of the Kainai people, in many ways Blood chief Red Crow would prove the most adaptable of the Blackfoot chiefs. As the fate of the buffalo became obvious, he turned to agriculture in an effort to demonstrate a means of survival for his people.

good ... be indulgent and charitable to them." He acknowledged the sound advice of the police and the evils of whiskey, concluding that if it had prevailed, "very few of us indeed would have been left today ... I trust that all our hearts will increase in goodness from this time forward ... I will sign the treaty."[13]

Medicine Calf assented, followed by Red Crow, who said: "Three years ago ... I met and shook hands with Stamix-oto-kan at Belly River. Since that time he made me many promises. He kept them all—not one of them was ever broken ... I will sign with Crowfoot."[14]

Jerry Potts watched it all, quietly and tersely interpreting the chiefs. Afterwards he would tell his officers that "he had never heard Indians speak their minds so freely before."[15]

Macleod, in a brief response, reminded the chiefs of how he had promised them that "nothing would be taken from them without their consent." He reiterated: "What I told you was true." He vowed that this day's promises would "be solemnly fulfilled" and assured the gathered chiefs: "I will always remember the kind manner in which you have spoken today of me."[16]

David Laird's most memorable moment may have occurred the next morning, when he was presented with reasonable doubt that the treaty would mean much of anything. "On Sunday the Indians fought a sham battle on horseback," he reported to his superiors. "They wore only breech cloths ... fired their rifles and sent bullets whistling past the spectators in such close proximity as to create most unpleasant feelings."[17] Cecil Denny recalled "600 mounted warriors ... a blanket round the loins and in war paint and feather headdresses ... armed with loaded Winchesters ... bullets whistling over our heads ... blood curdling whoops accentuated the unpleasantness."[18] Dr. Nevitt wrote to Lizzie that he had seen only part of the demonstration because he "had to go off and perform an operation on an Indian." During his week at Blackfoot Crossing he had been busy, he wrote, as the various tribes "had a good deal of sickness amongst them."[19]

On Monday, Denny and Inspector Winder started the three-day process of paying out over $58,000 to 4,842 claimants. They spent the following week teaching them how to use money and ensuring that the vulture-like traders would take no advantage.

With the treaty signed and only the administration, payments, and trading left to follow, Colonel Macleod's mind quickly turned south to the Cypress Hills. Jerry Potts was ordered to prepare himself and a small patrol to head for Fort Walsh, where an even more challenging council was to be held: between General Terry and the man who hated him—Sitting Bull.

Chapter 20

The Sitting Bull Quandary

Colonel Macleod was allowed no time to celebrate after the signing ceremony at Blackfoot Crossing. He had already sent Jerry Potts ahead to Fort Walsh with the southbound patrol when he and Dr. Nevitt broke camp and left to meet up with them. This was a new route, even for Potts, but the commissioner had given his orders and there was no time to return to Fort Macleod to take the more-travelled trail to the Cypress Hills.

The urgency of the trip to Fort Walsh had been established in mid-August when Prime Minister Sir Alexander Mackenzie's secretary of state, R.W. Scott, wired Macleod, stating the government's preference regarding Sitting Bull's large Sioux encampment north of the Medicine Line: "Important that Sitting Bull and other United States Indians should be induced to return to reservations." Macleod was told that U.S. commissioners were headed toward Fort Walsh to assure the Sioux no harm would be done to them if they returned south. Scott added, "Co-operate with Commissioners, but do not unduly press Indians. Our action should be persuasive, not compulsory."[1] This advice cautioning against a forced exit must have seemed a little superfluous to Macleod; anybody who believed that 50 redcoats could order 5,000 Sioux into the hands of the U.S. military had no idea of the current mood of the Sioux Nation and its powerful leaders.

The Canadian prime minister had no desire to assume a permanent caregiver role to the ever-growing refugee camp that the 600 Sioux lodges near Wood Mountain had become, so he sent an emissary, the minister of the interior, David Mills, to Washington to negotiate inducements to draw Sitting Bull south. Mills won the support of U.S. president Rutherford Hayes, who agreed to offer Sitting Bull and his followers a presidential pardon. Given Sitting Bull's recently expressed disregard for bluecoats, Hayes had trouble finding a man of substance to lead the U.S. contingent. As a final resort he turned back to the military and ordered a most substantial man, the six-foot-six-inch Brigadier-General Alfred Terry, to take the job.

The irony of Terry's appointment was not lost on historians, given that it was he who "as military commander of the Dakotas had directed the '76 campaign against the hostiles."[2] It was Terry's army that had joined in a plan with that of his subordinate, George Custer, to attack the Sioux at Little Bighorn. One of Sitting Bull's mortal enemies was now heading into Canada to entice the Sioux chief home.

General Terry requested in a telegram, sent September 11 from St. Paul, Minnesota, that "Canadian authorities be asked to induce Sitting Bull and his chiefs and headmen to come to Fort Walsh and meet the commission."[3] Macleod received his orders before heading to Blackfoot Crossing and he reluctantly asked Inspector James Walsh to try to do the impossible—bring Sitting Bull to meet with General Terry.

At Blackfoot Crossing, the weather had turned cold and there was fresh snow on the ground on September 28 when Inspector Denny, with his new staff sergeant Sam Steele, 28 other men, and Jerry Potts at the head of their column, broke camp and headed southwest. They left with horses and supplies shortly after dawn, planning to have a campfire ready when Macleod caught up with them around dinner time. Later that morning, with Inspector Crozier and Dr. Nevitt at his side, the colonel climbed into the saddle and started a day ride that would turn out to be most embarrassing.

Dr. Nevitt recalled their 11-hour adventure. "[We] got lost that day and rode from 10 a.m. to 9 p.m. without stopping and with nothing to eat ... we got back to the Crossing fearfully hungry and I can tell you made a hardy meal ... The next morning we started off with Jerry Potts, the guide who had come back to look for us that night."[4] Potts, who had by then gone 40 hours without sleep, made camp on their first night out beside the Bow.

The weather again turned cold and snow started to fall as he led the three officers across the Belly River at its junction with the Bow. Then, with the full party reconnected and snow falling steadily, Potts set out. "The policemen found themselves once more completely dependent upon the faultless sense of direction of Potts ... leaning into the blizzard, somehow guiding everybody through a white hell."[5] Out in front, day after day, alone and undisturbed, Macleod left Potts "unhindered, ahead of the column and just within sight ... a centaur, half man and half horse following some unseen guideposts."[6] Once again Potts defied the elements and found the way to Fort Walsh at the end of a five-day marathon.

Macleod waited three days for the Americans to arrive with their NWMP escort from the border; the escort returned alone. Impatient with the Americans' delay, the colonel ordered Potts, Nevitt, Denny, and Steele back in the saddle. On October 9, with Potts and Macleod out front as usual, the five men and their patrol headed toward the Sioux camp, where Inspector Walsh was committed to making a final effort to persuade the reluctant Sitting Bull to go with him to Fort Walsh and hold council with the hated General Terry. In his wildest dreams, Macleod could not have imagined the 24 hours his Inspector Walsh had just endured.

Walsh had moved his summer headquarters from the main Cypress Hills fort to Wood Mountain to be closer to the Sioux camp. By October he had spent enough time with Sitting Bull that the two men had achieved a mutual respect and trust, something unheard of south of the border. This unusual bond added to the mystique of both Bull and the Mounties and made Walsh an enigmatic character of great interest to the eastern press.

It was a summer of relative calm for the Teton Sioux, who had spent the previous decade either in battle or in some state of disruption at the hands of the U.S. government. Now, with the powerful Medicine Line reducing the threat of attack by bluecoats avenging Custer, Sitting Bull played with his children, organized the Looking-at-the-Sun dance, encouraged his followers to seek peace with their Métis neighbours, and policed his people to avoid offending Walsh and the Great White Mother. In addition, Bull made personal overtures to Crowfoot and pledged a desire for peaceful co-existence with all of the Canadian tribes.

The only bad news came from the south. Bull's trusted friend Chief Joseph and the Nez Percé Nation were suffering the same indignities inflicted upon the Sioux by the U.S. Cavalry the previous year. Joseph, for a long time the model of Indian co-operation with U.S. government regulators in the Oregon Territory, had abruptly been displaced from his reservation lands west of the Rockies and was now on an exodus to join Sitting Bull's Sioux in Canada. The Nez Percés spent the summer months evading capture despite relentless efforts to hunt them down. They wove their way through the mountains and valleys of Montana, successful in their escape until they entered the realm of the ambitious General "Bear Coat" Miles. Still smarting from Sitting Bull's success in getting to British lands the previous winter, and under explicit government orders to stay away from the Canadian border, Miles was not about to let a second legendary tribal leader elude his clutches. Daily runners brought the latest

After finding refuge on the perimeter of Blackfoot territory, Sitting Bull wisely sought a council with Crowfoot in the summer of 1877. The two chiefs smoked the pipe while pledging to end horse stealing and war forever. Bull further sealed the pact by naming one of his twin sons Crow Foot.

news to Sitting Bull about the progress and setbacks Chief Joseph was encountering.

Walsh knew of the cat-and-mouse game being played on the American side, and he could see in Sitting Bull a yearning to aid his brother. Walsh told Bull that if the Sioux were to go south, they would not be welcome back in Canada. It was a difficult situation. He was asking Sitting Bull to make peace with the bluecoat's head chief, Terry, while his bloodthirsty General Miles hungered to destroy Bull's ally, Joseph. In trying to get Sitting Bull to the Fort Walsh council, Inspector Walsh was up against difficult odds.

Adding to this already unfavourable state of affairs was a personal tragedy that befell the family-oriented Sitting Bull. When Walsh had arrived at the Sioux camp, he found Bull in mourning, practising the customary rites after the recent death of his nine-year-old son.

When word came to Wood Mountain that the Nez Percés were trapped, many of Sitting Bull's warriors chanted war songs through the night. The next morning Walsh again warned Bull and his chiefs of the consequences of going south. When a Sioux scout rode in to warn that an invasion of bluecoats had crossed the border, Walsh refused to believe it was Miles.

The warriors thought differently, and this time they prepared for battle, mounted their horses, and listened to the commands of Spotted Eagle. All Walsh could do was convince the band that he should ride with them, the Mounties out front, ready to confront any challenge to their sovereignty. "A more incongruous spectacle, in those times and on those plains, would be difficult to contrive," wrote one historian. Walsh started out with a small patrol and 200 warriors behind him, "a painted, feathered mob galloping full out with piercing yells and war cries to investigate reports of an American invasion."[7] The ranks swelled to a thousand Sioux as Walsh neared the border, knowing the potential consequences if Miles and his army really were headed their way. But they were not.

Instead, the pathetic column of "invaders" turned out to be a distraught band of 200 beleaguered Nez Percé followers of White Bird, the lone chief who escaped Miles' fury when the general laid siege to Joseph's main camp. "Many of them were wounded—men,

THREE YEARS OF ESCAPE

Although Nez Percé warrior White Bird never gained the notoriety of Sitting Bull, Inspector James Walsh, who had met both, described Bird as the greatest Indian soldier who ever lived. The adversity he endured over three years and his will to survive were unequalled.

In 1875, White Bird and other Nez Percé leaders found yet another reason to distrust the Indian Bureau when that body reneged on an agreement granting the followers of Chief Joseph (pictured here) a reservation in Oregon's Wallowa Valley. Two years later they were forced to move to a smaller reservation by an edict of the Indian Bureau. In May 1877, Joseph chose acquiescence over war, and his people grudgingly headed to the new reserve. En route, however, firewater helped determine the cruel fate of an indigenous people. Several unruly warriors made a drunken attack on settlers while Chief Joseph and his followers were making their way to their newly allotted home, and then the culprits killed more Whites while escaping south to join the lodges of a respected war chief, White Bird. A military response was assured, and the retaliation started when a battalion of soldiers under the command of one of General Otis Howard's officers ignored a Nez Percé flag of truce and fired on White Bird's peace party. The avengers wounded three Nez Percés, but in the ensuing hours the army was forced into full retreat, and by day's end 33 soldiers were dead.

Over the next month, Howard's army fought a series of skirmishes, always failing to diminish its enemy. White Bird, seeking to end the hostilities, joined other tribal leaders in their escape to Montana's buffalo plains, where they entered the Upper Missouri territory, still under the overall command of General Terry. They crossed the Great Divide in the first week of August before a three-day rest beside the Big Hole River ended with an attack from a new adversary. Colonel John Gibbon, the commander of Fort Shaw, raided the Nez Percé camp with no warning. White Bird rallied his warriors, and women and children escaped into the forest as Gibbon took control of the lodges. Then, in a counterattack organized by White Bird, the Seventh Infantry force was pinned down. Gibbon would later say, "At almost every crack of a rifle from the distant hills some member of the command was sure to fall."[14] Over the next day and night, White Bird's warriors held the bluecoats at bay while the women and children moved southeast. By the morning of August 10, all traces of the Nez Percés were gone and Gibbon was left to tally his 30 dead and count himself among the 40 wounded. Most of the 59 Native corpses they found amidst the lodges were women and children.

Chiefs Joseph, White Bird, and others managed to avoid all pursuers for another month while plundering horses and food as they moved farther northeast after their supplies gave out. General Terry turned the chase over to Bear Coat Miles, a man hungry for such a challenge. Miles deduced that Joseph and his allies were on their way to the Canadian border and finally caught up to them with his force of 400 men some 40 miles south of the Medicine Line. On the morning of September 30 (at the same time Colonel Macleod and Jerry Potts were en route from Blackfoot Crossing to meet with General Terry), Miles' forces struck hard at the Nez Percé village. He seized the main horse camp, isolating the warriors from their mounts but not their rifles. Trained and skilled, White Bird's marksmen took dead aim at anyone who wore an officer's coat. Soon only one officer of the Seventh Cavalry remained unscathed. Nine NCOs had also been shot, and all three first sergeants were dead. Fearing another military debacle, Miles prudently fell back and placed the camp under siege.

As snow fell and sharpshooters traded bullets, a few messengers filtered through the bluecoats and headed north toward Sitting Bull. Beyond the Milk River (the Hudson's Bay divide that separated all waters draining south to the Gulf of Mexico from those draining north to Hudson's Bay), Joseph's plea for help was taken to the camp of the Sioux sympathizers. On October 5, 1877, after Inspector James Walsh made his successful bid to keep the Sioux in Canada, Chief Joseph surrendered his rifle to Miles. "From where the sun now stands I will fight no more forever."[15]

That night, resolute as ever, White Bird and 104 of his warriors and their families fought their way through General Miles' army and escaped across the Canadian border.

women and children. Some were shot badly through the body, legs and arms," wrote Walsh in his official report.[8] Behind Walsh, the Sioux mood turned from ferocity to compassion as the wounded were tended to and children and women were given water and food. Walsh no doubt admired the still-proud White Bird, who had marched his people over 1,600 miles to freedom. Regarding the vindictive Miles, Walsh could only express his disgust and once again plead with Sitting Bull to honour his word to hold council with General Terry at Fort Walsh.

"We met Major Walsh about 60 miles east returning from the Camp and having Sitting Bull and various other Sioux chiefs along with him," wrote Nevitt.[9] Walsh was no doubt happy to see the quintet before him—Macleod, whom he had always admired; Steele, who was one of the first recruits Walsh had led out of Ontario four years earlier; "Texas Jack" Denny, the ever-entertaining fellow officer; and Nevitt and Potts, two men who had much to do with the fact that Walsh himself was still alive.

While Macleod was pleased to see Walsh, he was even more pleased to see Sitting Bull and the two dozen Sioux who rode with him. Scouts were reporting that the U.S. Cavalry had forced the complete surrender of Joseph, and with the arrival of General Terry pending, the commissioner knew he had his hands full.

Sam Steele, a keen observer of the Sioux party, later made an interesting observation. "When Major Walsh appeared he was accompanied by the Sioux chiefs, 20 in all, and one squaw, a tall powerful looking woman in the prime of her life ... these Chiefs were the most noted of the Teton Sioux, handsome in appearance, all having the dark and intensely piercing eyes of the Sioux."[10] The lone woman in the entourage was The One Who Speaks Once, a chief's wife whose presence went against the tradition of women not participating in councils. Steele would later speculate that her attendance was a symbolic slight orchestrated by Sitting Bull to insult General Terry.

General Terry sent word through a messenger to Fort Walsh that he would reach the border on October 14. Macleod got the notification only when he reached the fort with Walsh's escort for Sitting Bull and the 20 sub-chiefs who rode with him. Potts,

Macleod, and Inspector Denny made a quick turnaround and, with a patrol of two dozen horsemen, reached the boundary cairn in the Sweetgrass Hills in time to provide formal permission for Terry and an accompanying infantry to enter Canada. They made their way to Fort Walsh for the council with Sitting Bull on the evening of October 16. Sam Steele would later write, "It was a continual surprise to the Americans [that] we managed to control thousands of the most warlike Indians on the continent, there being only about sixty men all told at Fort Walsh."[11] Sitting Bull fulfilled his promise to Walsh to attend the council, but he would show nothing but spite for the U.S. generals.

The council was held in the officers' mess, the fort's largest room, where Macleod used Walsh's two resident scouts as interpreters. Sioux was not one of Jerry Potts' favoured languages, and he had no role in the dialogue, simply observing from a standing position. Macleod, seated at one table with journalists from the *New York Herald* and *Chicago Times*, offered introductory remarks, then gave the floor to his American guests. General Terry, seated at a second table with an aide and stenographer, was quick to the point: his government wanted Sitting Bull and his followers to return to the U.S. and lay down their arms. He would assure a full pardon for all Sioux warriors who took this action. They would trade in their horses and rifles for farm implements.

Walsh, who by this point had come to respect the Sioux leaders, knew that both the proposal and the choice of messenger to deliver it represented a ludicrous strategy. He and Macleod watched as Bull dismissed the offer outright and lectured General Terry on the deceits and ill will he had faced south of the border. He shook the hands of the Mountie observers, but refused to touch Terry. "You see me shaking hands with these people," Bull concluded. "I intend to stay here."[12]

Sitting Bull introduced two fellow chiefs, who further denounced the U.S. treatment of the Sioux, and then he gave the floor to The One Who Speaks Once. She rose, stared at Terry, and said, "I wanted to raise my children over there. You did not give me any time. I came over to this country to raise my children and to have a little peace. That is all I have to say to you. I want you to go back to where you came from."[13]

General Terry's overtures for a peaceful return of Sitting Bull's Teton Sioux followers are met with terse rejection, while Colonel Macleod patiently observes in this New York Graphic's *rendition of the Fort Walsh summit meeting requested by the U.S. government.*

After one more pronouncement, Terry had heard enough. Through the interpreter he asked, "Shall I say to the President of the United States that you have refused the offer he has made to you?" Bull responded, "That is all I have to say. This part of the country does not belong to your people. You belong on the other side."[14]

Two days later Major Walsh accompanied General Terry back to the border. Later accused by his Ottawa political bosses of being too interested in getting his name in the paper, Walsh had made time to host both of the eastern journalists while they conducted personal interviews with Sitting Bull.[15] It was those interviews and the ensuing news articles that "etched a portrait of a believable human being, a powerful leader less by rank than by wisdom ... true to his heritage, and possessed of unshakable principles and convictions."[16]

While Terry's overtures were seen by many as a failure, others in Washington were relieved. Sitting Bull was now a Canadian problem. Still, a winter war of words prevailed thanks to the persistence of the ambitious General Miles. He ridiculed the Terry Commission's efforts and pleaded for the power to deal personally with the threat that would hover over Montana and the Dakotas as long as Sitting Bull was nearby.

For his part, Macleod was most anxious to return to his home fort and his bride of slightly more than a year. Fine weather prevailed and, at the colonel's urging, Jerry Potts steered the column west, travelling one day from sunrise to sunset without even stopping for water.

Along the way, Colonel Macleod took one of his most dedicated officers, Dr. Barrie Nevitt, aside and shared with him a secret.

In 1875 a relatively unknown young English artist, D.B. Robinson, travelled west from Ontario to visit his friend, Colonel James Macleod. While there for about one year, his paintings and sketches included this ink-on-paper rendering entitled Jerry Potts and Friends. One of the friends was Dr. Barrie Nevitt, here portrayed with his head bowed and Jerry Potts to his left. Nevitt later used watercolours to complete the painting, which has been part of the Glenbow Collection for over 30 years.

Chapter 21

The Transition Years: 1878–79

Colonel Macleod's confidant was Dr. Barrie Nevitt, the only medical officer from the original march west to remain at Fort Macleod.

Nevitt was an American southerner who had left the turmoil of the Civil War to study medicine in Toronto. A graduate with limited prospects in his adopted country, he accepted an offer from the Force's senior medical officer, Dr. John Kittson, to join the march as assistant surgeon. While Commissioner French had seen fit to take Kittson east to Dufferin with his own party, Nevitt was left to tend to Mounties and any others who required his services. He was a devoted caregiver and quietly respected by his commanding officer.

Barrie Nevitt was a man deeply in love, ever writing to his sweetheart and always longing to complete his duty and return east to marry her. He had seen William Winder, other officers, and civilians bring their wives to settle at Fort Macleod, and most recently Colonel Macleod's hospitable bride had joined the community.

The NWMP recruiters had been unable to find a replacement for Nevitt, who by this time had been on the Canadian prairie for over three years with no chance to take leave in the east. Macleod was now in a position to grant Nevitt leave and have Fort Macleod fend for itself throughout the winter.

On the last day of October, Dr. Nevitt mustered the fortitude to write the first letter to his dear Lizzie in a month. "The Col. told me I could go when I liked—I determined to start at once—whenever the mail started to go with it [to Fort Benton] I packed up everything—made all my arrangements for leaving. I did all of this in pure selfishness thinking only of myself, of my great joy on seeing you again." Nevitt no doubt had great trouble adding, "I will tell you now my reason for changing my intention."[1] Nevitt swore Lizzie to secrecy, then explained his decision not to abandon his colonel: "Of course I have given the true reason [for staying put] to no one but yourself and Col. Macleod." He closed his letter "too homesick and heavy-hearted" to write any more.[2]

Dr. Nevitt's artwork and letters have provided many insights into life at Fort Macleod in its early years. Nevitt extended his stay of duty at the hospital there due to his concern for the health of Colonel Macleod's wife, Mary.

The mail system was a haphazard proposition in 1877. Letters were usually sent with the next departing trusted rider or scout heading toward Fort Shaw or Benton; sometimes it was Jerry Potts, more often it was one of Charles Conrad's people. To send a letter to the east and receive a reply would take a minimum of three months.

It promised to be a long winter at the fort for Nevitt. They had only been back at Macleod two weeks when the colonel announced he had to go to both Fort Calgary and Fort Edmonton and hold court. By the time he and Jerry Potts returned, they would have covered over 1,400 miles of trail since they had headed out to Blackfoot Crossing in mid-September. As it turned out, the lone prisoner in Edmonton was dead, so Macleod was able to return homeward sooner than expected.

In early December, word came to Fort Macleod that Chief Crowfoot was ailing and anxious to see the fort's doctor. Jerry Potts led Nevitt across icy rivers to the Blackfoot camp. They found the superstitious chief "in his lodge with three or four drums going and an old hag burning holes in his leg to drive away the pain and to deaden the Cree Medicine."[3] Jerry Potts interpreted for Nevitt and explained how Crowfoot was sure that his enemies, the Cree, had willed bad medicine upon him. After examining his patient, Nevitt diagnosed neuralgia and doled out his own medicine accordingly.

Nevitt had yet to reveal to his fellow officers the real reason he remained at Fort Macleod. His still-frequent letters home often mentioned the generosity of the colonel and described how Mrs. Macleod had fast become a favourite of the single officers at the fort since she often invited them to dinner and, in the case of Dr. Nevitt, even made curtains for his windows. At Christmas the Macleods were able to provide the officers adequate whiskey with which to make toasts (wearing his other hat, Magistrate Macleod conveniently issued a permit for spirits brought in from Fort Benton by the Conrads), along with a grand feast of turkey, mutton, and plum pudding. Even the weather co-operated. Sam Steele recalled a marvellous winter with "weather delightful during the whole of the season ... New Year's Day was like midsummer and cricket was played outside the fort."[4]

It was during this winter that Steele first got to know Old Jerry, a man he would come to admire during their lifelong friendship. An avid horseman, Steele was charged with assembling outgoing patrols regardless of the hour. Potts was at the head of all important missions, while Steele "paraded all parties and went with some of them ... the hours so uncertain that no one knew when he could get a night's rest."[5] By this time, enough Mounties had ridden with Potts that his talents were rubbing off on them. Potts rode with patrols "sent off to look for horse-thieves, to make sudden raids on Indian camps to capture lawbreakers, to lie in ambush at coulees ... to intercept whiskey outfits." All the while, Potts taught the men what to watch for, how to track, and how to hide. In Steele's estimate, as a result of the scout they had followed, "every man of two years' experience had so much [practice] that he could find his way to any point required for hundreds of miles around."[6]

Although Nevitt's closely held secret seems to have been based more upon professional courtesy than any real health concerns, the reasons for his commitment to Colonel Macleod and his wife, Mary, became more obvious with each passing week. The Macleods were about to have their first child. Eventually, a letter to Lizzie suggested that the good doctor was concerned about "complications"[7] when he swore her to secrecy the previous October, but the simple fact was, he was not going to ride away from Fort Macleod and leave Mrs. Macleod unattended.

Mary Macleod came to Fort Macleod from Winnipeg after her husband was named the new NWMP commissioner. She energetically assumed the role of "first lady" in the small community.

When duty called in mid-January and Macleod and Potts made another long journey to Helena to communicate with the east, Nevitt made daily visits to Mrs. Macleod. Concerned about his wife's condition, the colonel rode anxiously back into the fort three weeks later, at dusk on February 5, ahead of his wagons.

Potts arrived the next day, but had little time to rest. A messenger brought word to Dr. Nevitt that a man who had been hurt running buffalo had been carried on a travois 80 miles to Standoff, south and west of Fort Macleod on the Belly River. There he had asked his friends to ride up to Fort Macleod to get the redcoats' doctor who had been at the Blackfoot Crossing treaty signing. On February 7, 1878, Nevitt wrote to Lizzie, "I started for Standoff this morning at 9 sharp—the Colonel sent me over with his own wagon and team—I took Jerry Potts with me of course. We made capital time arriving at Standoff in two hours and a half."[8] Nevitt attended to the injured man, and Potts had the doctor back in his quarters before dark.

It was a busy week at Fort Macleod. With Major Walsh off to Ottawa to accompany new recruits back west, Major Irvine was dispatched to the Cypress Hills to tend to the growing camps of Sioux. Shortly after Dr. Nevitt took over Irvine's rented home at Fort Macleod, his mentor, Dr. John Kittson, arrived from Fort Walsh to be treated for a severely abscessed jaw. Colonel Macleod was also unwell, having been under the weather since his return from Helena four days earlier.

But on Saturday, February 9, all of these concerns paled in comparison to Nevitt's proudest moment. "Mrs. Macleod was delivered of a fine daughter at half past five this afternoon," he wrote to Lizzie. "I need hardly say that this is a great weight off my mind. I am so glad that she waited until the Colonel got home." The next day he added, "I naturally still feel slightly anxious for no one knows what symptoms might turn up."[9]

The doctor planned to spend at least a month attending to mother Mary and baby Helen before making a final trip to Calgary. After that, he wrote to Lizzie, all of his thoughts would be on returning home. The first boat of the season would reach Fort Benton in early May, where it would be laden with robes for the return trip to St. Louis. Nevitt planned to be on it.

In March, the gossip at Fort Macleod centred upon news that the colonel planned to move his headquarters to the Cypress Hills. With the traditional summer move of Crowfoot's lodges to the foothills, and the increasing concerns about both Sitting Bull's camp and the ever-posturing General Miles south of the border, Macleod knew that a stronger NWMP presence was required in the Hills. In the last week of the month, while awaiting the return of Jerry Potts, who was due in from Fort Walsh with the latest dispatches, he prepared for another trip to Helena, where the telegraph allowed him to communicate with the mandarins in Ottawa.

The latest indication that a new respectability was taking shape within the fort was a fundraiser aimed at starting a new school. "Mrs. Macleod and Mrs. Winder interested themselves in the school question and ... succeeded in obtaining about $360.00."[10] They arranged for a young schoolmarm, Miss Barrett, to move south from Reverend John McDougall's mission at Morley, near Fort Calgary. By the time school convened, D.W. Davis, the I.G. Baker store manager, had his three children enrolled, and respected carpenter William Gladstone's son, Bobby, and William and Julia Winder's little Georgie were also there. Rounding out the makeshift classroom were two of Jerry Potts' offspring, Willie Potts and a younger sister.

On Colonel Macleod's second trip of the year to Helena he had the company of his wife and baby daughter. Macleod was to confer with Major Walsh there before the latter carried on to Ottawa. Both men must have been astonished by the yarns Montana's news scribes, including the vociferous John J. Healy of Whoop-up fame, were unleashing to help nurture fear, sell newspapers, and ideally attract more military money to their towns. "Rumours of an alliance among the Northern Plains tribes in 1878 proved to be largely the invention of the citizens of Fort Benton," wrote a later observer. "The culprit was usually Sitting Bull, who allegedly darted around the region, hatching plots, forging agreements, acquiring weapons and supplies, and leading raids—a busy schedule."[11] Healy, who had witnessed Sitting Bull's encounter with General Terry at Fort Walsh the previous year, used his *Fort Benton Record* to keep the citizenry stirred up and occasionally to slander the NWMP officers he never forgave for putting him out of the whiskey trade.

On his way to Ontario, Walsh stopped long enough in Chicago to be interviewed by newsmen. Anxious to preserve the confidence of the Sioux in his own country, he distanced himself from any potential armed alliance with the Americans. "We have no interest in common," he stated. He told Chicago reporters: "The cost of an Indian war in such a country as ours would be enormous."[12] He singled out General Miles in particular, voicing his suspicions that Bear Coat would love to entice the Canadians to embrace his personal strategy. Sitting Bull's flat-out rejection of General Terry was still making news in the east. Walsh tried to dilute the fear-mongering. If the Sioux did move south, he said, "It would not only be a blessing for them, but [also] for the people on the frontier, and would cause a happy termination, for both Canada and the United States, of the hostile question."[13]

Of course some of his comments were taken out of context, and by the time Walsh reached Ottawa, he had to face bureaucrats who wished he were less vocal. Walsh, never one to shrink from confrontation, paid little heed. On his return trip he told a *Chicago Times* reporter of American confidantes who "freely state that the mistake their government has always made [was] in using force of arms rather than peaceful measures."[14]

Walsh confirmed that the more he heard about the tactics of Bear Coat Miles, the less impressed he became. "Miles claimed that 1,300 Sioux had been seen south of the boundary. Walsh dismissed this as impossible. Likewise, he was bemused on learning of Miles' letter to headquarters saying Walsh had ordered Sitting Bull out of his territory after a falling out. Finally he learned that Miles had arrested the Nez Percé leader, Joseph, while under a flag of truce. The more he heard about Miles, the more Walsh believed the general based a large part of his campaign on misinformation and desperation."[15]

Walsh forecast that starvation would eventually drive more and more Sioux and Nez Percé lodges south and the rate of flow would depend on how well the first returnees were treated. Before he left Chicago, Walsh's final prediction was that Sitting Bull would be the last to surrender.

James Walsh's return train trip had him back on the Missouri River at Bismarck, Dakota, with 65 recruits on May 25. Walsh had chartered the paddlewheeler *Red Cloud* for the two-week upriver journey to Fort Benton. Coincidentally, homeward-bound Barrie Nevitt was making a train connection in Bismarck during the same week. That he and Walsh actually made contact at Bismarck is unconfirmed, but it would have provided a serendipitous farewell reunion for both—for Nevitt, a final goodbye to the Force; for Walsh, a chance to toast the doctor's urgent winter journey to Fort Walsh in 1876.

It proved fitting that Dr. Nevitt's last case at Fort Macleod was his second delivery—another healthy baby girl. After reaching Toronto and marrying Lizzie that June, Nevitt announced that the two frontier births had inspired him to pursue a career in obstetrics. Richard Barrington Nevitt became the founder of Toronto Women's

Hospital and, as a leading proponent of women's medicine in Ontario, went on to deliver thousands more babies.

Jerry Potts once again relocated his large family to Fort Walsh in the summer of 1878 when the new NWMP headquarters was established there. On the journey he must have witnessed the impact that Treaty Seven was having on the prairie. With most of the non-reservation lands now officially managed by the North-West Council, free-range cattle were being brought in from Montana by former policemen. Observing how well some of the NWMP horses and cattle fared for themselves on the open range during the previous winter, a number of men sought their discharge from the Force and secured small herds, becoming the ranching pioneers of southern Alberta. By 1881, even Fort Macleod's long-serving commissioner, William Winder, would resign and settle down to a life of ranching, just north of what had been his command post for more than six years.

While the governing council was successful in nurturing ranching, it could not protect the buffalo from the growing influx of Montana-based, non-treaty Indians flowing into the Cypress Hills. After Commissioner Macleod had decided that the detachments at Fort Walsh and Wood Mountain, were too much for one senior officer to handle, he ordered Inspector Walsh to relocate permanently to Wood Mountain, closer to Sitting Bull's main camp. With Fort Walsh named the official Force headquarters, Colonel Macleod joined Assistant-Commissioner Irvine in time to watch the irrepressible General Miles make one more attempt to lure some Native exiles back to the U.S. This time Bear Coat sent one officer and three Nez Percé spokesmen from their Kansas reservation to persuade White Bird and the 25 Nez Percé lodges that followed him to surrender their arms. They would be allowed to rejoin Joseph and the other chiefs who had adopted their ways. But, like Sitting Bull's Sioux, White Bird chose to stay beyond the reach of the bluecoats.

In July, Jerry Potts accompanied Colonel Macleod and Inspector Denny to Blackfoot Crossing to begin the annual disbursement of treaty funds. Later they would visit the Bloods at their Belly River

After Colonel Macleod moved his headquarters to Fort Walsh, he posed (sitting between A.G. Irvine and Dr. Kittson) with his officers, including the recently married adjutant Captain Edmund Dalrymple "Frank" Clark (front). Tragically, Clark, a nephew of Sir John A. Macdonald, was the first Mountie to succumb to the typhoid fever that plagued Fort Walsh both before and during its short term as the Force's headquarters. In his memoirs, Cecil Denny (back row, right) would recall, "Clark was the first officer we had lost since coming to the country and he was most popular."

Camp, and the Peigans would come to Fort Macleod—to receive, like the others, an allowance of five dollars per person. It was a year when fire was the enemy of the buffalo hunt. "The summer of this year saw most of the country towards the Cypress Hills burnt over by great prairie fires," Cecil Denny recalled, "and [with] the feed being destroyed the buffalo moved south, many Indians following them."[16] Not only fire, but rain, too, proved a summer problem. At Fort Macleod Potts and the commissioner assessed the damage done when a combination of melting snow and torrential downpours swelled the Oldman River. The rogue runoff had created a second riverbed in a low-lying gully, leaving Fort Macleod an involuntary island. The flooding also brought on a new crisis as it contaminated water supplies, and typhoid outbreaks occurred at both Fort Macleod and Fort Walsh.

In many ways 1878 and 1879 were the defining years for southern Alberta's future over the next decade. At least 16 different ranchers set cattle loose on the open prairie, not knowing how their herds would winter. As the cows scattered and winter conditions worsened, any attempt to track the animals failed. Potts led patrols out to pacify ranchers as more and more complaints accused the Blackfoot tribes of rustling and killing stock to feed their families. Red Crow and Crowfoot dismissed the claims; their people far preferred buffalo meat to that of the lowly steer. Only a few were willing to admit this might be the last winter with any buffalo at all.

In November it was apparent that more and more Sioux hunting parties were ignoring the border in their search for food. Major Irvine reported to his government that in the Sioux camps "the women are urging the men to cross [into Montana] and save the children from starving."[17] Even Sitting Bull spent a week south of the Medicine Line trading and gathering food. When the chief returned, Walsh summoned Bull to Wood Mountain and asked him about his plans for the winter. In his last dispatch of the year to Irvine at headquarters, Walsh described Bull as patient, confident that "the Great Spirit would pity them and send the buffalo into the White Mother's country."[18]

Chapter 22

A Very Bad Year: Starvation, Mayhem, and Murder

The bitterly cold winter of 1878–79 and the absence of the buffalo from the Canadian prairie had added to the woes of the Blackfoot tribes. Crowfoot had opted to keep his winter camp to the north where the lack of game hit his people hard. "I have never seen them before in want of food," observed one missionary who knew the tribe well. "For the first time they have really suffered the pangs of hunger."[1]

The winter and spring patrols that Potts led out of the Fort Walsh headquarters found mixed messages in the tribal camps. The Siksikas at Blackfoot Crossing had fared the worst. From the Kainai or Bloods, Potts learned that Red Crow's lodges had found enough buffalo near their Red Deer River winter camp to sustain themselves. Game was sparse enough, however, that Potts knew the lodges would have to spread themselves more thinly across the prairie to survive future winters.

Hunger, too, had become the most pressing problem of the Sioux. Potts' forays north of the Cypress Hills, even before winter hit, had found small groups of lodges spread out in an effort to survive. Sitting Bull may have retained his faith in the Great Spirit as the new year began, but his trust in Inspector Walsh and the Canadian government was definitely beginning to waver. Although NWMP officers had been consistent in their message to Sitting Bull that the Sioux's asylum in Canada was considered temporary, he still hoped that his people would be granted a reserve. Inspector Walsh at Wood Mountain and Macleod at Fort Walsh wrote to Ottawa noting the scarcity of food, but the government held firm. The Sioux asylum was temporary; they would not gain the same privileges granted Canadian Indians. Bull persisted, but getting nowhere with his plea and with starvation looming, he returned to his old ways.

In midwinter, reports reached Inspector Walsh that Sitting Bull had resorted to seeking an alliance with his traditional enemies, the Crows, and that he had sent emissaries south of the border. Desperate to survive, he expressed willingness to make war upon the Americans and implied to his potential allies that the Canadians were his enemies too. In late January, Walsh sent word to Irvine

Removed from power shortly after the formation of the NWMP, John A. Macdonald was again Canada's prime minister at a time when Washington was insisting that he return Sitting Bull or move him farther from the border. Macdonald was relying on Major James Walsh to fix the problem, which would result in their being at loggerheads.

and Macleod that he had gone two miles south of the border in search of Bull. When he found the chief to be petulant and thankless, Inspector Walsh was forced to confront a grim reality. As a committed sponsor of Sitting Bull's sanctuary above the Medicine Line, he faced disaster if the Sioux went to war.

Along with Macleod and Irvine, Walsh assessed the fury that would erupt in the U.S. if a well-armed war party led by Sitting Bull descended upon Montana in one final act of defiance. Sitting Bull's verbal outburst resulted in a new sense of urgency that led to a spring of posturing and letter-writing by politicians on both sides of the border. Although Canada's first and now re-elected prime minister, Sir John A. Macdonald, was in favour of the Sioux voluntarily handing their arms over to the U.S. Cavalry, he ridiculed a suggestion by U.S. secretary of state William Evarts that the Canadian government invite Sitting Bull to Ottawa and then arrest him. Macdonald rejected the proposal outright, stating that "mere apprehension" on the part of the American government was "scarcely sufficient [evidence]" to dupe and incarcerate Sitting Bull.[2] Macdonald planned to give the Sioux less and less while suggesting that the Americans make some concessions to encourage Bull's return to their jurisdiction. Evarts, switching to a new ploy, not only rejected that overture but stated that the U.S. government "would henceforth regard the refugees as British Indians and the responsibility of Canada."[3]

At Fort Walsh, it was again time fo Colonel Macleod to survey the mood of the surrounding tribes. Hunger was an enemy to all. To his east, James Walsh was doing all he could to contain the Sioux problem, but west, toward Fort Macleod and Fort Calgary, he could only rely on the ongoing influence of commanding officers and Jerry Potts as they made their rounds.

The new American stance could not help but cause suspicion among the isolated NWMP officers in the Cypress Hills, and it raised some disturbing questions. Had the choice of Terry as a commissioner at the 1877 council been deliberately calculated to sustain Sitting Bull's fury? Was there hope in Washington that Canada would force Bull farther north, away from the border? A fledgling Canada had neither the budget nor the resources to finance a Sioux reserve, and, up until this point, Macleod's officers had balanced compassion for a starving people with consistent encouragement for them to return to an American reservation. Isolated as they were, the meagre NWMP force of less than 50 men had defied many skeptics to the south and kept a lid on a potentially disastrous situation. The thankless undertaking was well into a third winter, with 5,000 starving Sioux growing desperate for relief, and discontent among other nearby tribes growing daily, when the Force's worst fears were realized. The single thing that would add most to the volatile mood of the Sioux would be the reappearance of General Miles. Bear Coat obliged.

When the first roundup occurred in 1879, it was the beginning of a new era that would transform the region's economy over the next two decades.

By the summer of 1879, James Macleod and Jerry Potts not only shared significant mutual respect but were also bonded socially by a mutual affinity for Montana Redeye or any comparable liquid spirit. While Macleod and his redcoats had made their reputation by destroying the whiskey trade, communal imbibition was one of their favoured pastimes. "The lawmakers, almost to a man, had a perpetual affinity for grog that was officially embarrassing."[4] And in the case of James Macleod, his "passion for whiskey, and his ability to handle it, created a legend in every officers' mess he visited, Canadian or American."[5] The colonel enjoyed a drink, and if a drink was to be had, Jerry Potts would be there for the occasion. With drink comes conversation, and in the summer of 1879 there was much to talk about.

The need to overcome hunger among the Blackfoot tribes was a subject foremost in Macleod's mind. Reports from Cecil Denny at Fort Calgary or William Winder at Fort Macleod or any Potts-led patrol out of Fort Walsh confirmed that hard times lay ahead for the Blackfoot if they did not change their ways. From the Cypress Hills to Fort Macleod, beyond into the foothills of the Rockies, and north to Fort Calgary, ranching continued to grow, squeezing the nomadic Blackfoot more every day. Still they refused to adapt.

The demise of the buffalo created new grazing land that rapidly attracted naive cattle ranchers ready to take their chances with frigid winters and the open range. Livestock wandered freely across the grassland, and with every missing cow came a new complaint against the many Peigan families camped near Fort Macleod. In August, the first roundup of open-range cattle in southern Alberta was organized by 16 ranchers who had branded their animals but had little idea of the herd's breeding success. The cattlemen included many Americans who pointed accusatory fingers at the Natives when the count was done and then asked permission from Commissioner Macleod to shoot any Blackfoot warrior who entered their camp without invitation. Macleod would have none of it. There would be no armed violence against a hungry Indian, and any such killing would result in the culprit being hanged. No, the government would not compensate for loss. The land was not yet ready for rapid settlement, and ranchers whose animals grazed on open land in this territory did so at their own risk. Some of the cattlemen responded by fleeing south, but more than half the ranchers stayed on their homesteads.

On the advice of Potts, who had himself maintained lodges on the Peigan reservation, and endorsed by some of his Fort Macleod officers, Macleod had recommended the previous year that the government buy and release 1,000 head of cattle in the designated Porcupine Hills reservation lands. If the animals could survive the winter, they would multiply and supply a ready source of food to the Peigan lodges for years to come. "There is no question in my mind as to the investment," he wrote to Ottawa. "Utilize the magnificent domain lying idle in the West, and have at any moment such a supply of food as would meet any necessity that might arise."[6]

Among the ranchers who participated in the summer roundup were five discharged Mounties. Like other original enlistees, they had decided to set adventure aside and seek a more lucrative life when Ottawa suddenly announced that it was dramatically reducing members' daily pay. Sam Steele got a first-hand account of the ludicrous situation when he was ordered to Fort Benton to meet the latest batch of recruits who came up the Missouri from Bismarck. "When we got back to Fort Walsh we found that many changes had been arranged," Steele wrote. Officers were given new titles; inspectors were to be called superintendents, sub-inspectors became inspectors, and chief constables became sergeant-majors. The change was of little relevance to most of the officers, who preferred to use their established military titles—Colonel Macleod, Colonel Irvine, Major Walsh. Neither Steele nor the enlisted men would change how they addressed these officers; the contentious issue was that of pay. "Those who wished to re-engage when their time was up had been lowered to 50 cents a day. The recruits who had just arrived were being paid 75 cents; the next lot would receive only 40 cents. The consequence of this remarkable regulation was that none of the old hands would re-engage to get less pay than the recruits." The impact was calamitous, as "no high-spirited man would submit to such treatment."[7]

At a loss to fathom this decision, Steele speculated that Ottawa's powers that be had found the original Mounties too well-educated or opinionated. (Certainly the most prominent thorn in Prime Minister John A. Macdonald's side seemed to be the original Mountie, the man who had led the first column of recruits out of Ontario, James Walsh. Macdonald was ready to have Walsh removed from his post for challenging the actions of Ottawa's politicians and Washington's bureaucrats with moral arguments in his defence of the Sioux.) Ultimately, after the reaction led to many resignations, the pay returned to 75 cents. At this rate, members earned only a quarter of the monthly salary first paid to Jerry Potts five years earlier.

Steele, who like Colonel Macleod would become a lifelong friend of Jerry Potts, spent much of his summer in the scout's company dealing with the latest epidemic of horse thievery. They earned sincere gratitude and many toasts in their honour by returning American animals to their rightful owners after recovering them from assorted tribal camps north of the border.

Although Steele's strength and durability were legendary, in late summer he suffered a severe bout of typhoid fever when tainted water brought the disease to both Fort Macleod and Fort Walsh.

Steele recovered but Captain E.D. Clark, the Force's adjutant, became the first officer to die in the West. Steele experienced a relapse more severe than the first bout and was near death when Surgeon Kennedy, who had replaced Dr. Nevitt, came from Fort Macleod. The outbreak had now infected over 60 men and was devastating at a time when the Sitting Bull situation was sending new shock waves through the NWMP ranks.

In less than five years, the NWMP under Colonel James Macleod, both as assistant commissioner and then as the head Mountie, had curtailed the whiskey trade, had overseen the treaty negotiations with all Canadian tribes of the great prairies, had managed the Sioux and Nez Percé refugees in the Cypress Hills, and had maintained cordial relations with the American military to their south—all without the loss of a single man to violence. Now they had reached a totally untenable situation. The Canadian government would not feed the Sioux and their fellow refugees, and the U.S. government had announced that it, too, was rejecting all responsibility.

James Macleod was dealing with Blackfoot hunger, pay reductions and resulting morale issues among his men, the usual amount of horse thievery, the growing impatience of Sitting Bull, and the early signs of a typhoid epidemic; the last thing he needed was an ambitious American general. Bear Coat Miles had just returned to his Dakota posting from the east, where he had long made it a habit to seek influence and lobby Washington's power brokers to back his hawkish ways. Exploiting the fact that his wife was the niece of General William Sherman, he had confronted and even ridiculed his immediate superior, General Alfred Terry.

Miles had spent much of the previous winter in Washington, seeking authority to cross the Medicine Line and annihilate the Sioux once and for all. Sherman, exasperated by his nephew-in-law's audacity, wrote directly that any such undertaking would "most decidedly land him in serious trouble. Unless Sitting Bull came down in force, the Missouri River would be the northern limit of Miles' operations."[8]

Force was hardly an option for Sitting Bull's hunger-weakened Sioux. With their ponies too feeble to travel back and forth from their main encampment, tribal hunting parties stayed near the border along a Milk River tributary called Rock Creek. They then hunted south of the Line, where there were buffalo, with the sole intention of securing meat and robes. This limited presence was quickly interpreted as a threat to both White settlers and reservation tribes in the vicinity—at least in the eyes of Bear Coat Miles.

In mid-July the general made his move. After a successful hunt south of the Milk River, the entire camp of 600, including women and children, was busily butchering carcasses to travois north when an advance party of 80 Crow and Cheyenne scouts and two companies of Miles' Second Cavalry charged into view. Sioux warriors fought while their women and children forded the Milk River to reach the salvation of the Medicine Line. The Sioux warriors formed a line of defence while their families escaped; then they fell back into a new line of resistance. Largely outnumbered, the Sioux sent a significant message to one Crow warrior that would change the whole mood of battle.

In a brief lull in the exchange, a Crow, bearing a white flag of truce, rode forth awaiting a Sioux rival to meet him. The Crow spokesman, representing Magpie, one of their most powerful and respected warriors, challenged the Sioux to send their head chief forward to do one-on-one battle. Magpie, statuesque on a prized horse that was the envy of all warriors, had sensed that Sitting Bull himself was present. He had long boasted that, given the chance, he would destroy the Sioux leader.

As the two companies of cavalry and Magpie's fellow scouts looked on, Bull, then a man of average physique in his 40s, emerged to accept the challenge. In his biography of Sitting Bull, Robert Utley wrote: "The two spurred their mounts directly at each other. Magpie took aim first, but his rifle misfired. Sitting Bull took aim and blew the top off Magpie's head. Dismounting and taking what was left of his enemy's scalp, Sitting Bull mounted Magpie's horse ... and rode slowly away to his own lines."[9]

As Miles' main force arrived with its Hotchkiss machine guns, Bull's warriors hastened their retreat to Rock Creek. Six Sioux had died at the hands of the American scouts in what Miles would claim as a victory at the "Battle of Milk River." For those present, the only legend enhanced was that of Sitting Bull's prowess.

Four days after this clash, a frustrated Miles made camp beside the boundary of "Europe," as U.S. troops had taken to derisively labelling land beyond their jurisdiction. Two days later, Inspector Walsh showed up from his Wood Mountain detachment and listened to Miles' complaints about renegade hunting parties and Canadian traders who sold ammunition to Sitting Bull. Walsh gave no ground. He was adamant that Bull and his followers had no desire to fight unless they were left no choice; Miles had left them no choice.

To confirm his position, Walsh returned in a few days with Long Dog, a Sioux chief and spokesman Walsh had come to respect. The chief assured Miles that the Sioux, under Sitting Bull, intended to stay in Canada. Miles made it very clear that if they ventured south, he would be there waiting for them.

Walsh rejected a request to send a bluecoat messenger to Sitting Bull's camp, allowing, instead, one news correspondent to return with him to Bull's lodges. Reporter John Finerty of the *Chicago Times* confirmed for his readers the role of Sitting Bull as "all-powerful monarch. If he has not the sword, he has, at least, the magic sway of a Mohammed over the rude war tribes that engirdle him ... his present influence is undoubted. His very name is potent."[10]

Finerty noted no shortage of arms and ammunition, but food was scarce. Women foraged daily for berries and pine nuts; meat, thanks to Miles' cavalry, remained scarce. Aware of Canadian government policy, the reporter expressed surprise over the regular appearance of food wagons from Wood Mountain. In contravention of his government's policy, James Walsh was sharing his food with the Sioux.

It was only a matter of time before Walsh found himself in hot water with Ottawa. Macleod had chosen Walsh on two occasions as the officer most suited to run an isolated outpost. He had earned the trust of the Sioux because he deserved it, and, in the long run, his loyalty to them would be his downfall. Historians have come to paint Walsh as self-serving in his openness with the American press and his willingness to cater to their curiosity. At the same time, he is recognized for his passion. No doubt Walsh took pleasure in his own notoriety, but part of his astute vision included respect for the emerging influence of the press in bringing the callous U.S. treatment of its Plains tribes to the forefront.

Less than a year after Miles and Walsh met at the border in July 1879, John A. Macdonald's government, in a desperate effort to force Bull south, summoned James Walsh east and never again let him anywhere near Sitting Bull.

On leave back east, with a dying father, his wife, Elizabeth, and ten-year-old daughter, Cora, nearby, Walsh penned his report to the minister of the interior. "He is the shrewdest and most intelligent Indian living," he wrote of Sitting Bull. "He is respected and feared by every Indian on the Plains. In war he has no equal. In council he is superior to all. Every word said by him carries weight." Despite his admiration for Sitting Bull, Walsh had no trouble opposing a reservation for the Sioux, concluding that the Sioux would always breed trouble. "Bull's ambition is ... too great to let him settle down and be content with an uninteresting life," Walsh concluded.[11] He could have said the same about himself.

Chapter 23

The Murder of Marmaduke Graburn

As the typhoid epidemic ebbed and life appeared to return to normal at Fort Walsh, a final shock hit the detachment on November 17, 1879. Only two miles from the fort, one of the recent recruits Sam Steele had led into Fort Walsh that June was murdered in cold blood. The lad, Constable Marmaduke Graburn, had been dispatched to retrieve an axe and picket rope left behind where they had been feeding horses about three miles upstream. Graburn and a sergeant were monitoring the fort's horse herd closely in response to increased horse stealing. Several men guarded the pastureland during the day, and at night the horses were stabled in the fort.

The next morning, with still no sign of the missing Graburn and the mystery further complicated by fresh snowfall, Jerry Potts was summoned from his hillside lodge.

Other searchers spread out in different directions; Potts kept to Graburn's logical route back to the original grazing land. Near that camp he slowed, his eyes glued to the uneven ground as he watched his horse shuffle through the virgin snow. With every step, his gaze stayed riveted to the invisible track he sensed below. Drawn by intuition, he veered closer to the edge of a small ravine, still eying the snow his horse's feet kicked up. There! He had found it. Distinct flecks of red could be seen. He dismounted, brushed deeper into the snow, and confirmed that it was blood.

Potts moved down the slope and caught sight of the murdered recruit's pillbox cap hooked to a branch. Finally he located the body, rigid and blanketed in white, a single entry wound in the back of the head. In all the time since Jerry Potts had first led the red column to Fort Whoop-up, on frozen trails and in armed showdowns with whiskey traders or painted warriors, he had never lost a man. From the moment he saw the wound, Potts took the matter personally. He was looking at the first man killed on his watch.

Potts noticed next the prone shape of a snow-covered horse. It had been tied to a tree and shot. Whoever had killed the young constable was not stupid enough to be caught riding his horse. Potts sifted back through the snow, retracing the route from where the blood was found and eventually noting where other riders had joined the ill-fated Mountie. Called to the scene, the rest of the search party listened as Potts reconstructed the events that had led up to the murder.

Graburn had encountered two men who at first rode beside him. After riding a short distance, one fell behind the unsuspecting Mountie and shot him. The killers then pulled Graburn's body off the horse at the spot where the blood was found and dragged it into the ravine. In an attempt to hide the horse, they had tied its reins to a tree and shot it. Potts and everyone else were at a loss as to the motive.

Potts knew that in recent days a small party of Bloods had been seen camped near the police herd or lingering near the fort, pleading for food and ammunition, and he had his suspicions. Leading Sam Steele and a small patrol west onto the open plains, Potts was confident that he had picked up the killers' trail. Nature worked against him, though, when a chinook wind left a bare, thawed, and muddy ground with no clues to follow. It was obvious, however, that the pair had been making for the border.

A full year passed before the first break came in the case. When two Blood horse thieves were imprisoned at Fort Walsh, an intense interrogation, with Jerry Potts as the ever-present interpreter, established that the two had been camped near Fort Walsh at the time of Graburn's murder. Nervous that they might be accused of more than recreational horse theft, they attempted to escape. Their pathetic effort ended a half mile into their run for freedom; they were put back in the guardroom. Seeking mercy, they asked to speak with Inspector Crozier. Insisting that blankets cover the windows before they talked, the two provided the name of the man who had killed the redcoat.

From Fort Walsh, Inspector Crozier sent word to Colonel Macleod, whom he knew to be in Fort Benton after his return from eastern Canada. Crozier noted that a Blood troublemaker named Star Child was the alleged killer of Constable Graburn, and he was thought to be on the Montana side, somewhere in the Bear Paw Mountains. When Macleod sent Cecil Denny to Fort Benton to seek the aid of the local sheriff and justice of the peace, he was authorized to offer up to a $500 reward to gain support. However, when he arrived on the banks of the Missouri, the NWMP inspector

Many Mounties thought the infamous Star Child was able to escape the gallows only because the region's cattlemen did not want to trigger a backlash on the Blood reservation at a time when tensions were high between Natives and Whites. Ironically, the alleged murderer of Constable Graburn later was hired by a NWMP officer as a scout. Here the Blood recruit poses with his Winchester '73, the official weapon of the Force.

found himself talking to John J. Healy, the old whiskey trader and sometime newspaper man who had been at Fort Walsh with General Terry. Sheriff Healy did not have to remind Denny that he had little regard for anything British. His co-operation, he said, would cost $5,000. Denny opted to pass. The Mounties would wait for Star Child to reappear in a Blood lodge north of the Line sooner or later.

Potts had stayed closer to the Peigan camps than to the Bloods ever since his mother's death. Yet he still had contacts in most Blood camps. While it was not his way to offer Crozier or Macleod assurances, Potts knew that he would be informed when Star Child returned to his family's lodge near Fort Macleod.

At Fort Walsh, Colonel Macleod informed his men that he had made a personal decision to leave the Force and relocate to Fort Macleod, where he would continue to sit as magistrate. His commitment to his job had kept him in constant motion since the day he had married and now, with a young family, it was time to turn the reins over to his chosen successor, Major Irvine.

In late September the relaxed colonel bid adieu to his command in the Cypress Hills and headed west. Accompanying him was his nephew Donald, who was on his way to join his father, Norman Macleod, the recently appointed Blackfoot Indian commissioner. Also in the party were Cecil Denny, who was going on leave, and Jerry Potts, who was rejoining his family, recently returned to the Peigan reserve in the Porcupine Hills. Two constables, Claudius S. Hooley and A. Stewart, manned the wagon that carried supplies and the baggage of Colonel Macleod and Inspector Denny. The men, horses, and wagons made the first of two required crossings of the Belly River near Whoop-up. They managed the ford without incident in spite of high water and approached the second crossing, a further 20 miles distant, as the sun dipped below the Rockies. After Macleod and Potts crossed with Denny's horse, the wagon started to follow, but with dusk coming on and the river still high, Macleod ordered them to make camp on their side and cross over in the morning. Since they were only nine miles from Fort Macleod

James and Mary Macleod eventually had five children and settled at Pincher Creek after the commissioner resigned his post in late 1880. Helen (right), Norman, twin girls Roma and Mary, and Jean, in the arms of the governess, lost their father at a young age when he died of Bright's disease in 1894.

and anxious to see their families, the colonel and Potts headed in that direction.

Having endured a sleepless night plagued by the mosquitoes, Denny was up at daybreak, ready to get to Fort Macleod. He had Constable Hooley, one of the original members who had ridden west with Denny and Macleod, inspect the river ford while retrieving his horse and a second that had swum to the opposite shore. He and Stewart harnessed the front team and then the "wheelers," the second team that were closest to the wagon. With Stewart and young Donald in the rear and Denny and Hooley up front, the crossing was soon under way.

In midstream the front team balked, and Denny took those reins while Hooley tried to settle the wheelers. Together they got the horses restarted, but within seconds the front pair lost their footing and were swept away by the current. The wheelers followed and Stewart and young Macleod jumped aside as the wagon tipped. Denny barely got clear of the horses and reins, and soon everyone but the driver was ashore. For a short time the wagon remained in sight, and Denny tried to reach the panicked driver. Then the current carried the entire wreck away as those ashore watched helplessly. Hooley's body was only recovered a month later, 12 miles downstream. All four horses drowned and most of Denny's baggage and his three-month pay envelope were never seen again.

The tragedy brought a sombre end to James Macleod's police career. No doubt, given a second chance, Macleod, Denny, and Potts would all have done things differently. Certainly Macleod had crossed at the same river ford two springs earlier when he was anxious to reach home for the birth of his first child. At that time he had left the ever-capable Potts to cross the river with wagons the next morning. This time Macleod had ordered the wagon to forego the river crossing in the evening dusk, taking Potts with him and trusting Denny to lead it home the following morning. Did he rue not staying or at least leaving Potts behind to aid the crossing? In his later writings, Denny lamented the fact that they had not continued the crossing in the evening, but fell short of blaming Macleod. He took great pains to state that he tried to save the young constable, almost drowning himself in the process. Aside from the murder of Marmaduke Graburn, Hooley was the only man to perish while on active duty with Macleod as commissioner.

The colonel had been an outstanding leader during his two separate stints with the Force. He had come to love the new land that he had helped to tame, and he would continue to serve his chosen country as a member of the judiciary until his dying days. Although Jerry Potts would also stay close to the Force for the rest of his life, Macleod's departure had its impact—as did another tragic event that occurred at Fort Macleod only weeks after their arrival.

It had been a year since Macleod and his scout had officially transferred to the Cypress Hills, and the Fort Macleod they returned to was a much changed place. The river, which had changed its course due to flooding, continued to undercut both the fort and the town itself, forcing businesses and houses to relocate.

In the countryside, new settlement and bigger herds of cattle portended the immigrant invasion that lay ahead. Swept along with the tides of change were the hapless Blackfoot tribes, who would never fully recover from the disastrous, almost non-existent buffalo hunt of the previous fall. Many were on the verge of starvation, carrying their sick elders to the fort, where they begged food for them.

Although Potts would maintain a residence on the main street outside the fort's walls for many years, he spent much of his time in the nearby hills at the Peigan reserve lodges with his large family. By late October, either missing the comradeship of his Mountie drinking pals or summoned by the commanding officer, Potts returned to Fort Macleod. There a second fatal accident in as many months unfolded. "A tragedy occurred that would bring about a disturbing change in [Potts], although his inscrutable facade would not show it," wrote one historian. "On October 29, 1880, Potts was … examining the priming of an old fuke, [when] the dilapidated weapon exploded and killed a young child."[1] It is not known if the child was related to him or who owned the ancient Barnett, the single-shot weapon that had misfired, but his role in the death devastated him. "After the accident Potts did not seem to be himself anymore. He became more sullen, even morose, and shunned all company, except when he was summoned to do a job."[2] That winter he retreated to the Peigan reserve, where the bottle became his best friend.

Potts climbed out of his doldrums often enough that winter to comb both the Peigan and Blood reserves for any sign of Star Child, the man who had killed Graburn. It was spring before he was able to confirm that the renegade was somewhere near the Little Bow River but was constantly on the move. Patiently, Potts closed in on him. After he reported Star Child's location to Fort Macleod, an arrest warrant was issued and Potts led Sergeant Patterson and three other Mounties about 18 miles to the banks of the Little Bow River. Even though it was dawn and the patrol surrounded the fugitive's tipi quietly, the alert Star Child suddenly burst from the lodge with his rifle levelled at Sergeant Patterson. Patterson distracted Star Child by calling to one of his men and then pounced on him. As the two fell, Star Child's cocked rifle discharged, ending any hope of a quiet arrest.

In moments, armed Indians from other lodges rushed to the scene. By then Patterson had Star Child in handcuffs, while his three colleagues clutched their weapons as the throng of feisty Blood braves pressed closer.

Potts stepped forward to intercept their leader and explained the circumstance. As others crowded in to hear the respected Bear Child, the distraction allowed the redcoats to get to their horses and hoist the prisoner astride a spare mount. Invited by Potts to witness redcoat justice at work, a band of Blood warriors soon followed the lawmen on their return to Fort Macleod.

In custody in early 1881, Star Child confessed to murdering Constable Graburn but, after being brought before Magistrate Macleod, chose a trial by jury. The trial did not take place until October, when other evidence and his own words seemed to confirm the Blood's role in the murder. Despite what to the Mounties was an open-and-shut case, the all-White jury, largely composed of nearby ranchers, returned a "not guilty" verdict. Explanations of their decision simply fuelled the controversy. One juror rationalized that Star Child had confessed only to gain recognition as a great warrior, the first ever to kill a redcoat. In an odd leap of logic, and despite the resentment it caused in the NWMP ranks, the jury considered this reason enough to free the murderer.

Sam Steele later judged the mental state of those who acquitted the accused: "There is no doubt that the jurymen ... were afraid that conviction would bring on an Indian war." At the very least, Steele concluded, they were protecting their cattle, feeling that a guilty verdict would "cause the Bloods to kill their stock out of revenge."[3] Colonel Macleod, who observed the outcome from his bench, agreed that the verdict was spawned by fear. Cattle rustling was enough of a problem without more reprisals emanating from the Blood reserve should they have found Star Child guilty.

For Jerry Potts, it was another bitter pill best swallowed with a large gulp of whiskey and a dose of patience. Potts knew Star Child would never change and that there would likely be another opportunity to bring him to justice.

Within months of Potts and Macleod and their drinking habits leaving Fort Walsh behind, the appointment of Colonel Irvine as commissioner brought out of the closet what was seen by some as a widespread problem. Although he had tolerated Macleod's methods and respected his leadership, Colonel Irvine's sobriety was a distinct contrast to his predecessor's intemperance.

Soon after he was appointed commissioner, Colonel Irvine announced to his officers that "he earnestly trusted that he would receive their hearty support and co-operation ... to suppress intoxication within the Force."[4]

Irvine chose to set an example of new discipline at Fort Macleod with a reprimand of Inspector William Drummer Jarvis. Jarvis had led and survived the gruelling trek from Roche Percée to Fort Edmonton in 1874 and had built Fort Saskatchewan 20 miles northeast of that Hudson's Bay outpost the following year. Highly respected by those in his command, like Macleod he was known to both enjoy his whiskey and ignore its liberal use among the troops. In the spring of 1881, after seven years in his original posting, he had been transferred south into the judicial realm of his former commanding officer.

Certainly at Fort Macleod it seems that, in spite of his unbiased view from the bench, Magistrate Macleod may have joined in more than one celebratory toast with Jarvis, Potts, and the attending officers in the aftermath of the Star Child arrest. Irvine did not approve and soon registered his unfavourable impression when he wrote to Ottawa: "There is not the slightest doubt that illegitimate liquor traffic was carried on directly under his eyes."[5] Jarvis had his own response to the criticism; he resigned in June.

Not all of Ottawa was ready to condemn the redcoated heroes in the west, however. Prime Minister Macdonald, an embracer of the bottle himself, dismissed parliamentary accusations about police drinking habits, saying "it would be impossible to expect a corps of saints."[6]

In mid-summer Jerry Potts was asked to lead an escort patrol to Blackfoot Crossing to undertake a new duty. The Marquess of Lorne, son-in-law of Queen Victoria and Canada's Governor General, was touring the western plains. His party, which was being outfitted at Fort Qu'Appelle by Sam Steele, would soon cross the Carlton

Trail to reach the homelands of Chief Crowfoot. From there, Potts would escort them to Fort Macleod and then across the border to Fort Shaw.

Potts went north to the Bow River valley, arriving at Blackfoot Crossing before the Governor General's party in early September. After an exchange of greetings, Potts explained the significance of the Great Mother's son-in-law making a personal visit to Crowfoot and the other Siksika chiefs. A few days later the Marquess of Lorne arrived with a large police escort and Chief Poundmaker, the party's guide through Cree country. Amid gun

The Marquess of Lorne succeeded the Earl of Dufferin to become Canada's fourth Governor General in 1878. In 1881 he travelled across the West and made the acquaintance of Jerry Potts.

salutes and other festivities, the Governor General reaffirmed the commitment that the government had made in the treaty of 1877.

With the Qu'Appelle escort relieved and the Fort Macleod contingent ready to break camp, their diminutive guide galloped out ahead as he always did. The next morning the curious Governor General, who by then had observed the respectful relationship that Potts had with Crowfoot and, no doubt, had heard a few tales about Potts' uncanny sense of direction, watched the guide again head out into the morning sun, alone and seemingly content. The Marquess was a man who was always in the limelight and, perhaps piqued by the guide's solitude, he decided to ride out and join him. For his part, Potts had never appeared to be impressed by rank or the doting attention heaped upon eastern officials by the Mounties, and at first he tried to ignore him.

The intruder persisted, pointing to the horizon: "Up ahead there, what do we come to?" Potts stared silently ahead, apparently in no hurry to answer the question that every White man asked sooner or later. Suddenly impatient, the Marquess raised his voice a notch, "I

Here the government's special artist, Sydney Hall, portrays a cavalcade of local Natives crossing the Bow River to follow the mounted police who escorted the Marquess of Lorne south.

say, Mr. Potts, don't you hear? After that hill, what do we come to?" The answer was classic Potts: "'Nudder hill, ya damn fool."[7]

Potts' mood did not improve with distance. After formalities were completed at Fort Macleod, the entourage crossed into Montana, en route to Fort Shaw and the Sun River. Potts made sure that one night the cavalcade camped near a trading post operated by Alfred Hamilton, a man he had known since the days of Fort Whoop-up. Certain that his old employer would have a supply of whiskey, Potts sought out Alfred and secured ample quantities for himself and his redcoated friends. He also laid eyes on an old Piegan chief, a man with whom he had a score to settle. With each glass of rotgut Potts downed, the old wound seemed to fester more. Finally he told his drinking pals that the Piegan must die. Cooler, calculating heads concluded that the presence of Canadian police at the revenge killing by a drunken ally of a reservation Indian on American soil while guiding their Governor General to a U.S. Army reception might shorten their careers.

Potts was stubborn and strong. When he went for his rifle, his friends physically restrained him, wrested the gun away, tied him up, and posted a guard even after he slept. Scandal was avoided and the Marquess of Lorne completed his 1,229-mile journey in 35 days without incident. He described his NWMP escort and its scouts in glowing terms: "as fine a troop as I ever saw."[8]

It would be fair to say that when whiskey was tempting him, Jerry Potts leaned toward irresponsibility. Put another way, when whiskey smugglers were arrested, Jerry had a great affinity for the evidence. On his next adventure after the departure of Lord Lorne, he outdid himself.

In February 1882 he earned the wrath of his friend and former boss, Justice Macleod, after an uninitiated officer, Corporal Tom LaNauze, sent Potts and two of his constables, Callaghan and Wilson, to investigate reports of a suspected whiskey wagon heading north from Montana. Opting for the simplest solution to the matter, Potts led the young Mounties to the predictable border point where they could watch the smuggler cross.

The vista of the Rockies, seen here from a rise above the Bow River near Fort Calgary, provides a majestic backdrop as Potts leads his party south to Fort Macleod.

Constable Robert Wilson recalled the proceedings in his diary for February 20. "After arresting an ex-policeman named Cochrane [and an accomplice] at the border, [we] camped at St. Mary's River. The two prisoners and Jerry were soon howling drunk and the rest of us managed to keep from freezing by taking frequent doses of alcohol diluted in water which Jerry called 'mix.' About midnight a priest, who was camped not far from us, came over and was persuaded to take a drink for his stomach's sake. It was not long before he and Callaghan became very jolly and were toasting each other at every sip ... before morning I had the honour of being the only sober man in camp although I must admit that I took quite enough to keep the cold out. At daylight we saddled up and after each man had taken a cup of alcohol for his breakfast started off."[9]

Much of the evidence was gone. Though most Mounties saw their duty as protecting the various reserves and their inhabitants from the whiskey traders, they had a different set of rules for themselves. They lived an isolated, rugged life and one of their few pleasures was to share a bottle of hooch. Recollections of drinking with Old Jerry brought howls of laughter and fuelled many yarns among the enlisted men in different detachments. One keen observer of a Potts drinking spree seemed almost in awe. "Potts had an unquenchable thirst which a camel might have envied. He drank whiskey when he could get it. If he could not get it, he would take Jamaica ginger, or essence of lemon, or Perry Davis' painkiller, or even red ink."[10]

Historian Hugh Dempsey put Jerry's habits in an appropriate perspective. "Everyone who knew Potts admitted he was an unusual man and felt that his drinking was not uncommon on the frontier. With his virtues far outweighing his sins, he was considered to be a capable scout, guide and interpreter rather than just a drinker. Regardless of his condition, no one could question his honesty, bravery and faithfulness to the Mounted Police."[11]

During this time, after Dr. Barrie Nevitt left the NWMP and with much of the Force's medical staff based in the Cypress Hills, the medical staffing at Fort Macleod was sadly lacking. One episode, later recounted in a veterans' association magazine, *Scarlet and Gold*, portrayed Jerry Potts as second assistant in the operating room.

The story started with the murder of Old Mart Kelly, a bull puncher who was killed by a suspected army deserter from Fort Shaw while driving his wagon from Fort Benton to Fort Macleod. The killing had occurred on the Canadian side and the culprit, Judd Scott, made a run south toward the Milk River during a February storm. When Constable Leader from the Standoff detachment found him crawling out of a snowdrift he was "too badly frozen to walk ... The man was taken to Dutch Fred's [Standoff], where his boots were cut off and his feet and hands dipped in pails of snow and water. The pain was so excruciating that he had to be held but not a word would he utter."[12]

A wagon transported the frostbitten man to Fort Macleod that evening, into the care of hospital steward Teddy Farren. The anonymous observer recalled that Farren had one year of medical school and it was only because "the tough lot of roughs comprising 'C' troop needed very little medical attention [that he was able] to put up a bluff as a 'medicine man' ... He was never called 'Doc' by the boys."[13]

It was three days before Farren declared amputation a necessity and brought out his unopened bottle of chloroform. With no surgical instruments at hand, "Teddy borrowed the butcher's saw and a couple of knives, enlisted the aid of [a man] who had worked in a chemist's shop, and with old Jerry Potts, the interpreter, as second assistant, he got to work.

"I will draw a veil over the language used by the butcher when he had his saw and knives returned to him and heard what they had been used for."[14]

Scott pulled through and his future fate with judge and jury went unrecorded.

In 1883, after another winter on the Peigan reserve, Jerry Potts was once more summoned to Fort Macleod to assist in the arrest of the troublemaking Star Child for horse theft. "There was always someone to inform the police, very often one prompted by jealousy or a desire to even some old score. And Star Child's case was no different."[15]

Superintendent Crozier, then in charge of Fort Macleod, well knew that Jerry Potts would want to waste no time in again going after the Blood no-good whom he still believed had killed Constable Graburn four years earlier. When word of Star Child's latest deeds reached Crozier on July 5, he dispatched a sergeant, a constable, and Jerry Potts to arrest him. Ever since Star Child had been declared innocent at trial, Potts had blamed himself for being unable to track the horses that had left the original crime scene. Now he readied himself and led the two Mounties toward Standoff under cover of darkness. Two additional men were picked up at the Standoff detachment, and the patrol of five made its way to the Blood Indian agency where Peigan Frank, a non-admirer of Star Child, pointed out the shack where the wanted man was sheltered. Sergeant Ashe, the Mountie in charge of the patrol, said to the other four, "This fellow has told the world what he will do to us, so get your guns out, and if he touches a weapon of any sort, riddle him."[16]

When Ashe opened the door and slid in, he could see the sleeping Blood. Potts pushed forward and shook Star Child from his slumber. "Had he made a move for his weapons, Graburn would have been avenged then and there," recalled one observer.[17] Star Child was tied to a spare horse, transported to Fort Macleod, and soon put on trial. He was sentenced to four years in Manitoba's Stony Mountain Penitentiary for bringing stolen property into Canada. Within the ranks, most felt that young Graburn's murder had been at least partially avenged.

Chapter 24

The Autumn Years

When James Macleod resigned as NWMP commissioner and Jerry Potts returned to the Fort Macleod area to re-establish residence on the Peigan reserve in the Porcupine Hills, it was the beginning of the end of a remarkable era on the Canadian prairie. The feats of the Canadian redcoats would continue to spawn legends across North America and throughout the British Empire, but never again would the Mounties be pitted against such drastic odds. The peace that prevailed in the Canadian West in these years was to the credit and leadership not only of the Mounties under Macleod and his small band of officers, but also of the Blackfoot chiefs who kept their word and prepared their people as best they could for the changing world that lay ahead. And in the middle of this process was Jerry Potts, guide, interpreter, and advisor.

Macleod had formally commanded the Mounties for just over four years when he retired in late 1880, but he had been the *de facto* leader of the Force in the West ever since Jerry Potts had first signed on in September 1874, on the same day that Colonel French started his personal retreat to the province of Manitoba. The six-plus years that Potts and Macleod rode together would certainly cement James Macleod as the most important leader of the NWMP's formative years. "He must be singularly credited with the overall peaceful and generally violence-free settlement of the west," stated one biography.[1] At the time of his resignation, however, Macleod was not without his detractors amid the political land mines of Ottawa.

He became the political target of a tight-fisted government opposition that knew nothing of the challenges the NWMP faced daily. The most ludicrous detractors painted him as a reckless spendthrift, deserving of reprimand.

Had he survived to write his memoirs, James Macleod no doubt would have shared the historic accolades he received with his fellow officers and Jerry Potts. Macleod would die young in 1894, a victim of kidney disease, but he retained his friendship with Potts in their autumn years, often visiting Jerry and his family at his ranch on the reserve. Some of the folklore that grew up around Potts' ways and words over the

James Macleod and many of his felow "originals" are part of the heritage that is on exhibit in the modern-day displays at Fort Macleod, Alberta.

years has been credited to Macleod's stories. After telling and re-telling, the setting often varies, but the gist of the yarns remains intact. One such tale was the "chamber pot story," which Macleod would share with many.

It seems that one of the two Mrs. Potts had acquired a child's chamber pot while in Fort Benton, and the vessel was in the family's possession when they arrived at the Standoff Detachment, where Macleod was overseeing the issuance of treaty payments to the local Blood Indians. Upon completion, Macleod asked Jerry to show him the route to "the good water from Standoff spring." Jerry noted that he had just gathered water from that very spring and asked his nearest wife to fetch a drinking cup for the colonel. The best cup in the travois, as it turned out, was what Macleod knew to be a traditional English-made chamber pot. Sipping his water, Macleod explained the real purpose for the oversized cup while his good friend listened in silence.

"You white people are crazy," Jerry finally replied. "You got plenty of open prairie all around and yet you use a good cup like this for kids to piss in."[2]

Another Macleod yarn recalled one of the many river crossings that he and Potts had made together. Potts and another man were ensconced in the back of a lone wagon as it entered the swollen St. Mary's River. With Macleod sitting next to him, the driver urged his horses forward into the current until a front wheel of the wagon was jolted by a large underwater boulder. Hearing a sudden splash, Macleod yelled, "Hold on. I think Jerry has fallen in." Potts' voice was unmistakeable. "Not by a damn sight," he replied. "But your sergeant is drowned." All watched and laughed as the drenched man, an able swimmer, made his way to shore.[3] After Macleod's retirement from the Force this story lost some of its lustre as it immediately brought to mind the tragic drowning of Constable Hooley in the Belly River in the summer of 1880.

The Macleod era of the NWMP gave way to the Irvine regime, another six-year stint from 1881 to 1886 that shifted the spotlight from Alberta to Saskatchewan. Irvine's so-called first success resulted in Sitting Bull finally returning south to the United States.

By May 1882, Bull and about 300 old men, women, and children were all that remained of the proud Sioux Nation that had sought refuge in Canada five years earlier. Chiefs like Gall, Black Moon, Rain-in-the-Face, and Spotted Eagle had joined the steady march south to Fort Buford, only miles from the original Fort Union, base camp of the AFC invasion of White fur traders into the Upper Missouri valleys only five decades earlier.

In one last desperate act, having resisted the overtures of Irvine and all other Canadian government officials, Sitting Bull led his bedraggled followers north. Certain that his friend James Walsh would not abandon the Sioux, their chief had marched 160 miles to Fort Qu'Appelle, where Walsh had been transferred. Walsh, however, had been detained in the east, where the prime minister had insisted that his sick leave be extended, effectively quarantining him from any further role. The acting CO, Sam Steele, could offer Sitting Bull nothing and awaited the arrival of Indian Commissioner Edgar Dewdney to negotiate. Dewdney provided a small amount of flour and, restating federal government policy, refused the Sioux a reserve. Sitting Bull's determination to stay in Canada surprised Dewdney to the point where he told Ottawa that starvation itself might be the only thing that would see Bull yield his ground. If starvation was to be the motivator, Macdonald would not stand in the way; nor would his ally Lord Lorne, Queen Victoria's official representative, who was also anxious to see the end of the Sioux occupation on Canadian soil. "Leave hunger to do the work," wrote the Governor General.[4]

On July 20, 1881, eight weeks after his final rejection at Fort Qu'Appelle, Sitting Bull finally accepted the fact that Major James Walsh was not coming to his aid and surrendered his Winchester rifle in a formal ceremony at Fort Buford. In a final gesture the great Sioux chief "composed a song to connect what had been to what would be. 'A warrior/I have been/Now/It is all over/A hard time/I have.'"[5]

The focus of attention was shifting farther away from Fort Macleod with each passing year, and that was fine with Potts.

With few buffalo remaining, and tensions among the traditional enemy tribes who lingered in the Cypress Hills reduced, new priorities arose; a new headquarters was identified, one whose sole reason for being was tied to the coming of the railroad. In tribute to the Great White Mother it was called Regina.

The railroad itself would bring new problems and maintain old ones—like the abuse of alcohol. Much has been made of Jerry Potts' attraction to whiskey, but its appeal was common throughout the Force. Under Irvine's reign a growing list of incidents showed that the abuse was widespread. One year into the job, if a disgruntled Irvine had been in Winnipeg, he could have read for himself "The Invalid's Story" in the July 20, 1881, edition of the *Manitoba Free Press*. There, the confessions of a disillusioned recruit and recently discharged young Mountie, James Livingstone, who had spent his entire 237-day career in the hospital, publicized the misuse of spirits.

"They get it over from Fort Assiniboine on the Yankee side ... The Doctor writes a permit for so many gallons of alcohol for hospital purposes ... Then we have a lot of brandy for hospital use but ... invalids never get a taste of it ... the brandy is saved for the officers to drink on select occasions."[6]

Ironically, given the scolding Colonel Macleod had received for his alleged inefficiencies, it was decided to double the size of the Force headquarters beside the final route of the Canadian Pacific Railway (CPR) at Regina. There Commissioner Irvine's style did not work in the favour of many of the original officers. After his actions against Jarvis, next on Irvine's hit list was the vulnerable James Morrow Walsh, no longer "Sitting Bull's Boss." Walsh, who had earned the everlasting wrath of Macdonald for his efforts on behalf of Sitting Bull, languished under Irvine's command. Irvine no doubt gained points with his masters by suggesting that Walsh was "utterly incompetent and untrustworthy ... [without] respect from his men ... unfit to hold a commission."[7] A stubborn Walsh persisted for another few years, unwilling to yield to his unimpressed commissioner. He resigned on the 10th anniversary of becoming the Force's "original Mountie," the first officer to lead his division into the North-West Territories. Walsh's sole reward was 10 months' wages, part of which he used to pay $150 for his beloved horse.

Inspectors Winder and Walker turned in their red tunics for ranching gear in 1881. Cecil Denny lasted another year but he, too, bid Irvine adieu to act as Indian agent, first at Fort Walsh and then to administer Treaty Number Seven out of Fort Macleod.

With the old guard gone and new officers promoted to take their place, Potts worked intermittently for whomever was in charge at Fort Macleod. Need for his services waned to some degree and he spent more time maintaining his ranch. But Old Jerry would always be part of the detachment, his common appeal well depicted by historian John Peter Turner. "There was always about him, something of the humorous, the tragic and the mysterious. Held in deepest affection by all who knew him, his faithful service to the Force had become an institution in itself." Turner also painted him as "jovial or silent as occasion might demand" and "overly fond of liquor," the most likely reason for his chronic cough. "Yet liquor," he remarked, "never seemed to undermine his strict adherence to duty." Some might debate that latter conclusion, but anyone who ever saw him shoot agreed: "His ability with a rifle was proverbial."[8]

Like his aim, Potts' strength was legendary. Turner also recounted the observations of Norrie Macleod, son of Norman and nephew of the retired commissioner, who had chummed around with Jerry's son Willie in their youth. Norrie recalled an evening at the Potts' home when Jerry had suddenly been jarred from a deep sleep by Sergeant Spicer, sent to call him to the latest crisis at Fort Macleod. "In his rather befuddled state [Potts] seized an Indian bow from the wall and placed an arrow on the string. Drawing the arrow to the head, he held it within three feet of Spicer's face."[9] From the deep recesses of a dream the instincts of a youthful Bear Child were back. Fortunately for the young Mountie, Potts came to his senses, threw the bow in a corner, and went back to bed. "Anyone knowing the strength required to handle a Blackfoot bow," wrote Norrie Macleod, "which would drive an arrow through a buffalo back of the ribs, might well have wondered where Jerry, who was a slim man, got the strength to do this."[10]

Perhaps the most telling event to signal the end of an era for the NWMP occurred in May 1883 when Commissioner Irvine ordered the demolition of all buildings at Fort Walsh. Salvageable materials were taken to Maple Creek and Medicine Hat to be used in new police camps along the railway, camps that would fall under the supervision of Sam Steele.

And if police life was changing, reports on the final demise of the buffalo ensured the Blackfoot traditions were gone forever. One small herd of bison was spotted in the Chin Coulee east of Fort Macleod.

Steele's job with the railway would take him across the Rockies to B.C., but that summer he would concentrate mostly on maintaining peace between the hordes of rail navvies sent into the hills to cut wood for the track bed and the various Indian camps that coveted their horses. The Plains were forever changed when on June 10,

SAM STEELE

Samuel Benfield Steele was one of three sons of naval officer Elmes Steele. In the autumn of 1874 at Prescott, Ontario, he boarded a train with the first NWMP recruits. Before they had reached Collingwood barracks, their destination for the first step in the trip west, the officer in command, James Walsh, had made Sam his sergeant-major, one of two NCOs who would help lead "A" Troop to its winter base in Manitoba.

Sam Steele had already made that journey in 1870 as a 19-year-old member of the Ontario Rifles, part of the military force led by Colonel Wolseley sent to restore order and suppress the Métis uprising led by Louis Riel. Even at that point, young Sam, who had been orphaned at age 15, had four years' militia experience as the ensign of the 35th regiment.

After travelling by steamer across lakes Huron and Superior, Walsh and Steele led a troop of 75 men over a treacherous 450-mile trail to Lower Fort Garry, where they wintered. Sergeant-Major Steele became the official riding instructor, charged with preparing the recruits for the planned march west the following spring. "Our work was unceasing from six a.m. until after dark," he would later write. "I drilled five rides per day the whole of the winter ... if the temperature were not lower than 36 below zero the riding and breaking [went] on."[16]

Upon completing the epic 1,255-mile trek to Fort Edmonton with Inspector Jarvis in late 1875, Steele received a personal commendation from his CO and was promoted to chief constable at Swan River, where he was stationed when Colonel Macleod was made commissioner. When it was announced that headquarters would move to Fort Macleod, Steele joined his new boss on his treaty trail in the summer of 1876 and before year's end made the acquaintance of a man whose reputation preceded him, Jerry Potts. Steele would ultimately describe Potts as "one of the most important aids to [the NWMP] in our management of the Indians and the carrying out of our duties, both military and civil ... He was indispensable as a teacher of mysteries of the plains and the ways of the [Indians] ... The officers and men treated him with the greatest consideration and received in return the most loyal assistance and support."[17]

Steele was part of Colonel Macleod's patrol that went from the Blackfoot treaty signing to Fort Walsh and the aborted meetings of Sitting Bull and General Terry in late 1877. After wintering at Fort Macleod, Steele moved to Fort Walsh when it became headquarters the following May. At about the same time, new regimental numbers were issued; as the ranking NCO, Sam Steele was awarded New Series #1. Only months later he became the 40th commissioned officer in the Force's history.

In 1882 Steele was assigned a 25-man detachment to police all matters related to construction of the CPR's rails across the prairies. In 1883 he led a patrol of 27 men to Maple Creek, where 130 strikers were causing trouble. Steele got matters under control and "resumed his magisterial duties along the railway from Moose Jaw to the end of the line, several times trying cases while seated in a Red River cart with a plank laid in front of him, an impromptu desk for taking down evidence."[18]

In ensuing years his job took him through the Rockies into B.C., where he was stationed in 1885 at the time of the Northwest Rebellion. Summoned to Alberta, he assumed a militia appointment as major in the Alberta Field Force and organized Steele's Scouts (which included three of his brothers) to hunt down Big Bear, who was responsible for at least nine killings.

The following year Steele was promoted to superintendent, commanding "D" Division at Fort Macleod, but trouble in southeastern B.C. had him leading a troop to the site of present-day Fort Steele, where he managed to quell the unrest between settlers and the local Kootenay tribe. By mid-1888 Steele was back in Fort Macleod.

Later in his career he played a large role in bringing order to the chaos of the Klondike gold rush, establishing Customs posts in both the White Pass and Chilkoot Pass to restrict entry of those not fitted out to survive. He initiated vessel inspections on the Yukon River and sanitation rules in Dawson. Steele's energy was endless, and his next challenge took him to Africa as the military leader of Lord Strathcona's Horse. After serving in the Boer War, Steele took charge of the South African Constabulary and was in that position, with the blessing of his superiors in Ottawa, when he retired from the Force in 1903.

Both in Canada and in Great Britain he continued his military career through the First World War and published *Forty Years in Canada* in 1914. He died in England in 1919 and is buried in Winnipeg.

1883, the first locomotive, hauling cargo and new work gangs, pulled in to Medicine Hat.

Ten years after the Mounties arrived, both the Blackfoot and Métis peoples still had trouble adjusting to the disappearance of the buffalo and the ever-growing presence of White ranchers. An even worse problem was the tightening budget of Canada's Indian Department. Severe cutbacks in rations and staffing would cause a frustrated Cecil Denny to resign before the end of 1884.

Denny, who had witnessed it all from the beginning as a confidant of his fellow Mounties and Indians alike, could sense the growing tension. The month of May had seen the murder of a settler named Pollock, shot by thieves in the night as he investigated a disturbance in his horse corral. The resulting investigation exemplified one of the great frustrations of policing the Plains. While five Mounties and their guide, Louis Léveillé, tracked the culprits southeast for over 100 miles, once they reached the American border they were forced to abandon their chase. It was then left to Jerry Potts, with his contacts and wily ways, to make inquiries. "The artful guide gleaned conclusive evidence that Pollock's slayer, a Peigan named Big Mouth, was on the reservation in Montana."[11] If the murderer came north again, he was a marked man.

Despite the desertion of 11 men in March (an event that inspired the government to increase imprisonment for deserters from six months to a year), the summer of 1884 saw the NWMP at Fort Macleod resolutely celebrate the 10th anniversary of its presence on the Canadian prairie. It was also the first year in a new Fort Macleod; the relentless flow of the Oldman River had finally eroded enough of the original fort site that the town centre had been moved to higher ground a half mile away. To the pleasure of RCMP surgeon George Kennedy, a new hospital replaced the crumbling shelter where his predecessor, Dr. Barrie Nevitt, had delivered James and Mary Macleod's first child. With the new town came a new hotel and the resurrection of its owner, former whiskey smuggler Kamoose Taylor. It was a new watering hole where Jerry Potts could enjoy 50-cent drinks in the daytime or pay one dollar for the same hooch any night of the week. According to Taylor's house rules, "assaults on cooks [were] strictly forbidden; everything cash in advance; proprietor not responsible for anything; and all guests must rise by 6 a.m. as the bed sheets are needed for tablecloths."[12] New arrivals first encountered a bank of wash basins and a single roller towel. "When a guest complained about the condition of the towel, Kamoose was reported to have told him that 20 other fellows had used it, and he was the first to complain."[13]

The police desertions and other dissensions in the new NWMP headquarters at Regina said more about the future than did the frivolities at Taylor's Macleod Hotel. Seeds of discontent promised a new crop of problems, spore of the same prickly issues that originally had brought Canadian troops west in 1870. Then, the Red River district of Manitoba had been the centre of the Métis community and Louis Riel had made his first attempt to gain status for his people. Riel remained in exile in the U.S. 14 years later when Métis unrest resurfaced further west.

Ottawa, as had become a tradition regarding NWMP commissioners, ignored Irvine's recommendations to respect Métis pleas for fair treatment in their land claims and to address the concerns of their leaders. Along the South Saskatchewan, the resilient Métis, who had gradually been forced west from the Red River and then given nothing by the government to offset the disappearance of the treasured buffalo, had established farms in the dimensions defined by their French ancestors. As had been the case in Quebec along the shores of the St. Lawrence River, each farmer claimed only narrow river frontage but cultivated a long strip of land behind it. In Ottawa, the government was far more interested in the land interests and ambitions of railway builders than the petitions of troublesome Métis. Not only did it refuse to recognize the land rights of the South Saskatchewan farmers, but it also greatly underestimated where the resentment could lead.

The NWMP's latest relocation at Regina, on the Assiniboine River, meant that headquarters was now east of the hotbed of unrest at Batoche, where Métis leader Gabriel Dumont was growing more agitated with each passing day. Dumont was more warrior than ambassador, so in June he led a delegation south into Montana in an effort to recruit Riel. The schoolteacher resided in the community of St. Peter's, and in spite of his long absence from Canada, he was still

Louis Riel (left), in spite of his rhetoric, sought a peaceful solution to provide the Métis with a land settlement and government support and training to become farmers. After the rebellion started it was Gabriel Dumont (right) who became the field general.

the spiritual leader of the Métis people. The meeting was a success and on Canada's 17th birthday, July 1, 1884, Louis Riel embraced his Métis brethren at Batoche and agreed to represent them in their battle with Ottawa. Aside from fighting for land rights, Riel's strategy was to lobby on behalf of all Native peoples of the prairie to establish their own province and, in the process, establish an alliance with the various tribal chiefs around him. In their final form, Riel's demands to Ottawa also sought government aid to advance his people's farming skills. Prime Minister Macdonald stated only that he would investigate. Riel responded to the Ottawa slight by declaring himself president of a provisional government with Gabriel Dumont as his field general. Rebellion was in the air.

As they had been during their entire existence, the Mounties of Fort Macleod and other remote detachments were outnumbered at every turn. Riel and Dumont did have success among the Cree leaders, drawing the feisty chiefs Big Bear and Poundmaker to their winter camp in early 1885. Riel's fiery message of rebellion reached new levels at a council with the Cree chiefs on March 15. Using prior knowledge of a pending partial eclipse to impress his audience, Riel pointed to the darkening sun as an omen of his powers and the victories he would lead them to.

In a futile attempt to strengthen its presence in the region, the NWMP had rented Fort Carlton, only 20 miles from Batoche, as a regional detachment. The Force's most experienced officer, Superintendent Lief Crozier, was in charge. With trouble brewing in the vicinity and with the approach of spring, Crozier dispatched Sergeant Stewart and 17 men to secure ammunition and provisions that were stored with a local trader, Hilliard Mitchell, at the nearby outpost of Duck Lake. On March 25, 1885, Gabriel Dumont's force confronted Stewart's party along the trail, impeding the Mounties' route and using superior force to send them back to where they had come from with a message that demanded the surrender of Fort Carlton. At this point Lief Crozier made the biggest tactical error of his bold and courageous life when he led a force of almost 100 enlisted men and volunteers in the direction of the trading post at Duck Lake.

The next day Crozier's column confronted the Métis, and all hell broke loose while Crozier faced Gabriel Dumont's brother, Isidore, under a flag of truce. Crozier sensed that he was about to be ambushed and the police opened fire, killing Isidore Dumont and his scout in their saddles. Five Métis would die in the battle. On the Mounties' side, 9 Prince Albert Volunteers and 3 police were killed and another 11 men badly injured before Crozier retreated back to Fort Carlton. In his later account of the battle, Cecil Denny, the ex-Indian agent and active rancher, added one interesting footnote to this story: "I learned from Peter Hourie [a respected Métis guide and Denny confidant] that Gabriel Dumont, commander of the half-breeds, had given an order that Major Crozier was not to be fired upon while continually in plain view in front of the line. This order the half-breed leader explained as having been prompted by the admiration which the cool courage displayed by the officer had excited in him."[14]

Crozier was briefly joined by Colonel Irvine, who had arrived from the south with 80 men to reinforce Carlton, but upon receiving Crozier's report and assessing his losses, Irvine ordered a withdrawal to protect the citizenry of Prince Albert. Though forced to lead this evacuation northeast, Irvine and Crozier left nothing behind that would benefit the enemy. Whether by accident or intent, historic Fort Carlton, home of the Hudson's Bay Company, was burned to the ground.

A force of 225 Mounties and 300 male volunteers at Prince Albert awaited help from distant Ottawa. John A. Macdonald, apparently far more responsive to bloodshed than he had been to the peaceful petitions of Riel, took immediate action, sending three columns with a combined force of 5,000 armed men, 3,000 from the eastern provinces and 2,000 from British Columbia and the Rocky Mountain foothills. As historian Frank Rasky put it, "The Department of the Interior increased the Indians' rations and handed out money scrip for the Métis land claims. Then Macdonald mobilized the Dominion's first truly national army and fought a civil war that cost $5 million, killed 105 (70 whites and 35 rebels), wounded 141 and left racial scars that have not completely healed to this day."[15]

Both of the Cree chiefs who had aligned themselves with the Métis made their presence felt, fully ignorant of the likely response from Canada. Poundmaker, the adopted son of Crowfoot, had never adapted to reservation life and his forces soon laid siege to Battleford, where 500 White civilians crowded together while their town was ransacked over a three-week period. Farther north, Big Bear's band of malcontents proved more bloodthirsty when it massacred two priests and seven civilians at Frog Lake.

Dumont's poorly armed force of 350 soldiers, only two-thirds of which had rifles, briefly benefited from the questionable choice for leader of the Canadian force, Major-General Frederick Middleton. British-trained, like NWMP commissioner George French before him, Middleton alienated his officers, ignored any advice from the western Mounted Police, and managed an ill-conceived campaign. Unlike French, however, Middleton faced a determined resistance that helped magnify his ineptness. While Middleton's decisions cost lives and delayed the inevitable Métis surrender at Batoche, it was left to forces under one of his subordinates to relieve besieged Battleford. Farther west, General T.B. "Jingo" Strange, then retired to ranching, was re-commissioned to gather a force and pursue Big Bear. Unlike Middleton, as a rancher familiar with NWMP skills, Strange immediately sought out a man he greatly admired, Sam

Steele. The Mountie quickly brought together a patrol, aptly known as "Steele's Scouts," that headed for Fort Edmonton. It would be Sam Steele and his men who would induce the surrender of Big Bear.

The rebellion only lasted 48 days before potential all-out war on the Canadian prairie ended as quickly as it had begun. Despite the questionable competence of Middleton and the tactical skills of Gabriel Dumont, the government force prevailed. While the heroics of men like Steele and superior weaponry were key to success, another reason for the Canadian force's victory was that the Black-foot Nation stayed on the sidelines.

Big Bear was a thorn in the side of the NWMP from his earliest meetings with the Whites until his capture in 1886.

Louis Riel's attempt to bond with the various tribes of the prairies as allies against the eastern government was quelled more by détente than military action. In Alberta, the two men who were foremost in keeping peace were Cecil Denny and Jerry Potts.

From the summer of 1884 through the darkness of winter, restless sympathizers on the Blackfoot reserves around Fort Macleod were spreading tales of great Métis victories. A mood of unrest grew among many young braves who declared themselves ready to join the fight. Chief after chief, however, sought the counsel of the respected redcoats and, in particular, the senior officers who had first come west. Possibly upon the advice of Magistrate James Macleod, Fort Macleod's Superintendent Cotton asked Cecil Denny to resume his old job as Indian agent to the Treaty Seven tribes. Denny, who had quit in frustration at ration cutbacks, still held the trust of Crowfoot and other Blackfoot leaders, and he and Jerry

Potts were all that stood between the Blackfoot Confederacy and the war zone.

In camp after camp, Potts and Denny smoked the pipe and Potts reminded the chiefs that the hated Cree were Métis allies; to join Riel and Dumont was to join their traditional enemy. As was the case during the treaty talks and in all times of tension over the past decade, Potts' words, whatever he said, were crucial to maintaining peace. There would be no uprising along the Bow, Belly, or Oldman rivers or in the foothills of the Rockies.

Tensions continued through the summer, but with the capture of Big Bear and Louis Riel, members of Middleton's militia were rewarded with land grants of 160 acres. In contrast, the Mounties who had endured and overcome so much were in no way recompensed. Potts had done what had become expected of him and asked nothing in return. Cecil Denny was thanked along with others by John A. Macdonald in parliament and promised a promotion to inspector of Treaty Seven lands the following spring. The promise proved empty as Sir John assessed the future of his constituency.

With the uprising quelled, Dumont managed to escape to Montana; Riel was captured and imprisoned. Found guilty of treason by a Regina jury that recommended mercy, the impassioned Métis leader was sentenced to hang on November 16, 1885. By this time he was a citizen of the United States, but two appeals gained no leniency from Prime Minister Macdonald. Louis Riel stood on the gallows on the prescribed date. As a Catholic priest standing beside him uttered a final prayer, the trap door fell open and the hangman's noose snapped his neck.

The besieged Macdonald now wished to be delivered from the evil fallout that he blamed on Commissioner Irvine, who became his latest scapegoat. In March 1886 Irvine resigned, settling for a reassignment as Indian agent on the Blood reserve of Red Crow.

After he returned to the Fort Macleod area from Fort Walsh, Jerry Potts adapted his attire to the new surroundings. Here he is likely present at Fort Macleod to act as interpreter for the blanket-clad Blackfoot family, commanding officer of the day, Superintendent John Cotton, and Inspector Aylesworth Bowen Perry. Perry, who would become the Force's fifth permanent commissioner in 1900, distinguished himself throughout a career that spanned 41 years.

Early in 1886 the NWMP doubled in size to 1,000. The arrival of the railroad and telegraph changed the prairie forever. The Canadian Pacific Railway was the longest single railway in the world and linked Canada from coast to coast. The next year 104,000 cattle, 11,000 horses, and 24,000 sheep were grazing in Alberta, south of the Bow River. That winter one-quarter of the cattle herd succumbed to the harsh weather. Along with snow and cold, usury came to Fort Macleod in the form of a private bank that funded naive settlers at a rate of 3 percent per month and soon foreclosed on most of its portfolio.

At mid-year, the last of the original NWMP inspectors left the Force. Forty-year-old Lief Crozier, a brave and respected senior officer, realized that he could never come to grips with being passed over for promotion when Commissioner Irvine retired. Crozier had openly stated that his greatest aim in life was to command the Force. Denied that, he drifted south to Oklahoma and then back to

Ontario where he was buried at Belleville in 1901, "to a great extent a forgotten man."[16]

As might be expected, Jerry Potts had outlasted them all.

That year, however, ended in tragedy for Jerry and his family when his son Willie, one of the first students in the original Fort Macleod school, died two days before Christmas. The following year brought more grief as both of Jerry's heartbroken wives succumbed to illness. For Jerry, always a family man, some solace came from one of his long-time admirers.

In 1887 the recently promoted Sam Steele opened new headquarters in Lethbridge, then a thriving town of 2,000 residents who had been attracted to the rail line and substantial coal deposits that fuelled the flow of locomotives. No doubt aware of his friend's recent loss, Steele made a point to hire Potts' second son, Henry, engaging him as an interpreter ready to follow in the footsteps of his father.

Chapter 25

The Circle of Life

Throughout his life, Jerry Potts remained a believer in the strong medicine provided by the cat-skin amulet that he wore at all times. However, once he had resettled near the Belly River in 1889, either a convincing priest or his new bride encouraged Potts to broaden his concept of spiritual power to include the Roman Catholic religion. Jerry's young wife, Long Time Laying Down or Isum-its-tsee, was the daughter of Blood chief One Spot (also referred to as Netah-kitei-pi-mew or Only Spot in treaty documents[1]), and their union led to Potts returning to the permanent home of his late mother's people on the Blood reserve. It was in a Blood lodge that he had first won the name Bear Child.

The winter of 1887 had been a time of some turmoil. Red Crow, the politically astute head chief of his people and respected elder of the Fish Eater clan, was having trouble controlling young warriors in different factions of the Blood nation. The reserve itself was not the land originally earmarked for the Bloods in the treaty of 1877 but the land that Red Crow had asked for in its place, close to the Belly Buttes in what would become southeast Alberta. Red Crow had survived criticism from some of the other chiefs when they realized that he had accepted less land in the treaty revision of 1883 than they were entitled to. Always confident in his relationship with the redcoats, Red Crow's trust extended to all White officialdom at that time and he had endorsed the engineer's survey of reserve boundaries without question, even though the square mileage was less than treaty terms had called for. Jerry Potts had been the interpreter at the time and made it very clear, in a later review, that Red Crow was fully aware of the contentious southern border of the reserve. Neither Red Crow nor Potts thought in terms of square miles; their terms of reference were rivers, mountains, and hunting grounds.

When he moved to the reserve, Bear Child's new father-in-law, One Spot, was considered the heir apparent to Red Crow as head chief. At both the signing of the original agreement and again when the new reserve lines were drawn, One Spot had made his mark on the treaty documents as a band chief of the Fish Eaters. Like Red Crow, One Spot was viewed by the Mounties as willing to adapt to a new way of life, anxious to put horse thievery and cross-border raids in the past, and a loyal supporter during the Northwest Rebellion.

While the Fort Macleod NWMP detachment had no need to fear the Bloods going north to join Riel, unrest to the south was another matter. Small bands of Gros Ventres on the American side and Bloods and Peigans in Canada perpetuated intertribal warfare into the late 1880s. In mid-1886 exasperated Gros Ventre leaders, armed with letters from U.S. military officials, entered the Blood reserve under a flag of truce. Red Crow and One Spot accepted their peace offerings, located a number of stolen horses on their reserve, and sought the assistance of Jerry Potts, then on the nearby Peigan reserve, to do the same there. The Mountie scout delivered five American horses to Red Crow's corral. The next morning, to the Blood chief's embarrassment, all of the recovered horses were gone. The dissension made it impossible to pursue treaty talks. Red Crow gave the Gros Ventres ten of his own horses and sent them home.

A more serious concern for the Blood political chiefs came in August, after a small war party consisting of two zealous young warriors and four impressionable teenagers left the reserve for Montana. Within days rumours circulated that they had been killed by American cowboys or unknown Indians.

Red Crow's search for truth was first complicated by an early fall blizzard that deterred a search party. Then came word from local Indian agent William Pocklington that Red Crow and One Spot, along with Crowfoot and two other Blackfoot chiefs, had been invited east to meet Sir John A. Macdonald as a reward for

THE FISH EATERS

At the time that the Blood people first went to the Missouri River forts to trade with the American Fur Company in the 1830s, the head chiefs represented four separate subgroups. Numerically the Buffalo Followers were the dominant clan, but a series of strong leaders would move the Fish Eaters into a prominent political role by the time Treaty Seven was signed with the Canadian government four decades later.

Red Crow was still a young boy when his tribe made its first spring trip to Fort McKenzie to trade. Leading the expedition was his grandfather, Two Suns, the elderly leader of the Fish Eaters who would soon relinquish his head chief position to his son, Seen From Afar. This chief, in turn, would use his trading skills to make his followers the richest of all Blood tribes. The prestige gained in the 1840s by the Fish Eaters came not only from its warriors but more importantly from a marriage blessed by Two Suns when Alexander Culbertson, the head trader at Fort McKenzie, sought a union with his teenage daughter Natawista. At first the Blood elder hesitated, but the following spring, amid pomp and ceremony, the dowry-laden bride cemented the relationship between the two cultures.

After 1847, when Culbertson moved his trading base farther upstream, Natawista became the first lady of Fort Benton and then other forts after her husband's stature grew within the AFC. Earning great respect from her own people as well as White officials, she sat at the treaty table in 1855 when the Bloods first made peace with the Americans.

During the recurring waves of smallpox, in 1869, the Fish Eaters' leader, Seen From Afar, succumbed within a day of contracting the disease. Amid the dual scourges of disease and firewater, the Fish Eaters elected Red Crow's father, Black Bear, as their leader. The following spring he, too, was dead from smallpox and the tribe looked to 40-year-old Red Crow. A respected "veteran of the warpath," he was "shrewd, tough, proud, and rich ... merciless in dealing with an enemy, yet a good family man, an excellent hunter, and a capable provider ... He was, in every sense, a warrior."[19]

He was also a politician who emerged from the treaty process as the acclaimed voice of the Blood people in all talks with the Whites. When treaties were signed, Red Crow made sure that more Fish Eater chiefs had marked the document than any other clan. His friendship with Colonel Macleod and loyalty to the NWMP stood him in good stead with the Mountie hierarchy throughout his leadership.

It was in the Fish Eater clan that three strong personalities, each a distinct influence on the recent history of the Blood people, spent their final years. Each of the three—Red Crow, Natawista, Bear Child—had become a legend in their own way.

their loyalty during the rebellion. All that Red Crow could do before starting his trip east in October was gain promises from the missing boys' relatives to await his return before seeking revenge.

By the time he got home, Red Crow found that the Gros Ventres were being blamed for the deaths of the missing Blood party, which had been traced to the border country near the Sweetgrass Hills. It was January 1887 before remains of the six scalped bodies were located near Dead Horse Coulee just north of the border. Within days, up to 400 Blood warriors vowed they would wage war on the Gros Ventres as soon as spring arrived. By March four war parties had gone south, and in April another Blood returned from a skirmish wounded. NWMP patrols, some led by Potts, policed the boundary country but were spread too thin to stop the horse theft. In May, when they did intercept a Blood raiding party returning north with a dozen Gros Ventre horses, gunfire broke out.

On May 22 a retaliatory raid from the south scored a major coup when the Gros Ventres infiltrated the Fish Eaters camp and made off with 40 horses from Red Crow's personal herd. Wisely, Red Crow sought out Indian agent Pocklington to propose a treaty process as the only way to avoid an Indian war. Through government channels, meetings of tribal heads of the Bloods and Gros Ventres were set to be held in Montana. On June 3 a Canadian delegation of three Mounties, agent Pocklington, and four Blood chiefs, including Red Crow and One Spot, rode with Jerry Potts out of Standoff for the American border.

When they reached the site where the misguided Blood youths had died the previous fall, Potts and the others spread out over the battleground, searching for clues of exactly what had happened. Numerous empty shell casings indicated a fierce encounter. One skull was retrieved. The Canadians were met at the border by a U.S. Cavalry escort that led the trek southeast to Fort Assiniboine on the south bank of the Milk River. There his hosts made sure that the sight of 35 of his recovered horses put Red Crow in an amiable frame of mind before they continued 30 miles downriver to Fort Belknap, where the treaty talks were held.

Speeches were made, papers signed, and mutual forgiveness was celebrated in a late-night feast on June 9. Red Crow and the others

STANDOFF, ALBERTA

Standoff, approximately 30 kilometres or 20 miles south of Fort Macleod, has been the administrative centre of the Blood Indian reserve since the 1880s. The reserve is the largest in Canada and is bound on three sides by rivers. It lies between the Belly and St. Mary rivers to the point where both of these tributaries flow northeast into the Oldman River. The southern limit of the reserve runs parallel to and about 15 miles north of the international border. Standoff got its name after whiskey trader Joe Kipp and his allies were confronted by U.S. marshal Hand near the Medicine Line in 1870. When the Montana-based marshal announced that he was placing them under arrest, they claimed to be north of the Line, standing on ground where he had no jurisdiction. In a frontier land without law, they threatened to kill him if he didn't back down. Marshal Hand did the prudent thing; Kipp and his crew celebrated by giving the name Fort Standoff to the new whiskey fort they built nearby.

returned to Canada and peace reigned—until the following spring of 1888. Red Crow demonstrated no tolerance for a Blood raiding party that broke the treaty, going so far as to allow the arrest of his own son. "The firm stand taken by the chief cooled the spirits of the young warriors for the rest of the year."[2]

By that time the recently wed Jerry Potts was living on the Blood reserve, establishing a new ranch and spending some time training scouts for the NWMP Macleod detachment. It was there that he heard, in December 1888, that a man 11 years his junior, an able horseman who had earned his respect, had risen through the ranks to be named the new CO at Fort Macleod. When he arrived there from the Kootenay district of British Columbia, 38-year-old Superintendent Sam Steele was returning to his favourite of the many detachments he had called home over the 15 years since he had marched out of Ontario to police the West. The original Mountie fort was, at that time, the only detachment outside of the Regina headquarters to command two separate divisions, led by Inspector Zack Wood and Superintendent A.R. Macdonnell. Both were "hard working, loyal officers, great favourites throughout the country," stated Steele, "and better comrades could not be desired."[3]

In 1889, Steele had received word from military officials to the south that a band of Bloods had moved far into their jurisdiction and run off about 100 horses belonging to the Crow Indians. Red Crow set out to both demonstrate his co-operation to Steele and make an example on the reserve; he took the first thieves of the season, on their return from Montana with stolen horses, to Fort Macleod for arrest. When the dust had settled on this adventure, it was learned that these three were half of six young men led by a young buck, Prairie Chicken Old Man, who had 40 horses in their possession when a war party of Gros Ventres intercepted them near the Bear Paw Mountains. They had to abandon most of their rustled horses and, during the escape, ran into a new enemy in the form of two rival Assiniboines before reaching the safety of the border. During this encounter one of the enemy was killed and scalped by the Bloods' leader. The three were released a month later, and a fourth confessor was severely scolded by a frustrated Sam Steele when nobody came forward to press charges.

Later that summer there was further fallout. During a Sun Dance ceremony, when all the young Bloods who had fought the Assiniboines were on the reserve, Calf Robe, one of the two culprits who had avoided a hearing in the spring, was singled out for arrest by Staff-Sergeant Chris Hilliard. He and two young Mounties went to the Blood reserve to make the arrest, but after locating the accused, the policemen were obstructed by an angry mob of 200 Sun Dance revellers. When the resistance was reported to Sam Steele, Jerry Potts was again called into action. Potts was handed the delicate task of informing Red Crow that not only did Steele and Inspector Zack Wood want Calf Robe, but they also wanted the chief to surrender all who had opposed Hilliard. Potts led a patrol south toward Standoff, met alone with Red Crow, and then left the old chief to ponder the dilemma. Wood planned to have his prisoners within the hour. Exactly how Potts delivered this dictate and what tact he used to help the Blood chief save face with his people will never be known. Historian J.P. Turner wrote, "With numbers strongly in their favour, the young bucks were eager for a fight, and as the stipulated time drew near, the prospect was a desperate one."[4] Just as Wood readied his men to confront the Blood encampment, Calf

Robe and four followers surrendered their weapons. As Potts and his party headed for Fort Macleod, Red Crow and a solemn band of Bloods rode at their heels, some still not convinced that justice would prevail. But after the detainees had been processed at the detachment, a tongue-lashing of the Blood leaders by Sam Steele was the extent of the punishment. Possibly based more on prudence than the declared technicalities, the courts released all five men Red Crow had delivered to the Mounties.

The final outcome of the whole episode was one positive statistic. The Assiniboine scalp at the centre of the melee was the last one ever taken by a Blood warrior. Like the buffalo, the ways of war had become a thing of the past.

Co-operation between American and Canadian authorities continued to improve as both sides sought to end the north-south raiding. Late in 1889 Jerry Potts, acting on Steele's directive, demonstrated the merits of White justice to the Blood people when he led Blood chief Eagle Tail, along with NWMP representatives, south to Chinook, Montana, to bear witness to horse theft. The guilty party, another Blood, was soon in Fort Benton's jail and Jerry was asked to act as interpreter at a hastily called evening trial. The next day the *Benton River Press* wrote, "Under the glare of the electric light, Jerry, with his wrinkled front of thought, seemed an ancient Aztec come to judgement, and the Blood looked something like the last of the Mohicans lamenting the doom of his horse-stealing race."[5] The rightful Bloods regained their horses and returned with Potts to Canada.

One character who returned to the scene in 1889 was Potts' nemesis, Star Child. It had been a decade since the death of Constable Graburn and for many, with the exception of old-timers like Jerry Potts, the significance of that murder had faded. Potts had gained some solace from helping put Star Child in the penitentiary for horse theft, but the "not guilty" verdict in Star Child's murder trial still rankled. Imagine the surprise, then, when word came from Lethbridge that the local commanding officer had not only retained him as a scout but was even singing his praises, calling him the best scout he had. At Stony Mountain Penitentiary, Star Child had "followed the pattern of other convicted horse thieves by learning

English and becoming a Mounted Police scout at the end of his prison term."[6]

Happy with his reversal of fortune, the Blood loner told anyone who would listen that he believed he had "a charmed life because he had never taken a woman."[7] His priorities were to change, however: he was soon facing dire consequences after making off with another man's wife. "His 'medicine' left him, and within a year he was fired by the Mounted Police and died of tuberculosis."[8] He was only 29, but few grieved his loss, including Jerry Potts.

Life looked brighter for Sam Steele. At year's end, after a career of steady movement, he had settled into Fort Macleod with some assurance of stability. Many of his officers and long-time retired Mountie friends, Macleod, Winder, Denny, Irvine, and, of course, Jerry Potts, raised a glass or two in Steele's honour before he headed east on leave. When he returned from Montreal, bride Marie Elizabeth Harwood would be with him.

As the final decade of the 19th century got underway, it became more and more clear that an incredible era was near its end. In Canada the death of Crowfoot on April, 25, 1890, was symbolic of the passing of a way of life. Although a lifelong leader of the Siksika, Crowfoot had been born the son of a Blood warrior. After his father's death, his mother remarried and he moved to the Blackfoot lodge of a stepfather.

By this time, Red Crow, too, had relinquished his title as head chief to a younger man. As late as 1888 it was assumed that One Spot, father of Jerry Potts' wife, would be Red Crow's choice. Instead, impatient that One Spot had not grown into the position, Crow opted for "Day Chief, a forty-five year old man who had considerable influence with the young people."[9] At age 60, Red Crow was prepared to live out his final years as a farmer, setting an example to others.

Jerry Potts, like all other ranchers in southern Alberta, was working at restoring his stock. They had suffered huge cattle losses during the severe winter of 1889-90 when 25,000 animals froze to

Pictured here in December 1890, Potts (right) stands with Scout Hunbury, while ex-Mountie Cecil Denny, Staff-Sergeant Chris Hilliard, and Sergeamt George Cotter sitting (left to right) behind two influential Bloods, Black Eagle and Elk Facing the Wind.

death. Potts and his family lived near the Fish Eaters camp, an active part of that community. In the summer, Old Jerry helped Steele and Fort Macleod organizers plan events where Whites, Peigans, and Bloods assembled for a day of bronco riding, steer roping, and running events. "Horse races were arranged for the Indians, both men and boys. [They] were real sports and rode to win; Jerry Potts was always the starter, and decided many disputes. He was a leader amongst them and remained so until the day of his death."[10]

If Pòtts made the best of his autumn years, it was not without some yearning for the prairie of his youth. In the early spring of 1890 he had just returned from Fort Benton, where the White justice system had proven a peaceful alternative to the old ways. Superintendent Sam Steele, who had encouraged Potts to make the trip, was on leave to be married in the east, so a visit with him would have to wait. Along the main street, Jerry did encounter Indian agent Irvine in Fort Macleod, and the two "engaged in idle conversation ... Potts told Irvine about his latest trip to Benton and his first encounter with electric lights."[11] While the appealing landscape on the edge of the Rockies foothills may have been "God's Country" to Irvine, he found that his old scout was in a restless mood. Potts asked the well-travelled Mountie if he knew "any other country where buffalo roamed ... and Indians lived a life of uncurbed freedom." When Irvine wondered aloud why he would ask such a question, Potts answered, "This country is getting too damned soft for me."[12]

It is likely that at least one social gathering in the summer of 1890 or 1891 included five people whose personal accounts, taken together, would cover most significant historic events of the Upper Missouri basin and the Canadian West as they had evolved over the previous half century.

On the White side, both James Macleod and Sam Steele had first reached Manitoba in 1870 and returned west four years later to bring law and order to the prairies. The other three lived on the Blood reserve, and their lives were marked by contrast. First there was Red Crow, the great warrior and able chief. He had largely avoided violence and whiskey after the redcoats had found his land, yet revelled in war, the buffalo hunt, and firewater in his earlier years. Secondly, Bear Child, or Jerry Potts, was born of two bloods into the Upper Missouri fur trade, a survivor from his birth. After the arrival of the redcoats, he spent his adult life helping others survive. And equally at home on the Blood reserve, in this trinity of elders, was the widely respected aunt of Red Crow, Natawista (Holy Snake), former wife of Alexander Culbertson. When still in her 20s, she had been the respected spokeswoman for Native interests at treaty tables during the era of the fur trade. While the demise of her well-intentioned husband had been tragic, her personal resilience

While bureaucrats would later do their utmost to eliminate the Sun Dance on the Peigan and Blood reserves near Fort Macleod, the Mounties were far more relaxed about Native ritual and ceremony. Here, in 1886, a number of NWMP members join Jerry Potts (centre row, light suit) and his Peigan brethren at the summer solstice celebration.

and lifelong dignity symbolized what the Blood Nation would always be—the chosen ones.

Now 65 and living with Red Crow's son Chief Moon, Natawista had long impressed those who met her. In 1843, naturalist John James Audubon, who had met her at Fort Union, called her "an Indian princess ... possessed of strength and grace in a marked degree." Dr. Barrie Nevitt "expressed amazement at seeing an Indian woman wearing a 'Dolly Varden style' dress and balmoral petticoat over beaded leggings and moccasins."[13]

Jerry Potts was over 50 when he came to the Blood reserve, and one of the great joys of his return to the home of his mother's people was the gift of birth. When Isum-its-tsee presented him with a baby son, he proudly named the child Blue Gun and bequeathed to him the blue steel rifle he had taken from a Crow rival long ago after being ambushed near the Sun River.

Like Red Crow, Bear Child had proved invincible in play and on the field of battle. Neither man had ever been so much as wounded by an enemy bullet—until the day Jerry was shot from behind. It was a story Potts would tell and retell among his drinking mates until they rued it ever happening. In 1891, while out duck hunting with a young constable, Tom Clarke, Potts was knocked to the ground by an errant shotgun blast. An anxious Clarke found Potts sitting in the reeds muttering, "I thought somebody hit me in the head and knocked my damn block off."[14] Potts seemed unconcerned when it was discovered that a single lead pellet remained embedded just behind his ear. Calling it a new good-luck charm, he insisted on leaving it there.

It was 1896 before the recurrent story, told largely at Tom Clarke's expense, led to an act of spontaneous surgery. As the whiskey flowed and Old Jerry finished his buckshot story, a Mountie friend asked him to lean forward and show off the charm. When a foggy-headed Potts obliged, the quick flip of a sharp penknife removed the pellet for good. "In the morning, when Potts unfogged his head and realized what had happened, he bemoaned the loss ... and voiced concern for the future."[15]

Within months he was on his deathbed.

A resident of the Blood reserve, Jerry Potts is seen here beside a ceremonial tipi, most likely on his own property.

Biographer Bruce Sealey describes his later days when his wife, Long Time Laying Down, cared for the ailing Potts. A local officer who visited his bedside reported: "He most keenly felt the need for his old friend, George Star ... When asked if he needed anything Jerry replied, 'Sure, a big bottle of whiskey and George Star. I haven't had my moustache trimmed in years."[16]

When Potts was finally transferred to the Fort Macleod hospital and word spread that he was nearing the end, many of his Métis and Mountie friends paid a final visit. They recalled the good times more than the bad, and each forgave Potts any indiscretion that might have been fuelled by inebriation. Potts still took pride in his days as an invincible warrior, all the time clutching the good medicine contained in the cat-skin amulet at his side. Jerry Potts returned home to spend a final few days with his family and died at the estimated age of 56.

He was buried at Fort Macleod the next day. Six red-coated Mounties carried him from the Roman Catholic church to their members' graveyard, near the banks of the Oldman River. Volleys of rifle fire rang and bugles sounded as he was laid to rest. Today a stone marks his grave with the words "Spl/Const. Intpr-Guide Jerry Potts 13th July 1896." A second marker for his son Willie, who had died 10 years earlier, is set beside his. The town's three-year-old newspaper, *Macleod Gazette*, wrote a stirring obituary on Jerry's life: "For years he stood between the police on one side, and his natural friends, the Indians, on the other, and his influence has always made for peace. Had he been other than he was ... it is not too much to say that the history of the North West would have been vastly different to what it is ... his influence could always be relied upon ... Of late years ... he was still and always the Jerry Potts who could ever be trusted to act squarely, and do the right thing."[17]

While his contribution is known to many historians, it seems strange that this man, who chose Canada as his homeland and served the country so well, remains largely without public recognition. In the United States he is relatively unknown. Only an informally christened mountain along the Great Divide and the name of a school in Calgary honour his life. Three of his descendants have served in red coats and many others, fittingly, live on both sides of the Medicine Line.

Of the 41 graves in the NWMP pioneer cemetery on the banks of the Oldman River in Fort Macleod, Alberta, there are 33 for Mounties, 5 for civilians, a lone unknown grave, and the 2 picured in the foreground for Jerry Potts (right) and his son, Willie.

Bear Child's Century

1803   President Thomas Jefferson purchases all lands between Mississippi and Rocky Mountains from Napoleon (the Louisiana Purchase) and embarks upon a plan to reach the Pacific.

1808   John Jacob Astor establishes the American Fur Company (AFC) and, three years later, builds Fort Astoria, a trading fort at the mouth of the Columbia River, establishing a brief U.S. presence on the Pacific.

1812   War between British and American armies, fought largely near the Upper and Lower Canada boundaries, yields a setback to American expansionism.

1813   Fort Astoria is taken over by the North West Company.

1821   The North West Company merges with its hated rival, the Hudson's Bay Company.

1827   The Astor empire east of the Mississippi buys management talent (Kenneth McKenzie and Pierre Chouteau Jr.) in two business acquisitions.

1830   McKenzie moves into new residence at Fort Union, making it the AFC headquarters for the Upper Missouri fur trade.

1832   Justice John Marshall's Supreme Court decision in the case of Worcester vs. Georgia seeks to protect Indians and uphold treaty obligations while the White House ignores continued encroachment. President Andrew Jackson tells Marshall it is his decision so he can enforce it.

1833   Prince Maximilian of Wied leads expedition to Fort McKenzie, the farthest inland American presence on the Upper Missouri.

1836   Andrew Potts takes employment with the American Fur Company at Fort McKenzie and is present there the following summer when the dreaded smallpox virus travels upriver aboard AFC cargo boats.

1839-40   Andrew Potts killed, leaving infant son Jeremiah and his mother, Crooked Back, to survive among the traders.

1844   Fort McKenzie burned to the ground, the site thereafter known as Brulé (Burnt) Bottoms. Replaced upriver by Alexander Culbertson, who eventually establishes a permanent base at Fort Benton.

1845-46   Despite the expansionist rhetoric of U.S. president James Polk ("54-40 or fight!") the U.S. and Great Britain agree that their common boundary west of Lake Superior will be at the 49th parallel.

1853   Future English prime minister Benjamin Disraeli dismisses the British holdings in North America as "a millstone around our necks."

1854   Andrew Dawson becomes head of Fort Benton and "adopts" Jerry Potts.

1855-56   First U.S. treaty with Blackfoot Confederacy is closely followed by gold discoveries in Montana.

1861-65   American Civil War leads to exodus west.

1864   Abraham Lincoln signs act officially making Montana a U.S. territory.

1866   American Fur Company sells Fort Benton, yielding its monopolistic hold on the territory and leaving the fur trade to an influx of independents.

1867   Canada becomes a nation, overseeing the North-West Territories west of Ontario.

1869   Fort Whoop-up built north of U.S. border by Montana-based traders led by John J. Healy. Smallpox and famine devastate Blackfoot peoples.

1870   Baker Massacre of South Piegan village occurs along Montana's Marias River while north of the border, Manitoba becomes Canada's fifth province. The federal government-sponsored Red River Expedition establishes civil order for settlers and the Métis gradually move farther west.

1873 Cypress Hills Massacre occurs and Prime Minister Sir John A. Macdonald announces the formation of the North West Mounted Police (NWMP). Canadian and U.S. governments send the Boundary Commission to mark their common 49th parallel border across the West.

1874 In September the first Mounties, under Commissioner George French, arrive in Fort Benton. In the next two years they establish Fort Macleod, Fort Walsh, and Fort Calgary.

1876 Custer's Seventh Cavalry defeated by Sioux at Battle of Little Bighorn and Sitting Bull leads his followers toward Canada. Colonel George French dismissed as commissioner of the NWMP, to be replaced by James Macleod.

1877 Treaty Seven signed between the Canadian government and chiefs representing the nations of the Blackfoot Confederacy. To the south, John Healy is named county sheriff in Montana.

1878 John A. Macdonald re-elected as prime minister in October. Dr. Richard Barrington Nevitt leaves Fort Macleod for Toronto, where he helps establish Toronto Women's Hospital and is instrumental in the founding of Women's Medical College and Toronto Hospital for Sick Children.

1880 Nelson Miles made brigadier general and placed in charge of U.S. Army's Department of the Columbia, later transferred to Department of the Missouri.

1881 Sitting Bull returns to the U.S.

1883 Crowfoot and 700 warriors confront Canadian Pacific railroaders laying track up to their reserve. Peaceful land swap occurs and Crowfoot gets lifetime pass on CPR.

1884 Harry "Kamoose" Taylor builds Macleod Hotel, fittingly located on Fort Macleod's main street between residences owned by two reputed imbibers, local magistrate Col. James Macleod and Jerry Potts. The first railroad is built across Montana. Louis Riel returns to Canada after exile in the U.S.

1885 Northwest Rebellion pits Métis and Cree leaders against Canadian troops after 12 men led by Major Lief Crozier were killed at Duck Lake. Louis Riel hanged.

1887	Rejecting the Natives' tradition of communal land ownership, U.S. Congress imposes the Dawes Severalty Act and a system of private land ownership on all Native American tribes. Individual allotments are restricted to 160 acres and any reservation territory in excess of allotments can be sold.
1889	Montana becomes the 41st U.S. state. Washington and the Dakotas also join the Union.
1890	Crowfoot dies. Sitting Bull killed by tribal police on Sioux reserve. The holocaust of Wounded Knee sees the slaughter of 180 Sioux, and General Miles condemns his commanding officer of the Seventh Cavalry for avenging Custer in an "outrageous blunder."
1892	Under the Dawes Act, 2 million acres of Crow reservation land are made available to White settlers in Montana.
1894	Supreme Court judge James Macleod dies at age 58. Reputedly never a seeker of wealth, he leaves behind "a wife, five children and eight dollars" (University of Calgary website).
1896	Jerry Potts dies of tuberculosis or throat cancer at Fort Macleod.
1897	A resurrected James Walsh is sent by the Canadian government to the Yukon goldfields as "administrator," with the powers of governor, NWMP superintendent, and supervisor of Customs and mail services. He lasts only a year but establishes order out of chaos. He is assisted by various NWMP originals including Sam Steele, William Jarvis, and Robert Belcher.
1899	Sam Steele returns from northern posting amid Yukon gold rush and accepts invitation to command a mounted regiment (Lord Strathcona's Horse) during South Africa's Boer War.
1904	Prefix "Royal" conferred on NWMP by King Edward VII.
1905	Alberta and Saskatchewan become Canadian provinces. James Walsh dies in Brockville, Ontario, at his retirement home, Indian Cliff (named after his favourite place in the Cypress Hills).
1906	Earthquake devastates San Francisco.

Notes

Chapter 1: The Lure of Fur

1. Fardy, 19.
2. Lavender, 38.
3. Chittenden, 385.
4. Fardy, 19.
5. Chittenden, 384.
6. In the rendezvous system designed by Rocky Mountain Fur Company founder William Ashley, the independent traders of the company would come out of the mountains to a predetermined point every spring to meet a pack train of new supplies sent from St. Louis. The rendezvous was an annual event from 1825 to 1840.
7. Blevins, 25.
8. Ewers et al., 25
9. Quoted in Wischmann, 42.
10. Excerpted from Catlin, *Campfire Stories with George Catlin: An Encounter of Two Cultures*, <http://catlinclassroom.si.edu/searchdocs/catlinletter2.html>.

Chapter 2: The Missouri

1. Information about Chouteau's *Assiniboine* is derived from Robertson, 59.
2. Ewers et al., 14, quoting Maximilian diary entry of June 18, 1833.
3. Terrell, *Furs by Astor*, 391.
4. Ibid., 417.
5. Chittenden, 340.
6. Terrell, *Land Grab*, 153.
7. Ibid.
8. Larpenteur, 84.
9. Robertson, 251.

Chapter 3: Four Years of Turmoil

1. Robertson, 169.
2. Dempsey, *Jerry Potts*, 4.
3. Fardy, 8.
4. Email correspondence to R. Touchie from L. Wischmann, author of *Frontier Diplomats*, Feb. 3, 2003.
5. Ibid.
6. Fardy, 8.
7. Chittenden, 684.
8. Ibid.
9. Robertson, 174.
10. Ibid.
11. Ibid.

12. Sealey, 8.
13. Cruise, 73.

Chapter 4: Last King of the Missouri

1. Dempsey, *Jerry Potts*, 4.
2. Ibid.
3. Unedited paper written by James Dawson and the basis for an article appearing in the *Montana Lookout*, Dec. 26, 1908.
4. Andrew Dawson file, Montana Historical Society.
5. *Montana Lookout*, Dec. 26, 1908.
6 *Montana Lookout*, Jan. 16, 1909.
7. Ibid.
8. Dempsey, *Jerry Potts*, 8.
9. Fardy, 13.
10. Ibid.
11. Ibid.
12. Ibid., 12.
13. Ibid., 15.
14. In spite of Morgan's abandonment of Dawson as they made their way west 20 years earlier, the two Scots remained friends.
15. From copy of entry in the County of Edinburgh Register of Deaths provided by the Montana Historical Society.

Chapter 5: The Warrior Years

1. Fardy, 22.
2. Dempsey, *Jerry Potts*, 5.
3. Ibid.
4. Fardy, 23-24.
5. Dempsey, *Jerry Potts*, 6, quoting W.S. Stocking, *Fort Benton Memories*, Montana Historical Society files.

Chapter 6: The Kainai: Bear Child's People

1. Middleton, 38.
2. Ibid., 39.
3. Donald.
4. Ibid.
5. Berry, 14.
6. Ibid., 13.
7. Ibid.

Chapter 7: The Whiskey Scourge

1. Dempsey, *Firewater*, 27-28, details this event.
2. Ibid., 21.
3. Athearn, 257.
4. Ibid., 242.
5. Dempsey, *Firewater*, 30.
6. Ibid., 30.
7. Ibid., 27-28.
8 Ibid., 33.
9. Ibid.

Chapter 8: Fort Whoop-up

1. Dempsey, *Firewater*, 49.
2. Baker's military career came to an abrupt end after he embarrassed the army in

an encounter with Sitting Bull in 1872. In a Sioux challenge to the building of the railway, a brief skirmish known as the Battle of Arrow Creek led to the army withdrawing back up the Yellowstone Valley away from further confrontation. Then Major Eugene Baker was in command, but the August 22, 1872, *Helena Daily Herald* portrayed him as "so drunk he could not direct the fight and was superseded by a subordinate," Utley, *The Lance and the Shield*, 355.

3. Dempsey, *Firewater*, 49.
4. Berry, 15. It is unknown if the Evans referred to by Gerald Berry in this reference is the same John Evans who would later gain infamy for his role in the Cypress Hills Massacre.
5. Ibid.
6. Chittenden, 386.
7. Wischmann, 82.
8. Email correspondence from L. Wischmann to R. Touchie, Feb. 3, 2003.
9. Ibid.
10. Quoted in Dempsey, *Firewater*, 228, footnote 52, chapter 3.
11. Email correspondence from L. Wischmann to R. Touchie, Feb. 3, 2003.
12. Middleton, 176.
13. Dempsey, *Firewater*, 66.
14. Ibid.

Chapter 9: The Last Great Battle

1. Fardy, 41.
2. Ibid.
3. Dempsey, *Jerry Potts*, 10.
4. Fardy, 43.

Chapter 10: The Tragedy of Crooked Back

1. Dempsey, *Firewater*, 224.
2. Ibid.
3. Middleton, 169.
4. Berry, 98.
5. Ibid.
6. Dempsey gives a descriptive account of the tragedy in *Firewater*, 141-143.
7. Dempsey, *Firewater*, 141, and footnote 22, chapter 10, 234.

Chapter 11: A Defining Year

1. Athearn, 229.
2. Ibid., 277.
3. Ibid., 278.
4. Dempsey, *Firewater*, 116.
5. Ibid., 116-121. Dempsey provides a detailed account of the events leading up to the murderous confrontation and specifics of the many atrocities committed. The deeds and words attributed to "Chief" John Evans by Dempsey and his sources certainly support the likelihood that Gerald Berry's "Evans" character, described in chapter 8 as avenging the death of a partner by spreading smallpox among the Blackfoot tribes, and the Cypress Hills "Evans" are the same man.
6. Ibid., 121.
7. Ibid.

Chapter 12: French's Folly

1. Denny, *The Law Marches West*, 20.
2. Cruise and Griffiths, 228.
3. Ibid., 241.

4. MacBeth, 51.
5. D'Artigue, 55-57.
6. Denny, *Denny's Trek*, 46.
7. Ibid., 48.
8. Ibid., 47.
9. Ibid.
10. Ibid., 49.
11. Ibid.
12. Ibid.
13. Cruise and Griffiths, 346, quoting from Colonel French's diary.
14. Ibid., 350.
15. Denny, *Denny's Trek*, 53.
16. Fardy, 58.
17. Cruise and Griffiths, 367.
18. Fardy, 59.
19. Denny, *Denny's Trek*, 58.

Chapter 13: Crossing Over

1. Berry, 31.
2. A colourful account of the Baker Massacre and the Joe Cobell story is included in Cruise and Griffiths' epic account of the early Mounties, *The Great Adventure*, 164-178.
3. Berry, 27. Gerald Berry writes in *Whoop-up Trail* that the 272 white males greatly outnumbered the 63 "coloreds, halfbreeds, quarterbreeds and Chinese" males who called Benton home. On the other hand, he claims that the 13 single white females were greatly outnumbered by "6 colored, 14 Indian, 62 halfbreed, and 3 quarterbreed females." While none of their occupations were noted, 40 identified themselves in one form or other as Canadians.
4. Dempsey, *Firewater*, 186.
5. Cruise and Griffiths, 388, quoting Sub-constable James Finlayson.
6. Denny, *Denny's Trek*, 56.
7. Ibid., 54.
8. Cruise and Griffiths give a more complete account on 385-397.
9. Denny, *Denny's Trek*, 60.
10. Ibid., 61.
11. Ibid.
12. Steele, 76. It is interesting to note that Steele had obviously discussed Potts' feats with Macleod and other Mounties over the years, because on the day this event occurred, he was still more than three weeks short of Fort Edmonton on the three-month, 900-mile journey with Inspector Jarvis.
13. Ibid.
14. Anderson, 46. Macleod, like other former army officers and militia members, was referred to by his former rank.
15. Steele, 76-77.
16. Ibid.
17. Cruise and Griffiths, 403.
18. J.P. Turner, vol. 2, 160.
19. Dempsey, *Firewater*, 187.
20. Ibid.
21. Berry, 79.
22. Steele, 76.
23. MacBeth, 57-58.
24. Denny, *Denny's Trek*, 63.
25. Dempsey, *Firewater*, 208.
26. MacBeth, 58.

Chapter 14: A Trusted Voice

1. Dempsey, *Firewater*, 177, quoting from a letter sent from T.C. Power to John Kerler, July 25, 1874.
2. Ibid., 191.
3. Fardy, 68.
4. Dempsey, *Firewater*, 18.
5. Dempsey, *Red Crow*, 85.
6. Ibid., 53. "When Natawista learned of the mission, she demanded that her husband include her: 'My people are a good people, but they are jealous and vindictive ... I am afraid that they and the whites will not understand each other; but if I go I may be able to explain things to them. I know there is danger, but my husband, where you go I will go, and where you die, I will die.'"
7. Fardy, 74.
8. Ibid.
9. Dempsey, *Firewater*, 145.
10. Fardy, 76.

Chapter 15: The Winter Of 1875

1. Fardy, 79. Booze, although unlawful, was not unknown.
2. Dempsey, *Firewater*, 194, quoting from a letter sent from Macleod to G.A. French, Feb. 2, 1875.
3. Fardy, 79.
4. Ibid.
5. Dempsey, *Firewater*, 197.
6. Ibid.
7. Ibid.
8. Fardy, 80.
9. After the Hudson's Bay Company territory was transferred to Canada in 1870, a force of 400 British regulars and 800 Ontario militiamen was sent to Manitoba to quell Louis Riel's provisional government. It arrived in August to find Fort Garry deserted, Riel having fled to the U.S., and Colonel Wolseley decided to return the British to Ontario, leaving a force of militiamen, including A.G. Irvine as battalion commander.
10. Denny, *Denny's Trek*, 83.
11. Ibid.
12. Ibid.
13. Ibid.
14. Ibid., 84.
15. Ibid.
16. Ibid., 85.
17. Ibid., 87.
18. Ibid., 87-88.

Chapter 16: Into the Cypress Hills

1. Dempsey, *Jerry Potts*, 18.
2. Denny, *Denny's Trek*, 89.
3. Sealey, 33.
4. Anderson, 66.
5. Fardy, 87.
6. C. Frank Turner, 32.
7. Ibid.

Chapter 17: A Change of Command

1. Utley, *Frontier Regulars*, 413.
2. Ibid.
3. Ibid., 410.
4. Denny, *Denny's Trek*, 94.
5. Dempsey, *Red Crow*, 100-101.
6. Steele, 112.
7. Denny, *Denny's Trek*, 108.
8. Letter from Richard Barrington Nevitt to Elizabeth "Lizzie" Beatty, Feb. 20-29, 1876. All letters January to August 1876 found in Folder M893/9, Glenbow Museum, Calgary.
9. Ibid. This account is described in detail in a letter sent from Helena, Montana Territory, dated March 31, 1876.
10. Ibid.
11. Ibid.
12. Ibid.
13. Ibid.
14. Ibid.
15. Ibid., April 12, 1876.
16. Ibid.
17. Ibid.
18. Ibid.
19. Steele, 115-116.
20. Ibid., 277.
21. Hulgaard and White, 68.

Chapter 18: A Study in Contrast

1. Quoted in MacBeth, 80.
2. Steele, 101.
3. Ibid., 106. Big Bear would lead the massacre of nine people at Frog Lake, only 28 miles from Pitt, and it would be Sam Steele, then recruited into the army militia, who would hunt Big Bear down and overcome his resistance at Loon Lake.
4. Denny, *Denny's Trek*, 104.
5. Ibid., 105.
6. Ibid., 106.
7. Anderson, 88.
8. Utley, *Frontier Regulars*, 289.
9. Ibid., 273.
10. Dempsey, *Red Crow*, 100.
11. Ibid., 103.
12. Ibid.
13. Ibid., 104.

Chapter 19: The Pursuit of Lasting Peace

1. Anderson, 112.
2. Sealey, 44.
3. Dempsey, *Red Crow*, 104.
4. Ibid.
5. Ibid., 103.
6. Hulgaard and White, 21-22.
7. Denny, *Denny's Trek*, 111.
8. Steele, 127.
9. Ibid., 128.
10. Ibid., 129.

11. Dempsey, *Red Crow*, 111.
12. Ibid.
13. Steele, 120.
14. Dempsey, *Red Crow*, 114.
15. Steele, 121.
16. Ibid., 122.
17. Denny, *Denny's Trek*, 113.
18. Ibid., 114.
19. Letter from R.B. Nevitt to Elizabeth "Lizzie" Beatty dated Sept. 28, 1877, Blackfoot Crossing. Folder M893/9, Glenbow Museum, Calgary.

Chapter 20: The Sitting Bull Quandary

1. C. Frank Turner, 120.
2. Ibid., 121.
3. Ibid., 121-122.
4. Letter from R.B. Nevitt, November 14, 1877. Folder M893/9, Glenbow Museum, Calgary.
5. C. Frank Turner, 123.
6. Ibid.
7. Ibid., 112.
8. Utley, *The Lance and the Shield*, 193.
9. Letter from R.B. Nevitt, October 18, Cypress Hills.
10. Steele, 128.
11. Denny, *Denny's Trek*, 118.
12. Steele, 129.
13. Ibid., 130.
14. Ibid.
15. The two eastern journalists were Jerome Stillson of the *New York Herald* and Charles Diehl of the *Chicago Times*. The former also sketched and announced to Dr. Nevitt that he was preparing a piece for *Harpers Weekly*. According to correspondence Nevitt wrote to his fiancée, Stillson asked for and received some of Nevitt's sketches of Sitting Bull, saying he preferred them to his own and that he would submit them to *Harpers Weekly*. Most references that identify a sketch of Sitting Bull that appeared in the December 8, 1877, issue of the periodical attribute it to Stillson, but it is not signed by him.
16. Utley, *The Lance and the Shield*, 197.

Chapter 21: The Transition Years—1878-79

1. Letter from R.B. Nevitt, Oct. 31, 1877. At this point in the Nevitt letters, which are archived in Alberta's Glenbow Museum, an asterisk appears in the transcript, indicating a portion of the letter was deleted out of respect for medical confidentiality.
2. Ibid.
3. Ibid., Dec. 8, 1877.
4. Steele, 130.
5. Ibid., 131.
6. Ibid.
7. Letter from R.B. Nevitt, Jan. 15-22, 1878.
8. Ibid., Feb. 7-10, 1878.
9. Ibid.
10. Ibid., March 21, 1878.
11. Manzione, 125.
12. C. Frank Turner, 150.
13. Ibid.

14. Ibid.
15. Anderson, 159.
16. Denny, *The Law Marches West*, 135.
17. Manzione, 129.
18. Ibid.

Chapter 22: A Very Bad Year: Starvation, Mayhem, and Murder

1. Dempsey, *Red Crow*, 123-124. As reported by Catholic priest Constantine Scollen in a letter to Assistant Commissioner A.G. Irvine, April 18, 1879.
2. C. Frank Turner, 167.
3. Manzione, 134.
4. C. Frank Turner, 28.
5. Ibid.
6. Brado, 37.
7. Steele, 143-144.
8. Utley, *The Lance and the Shield*, 204.
9. Ibid., 208.
10. Ibid., 210.
11. Ibid., 218.

Chapter 23: The Murder of Marmaduke Graburn

1. Fardy, 120.
2. Ibid.
3. Atkin, 146. It is interesting to note that while such timidity was expressed by this Canadian jury, outright lynching and gunfights were settling matters south of the border. Reportedly one outbreak of vigilante law led to 40 hangings of alleged Native rustlers, and in the same month that Star Child was set free, Marshal Wyatt Earp and his brothers were outgunning the Dalton gang in their famous showdown at the OK Corral.
4. Ibid., 193.
5. Ibid., 194.
6. Ibid.
7. Fardy, 122.
8. Steele, 264.
9. Atkin, 191-192.
10. Fardy, 124.
11. Dempsey, *Jerry Potts*, 20.
12. Fryer, 58-59.
13. Ibid.
14. Ibid.
15. J.P. Turner, vol. 2, 10.
16. Ibid.
17. Ibid.

Chapter 24: The Autumn Years

1. Hulgaard and White, 108.
2. Dempsey, *Jerry Potts*, 19, from an interview with Harry Mills, Dec. 26, 1953.
3. J.P. Turner, vol. 1, 516.
4. Atkin, 153.
5. Utley, *The Lance and the Shield*, 233.
6. Atkin, 194.
7. Ibid., 154.
8. J.P. Turner, vol. 1, 530-531.
9. Ibid.

10. Ibid.
11. Ibid.
12. Fardy, 47.
13. Berry, 70.
14. Denny, *Denny's Trek*, 169.
15. Rasky, 233.
16. J.P. Turner, vol. 2, 293.

Chapter 25: The Circle of Life

1. Middleton, 170 (copy of Treaty Seven reproduced).
2. Dempsey, *Red Crow*, 212
3. Steele, 256.
4. J.P. Turner, vol. 2, 10-11.
5. Fardy, 141.
6. Dempsey, *Men in Scarlet*, 61.
7. Ibid.
8. Ibid.
9. Dempsey, *Red Crow*, 222.
10. Steele, 271.
11. Fardy, 141.
12. Ibid.
13. Dempsey, article on Natawista, Dictionary of Canadian Biography Online, Library and Archives of Canada, <www.biographi.ca/EN/>
14. Fardy, 142.
15. Ibid.
16. Sealey, 58.
17. Ibid., 63.

Sidebar Endnotes

1. Crutchfield, 49.
2. Ewers et al., 14.
3. Ibid., 17.
4. Chittenden, 383.
5. Larpenteur, 65.
6. Chittenden, 383.
7. Ibid.
8. Fardy, 18.
9. Dempsey, *Firewater*, 34.
10. Ibid., 35.
11. Ibid.
12. Dempsey, *Firewater*, 30.
13. Ibid. p 69.
14. Utley, *Frontier Regulars*, 307.
15. Berry, 87.
16. Steele, 60-61.
17. Ibid., 115-116.
18. J.P. Turner, vol. 2, 7.
19. Dempsey, *Red Crow*, 79.

Bibliography

Anderson, Ian. *Sitting Bull's Boss: Above the Medicine Line with James Morrow Walsh.* Surrey, BC: Heritage House, 2000.

Aspects of the Fur Trade: Selected Papers of the 1965 North American Fur Trade Conference. St. Paul: Minnesota Historical Society, 1967.

Athearn, Robert G. *Forts of the Upper Missouri.* Englewood Cliffs, NJ: Prentice-Hall, 1967.

Atkin, Ronald. *Maintain the Right: The Early History of the North West Mounted Police, 1873-1900.* Bristol: Macmillan, 1973.

Berry, Gerald L. *Whoop-Up Trail: The Alberta–Montana Relationships.* Edmonton: Applied Art Products Ltd., 1953.

Blevins, Winfred. *Give Your Heart to the Hawks.* Los Angeles: Nash, 1973.

Brado, Edward. *Cattle Kingdom: Early Ranching in Alberta.* Surrey, BC: Heritage House, 2004

Brown, Dee. *Bury My Heart at Wounded Knee: An Indian History of the American West.* New York: Bantam Books, 1970.

Brown, Wayne F. *Steele's Scouts: Samuel Benfield Steele and the North-West Rebellion.* Surrey, BC: Heritage House, 2001.

Catlin, George. "Mouth of Yellow Stone, Upper Missouri, 1832." Letter No. 2 in *Letters and Notes on the Manners, Customs, and Conditions of North American Indians.* First published in London, 1844. Available on the website *Campfire Stories with George Catlin: An Encounter of Two Cultures.* http://americanart. si.edu/catlinclassroom/searchdocs/catlinletter2.html

Charters, Dean. *Mountie 1873-1973: A Golden Treasury of Those Early Years.* Don Mills, ON: Collier-Macmillan, 1973.

Chittenden, Hiram Martin. *The American Fur Trade of the Far West*, vols. 1 and 2. New York: Press of the Pioneers, 1935.

Cruise, David, and Alison Griffiths. *The Great Adventure: How the Mounties Conquered the West.* Toronto: Penguin, 1997.

Crutchfield, James A. *Mountain Men of the American West*. Boise, ID: Tamarack Books, 1997.

D'Artigue, Jean. *Six Years in the Canadian North-West*. Toronto: Rose and Co., 1882.

Dempsey, Hugh A. *Big Bear: The End of Freedom*. Toronto: Greystone Books, 1992.

———. "A Blackfoot Winter Count." Calgary: Glenbow Museum, 1965. <http://www.telusplanet.net/public/mtoll/winter.htm>.

———. *Charcoal's World*. Saskatoon: Western Producer Prairie Books, 1978.

———. *Crowfoot: Chief of the Blackfoot*. Edmonton: Hurtig Publishers, 1972.

———. *Firewater: The Impact of the Whisky Trade on the Blackfoot Nation*. Calgary: Fifth House, 2002.

———. *Indian Tribes of Alberta*. Calgary: Glenbow-Alberta Institute, 1979.

———. *Jerry Potts: Plainsman*. Occasional Paper No. 2. Calgary: Glenbow Museum, 1989.

———, ed. *Men in Scarlet*. Calgary: McClelland and Stewart, 1974.

———. *Red Crow: Warrior Chief*. Saskatoon: Fifth House, 1985.

———, ed. *William Parker: Mounted Policeman*. Edmonton: Hurtig Publishers, 1973.

Denig, Edwin Thompson, ed., with introduction by John C. Ewers. *Five Indian Tribes of the Upper Missouri: Sioux, Arickaras, Assiniboines, Crees, Crows*. Norman, OK: U of Oklahoma Press, 1980.

Denny, Sir Cecil E. *Denny's Trek: A Mountie's Memoir of the March West*. Surrey, BC: Heritage House, 2004.

———. *The Law Marches West*. Toronto: J.M. Dent & Sons, 1972.

Donald, Dwayne T. "Elder, Student, Teacher: A Kainai Curriculum Métissage." Master's Thesis. U of Calgary, 2003.

Ewers, John C., Marsha V. Gallagher, David C. Hunt, and Joseph C. Porter. *Views of a Vanishing Frontier*. Omaha, NE: U of Nebraska Press, 1984.

Fardy, B.D. *Jerry Potts: Paladin of the Plains*. Langley, BC: Mr. Paperback, 1984.

Fetherstonhaugh, R.C. *The Royal Canadian Mounted Police*. New York: Carrick & Evans, 1938.

Fort Macleod History Book Committee. *Fort Macleod—Our Colourful Past: A History of the Town of Fort Macleod from 1874 to 1924*. Fort Macleod, AB: 1977.

Fryer, Harold. "Jerry Potts: Orphan of the Fur Trade." In *Canadian Plainsmen*. Surrey, BC: Heritage House, 1982.

Gattinger, Marie M. "Hero in Buckskins." In *The History of the Canadian West*, vol. 2. Langley, BC: Mr. Paperback, 1982.

Haydon, A.L. *The Riders of the Plains: A Record of the Royal North-West Mounted Police of Canada, 1873-1910.* Edmonton: M.G. Hurtig Ltd., 1971.

Horrall, S.W. *The Pictorial History of the Royal Canadian Mounted Police.* Toronto: McGraw-Hill Ryerson, 1973.

Hulgaard, William J., and John W. White. *Honoured in Places: Remembered Mounties Across Canada.* Surrey, BC: Heritage House, 2002.

LaDow, Beth. *The Medicine Line: Life and Death on a North American Borderland.* New York: Routledge, 2001.

Larpenteur, Charles. *Forty Years a Fur Trader on the Upper Missouri: The Personal Narrative of Charles Larpenteur, 1833-1872.* Lincoln, NE: U of Nebraska Press, 1989. Originally edited by Elliott Coues and published in 2 vols., New York, 1898; then re-edited by Milo M. Quaife and published as a Lakeside Classic by R.R. Donnelly & Sons, Chicago, IL, 1933.

Lavender, David. "Some American Characteristics of the American Fur Company." In *Aspects of the Fur Trade: Selected Papers of the 1965 North American Fur Trade Conference.* St. Paul: Minnesota Historical Society, 1967.

Leeson, Michale A., ed. *History of Montana 1739-1885.* Chicago: Warner, Beers & Co. 1885.

Loew, Franklin M., and Edward H. Wood. *Vet in the Saddle: John L. Poett: First Veterinary Surgeon on the North West Mounted Police.* Saskatoon: Western Producer Prairie Books, 1978.

MacBeth, R.G. *Policing the Plains.* New York: George H. Doran, 1931.

MacEwan, Grant. *Fifty Mighty Men.* Vancouver: Greystone Books, 1995.

Macleod, R.C. *North-West Mounted Police and Law Enforcement, 1873-1905.* Toronto: U of Toronto Press, 1976.

Manzione, Joseph. *I am Looking to the North for My Life: Sitting Bull 1876-1881.* Salt Lake City: U of Utah Press, 1994.

McKee, Sandra Lynn, ed. *Gabriel Dumont and Jerry Potts: Canadian Plainsmen.* Frontier Series No. 14. Surrey, BC: Frontier Books, 1982.

———, ed. *Gabriel Dumont: Indian Fighter.* Frontier Book No. 14. Aldergrove, BC: Frontier Publishing, 1973.

Middleton, S.H. (Chief Mountain). *Indian Chiefs: Ancient and Modern.* Lethbridge: Lethbridge Herald, 1951.

Nevitt, R.B. *Winter at Fort Macleod.* Ed. Hugh A. Dempsey. Calgary: Glenbow-Alberta Institute, McClelland and Stewart West, 1974.

Overholser, Joel. *Fort Benton: World's Innermost Port*. Helena, MT: Falcon Press, 1987.

Paterson, T.W., ed. *The History of the Canadian West*. Langley, BC: Mr. Paperback, 1982.

Rasky, Frank. *The Taming of the Canadian West*. Toronto: McClelland and Stewart, 1967.

Robertson, R.G. *Competitive Struggle: America's Western Fur Trading Posts, 1764-1865*. Boise, ID: Tamarack Books, 1999.

Sealey, D. Bruce. *Jerry Potts*. The Canadians series. Don Mills, ON: Fitzhenry & Whiteside, 1980.

Sharp, Paul F. *Whoop-Up Country: The Canadian West, 1865-1885*. Minneapolis: U of Minnesota Press, 1955.

Steele, Samuel B. *Forty Years in Canada: Reminiscences of the Great North-West with Some Account of His Service in South Africa*. Toronto: McGraw-Hill Ryerson, 1972.

Tanner, Ogden. *The Canadians*. Eds. George G. Daniels, et al. *The Old West*. Alexandria, VA: Time-Life, 1979.

Terrell, John Upton. *Furs by Astor: The Full Story of the Founding of a Great American Fortune*. New York: William Morrow & Co., 1963.

———. *Land Grab: The Truth About "The Winning of the West."* New York: Dial Press, 1972.

Turner, C. Frank. *Across the Medicine Line: The Epic Confrontation Between Sitting Bull and the North-West Mounted Police*. Toronto: McClelland and Stewart, 1973.

Turner, John Peter. *The North West Mounted Police: 1873-1893*, vols. 1 and 2. Ottawa: King's Printer, 1950.

Utley, Robert M. *Frontier Regulars: The United States Army and the Indian, 1866-1890*. New York: Macmillan Publishing Co., 1973.

———. *The Lance and the Shield: The Life and Times of Sitting Bull*. New York: Ballantine Books, 1993.

Wischmann, Lesley. *Frontier Diplomats: The Life and Times of Alexander Culbertson and Natoyist-Siksina*. Western Frontiersmen Series. Spokane: Arthur Clark, 2000.

Woodcock, George. *Gabriel Dumont: The Métis Chief and his Lost World*. Edmonton: Hurtig Publishers, 1976.

Index

Photo Credits

Glenbow Archives: pp. 43 (NA-1274-5), 68 (NA-1274-12), 77 (NA-568-8), 78 (NA-568-5), 85 (NA-1274-13), 92 (NA-360-14), 98 (NA-278-2), 101 left (NA-360-7), 101 right (NA-360-16), 103 left (NA-568-3), 103 right (NA-568-4), 112 (NA-550-11), 120 (NA-1274-14), 128 top (NA-1376-4), 128 bottom (NA-843-37), 151 (NA-2446-11), 165 (NA-550-18), 169 right (NA-343-1), 175 (NA-29-1), 186 (NA-1225-1), 195 (NA-98-24), 199 top (3056), 203 (1382), 206 (1386), 214 top (NA-23-2), 214 bottom (NA-2221-1), 221 (NA-1434-28), 231 (3073), 242 (NA-5091-1), 244 (P0005331), 246(NA-2859-1), 248 (NA-684-2), 253 (3057), 267 (NA-451-1), 269 (NA-3690-1), 274 (NA-900-1), 275 (NA-1190-9), 276 (NA-1041-14), 286 (NA-1506-1), 295 (NA-3811-2A), 305 (NA-556-1), 307 (NA-2928-53), 308 (NA-668-47)

Heritage Collection: pp. 18, 23, 25, 33, 34, 35, 47, 59, 118, 169 left, 188, 199 bottom, 204, 218, 219, 238, 256, 258, 281, 287, 290 right, 293, 310

Montana Historical Society: pp. 48 (3001), 55, 67 (941-913), 75, 100 (941-817), 106 (3007)

National Archives of Canada: pp. 136 (3011), 144, 147 top, 147 bottom (62688), 190 (PA204295), 228 and front cover (3050), 236

RCMP Museum: pp. 147 middle, 153 and front cover (3022), 202

Saskatchewan Archives Board: pp. 135 (71-870-43), 290 left

www.fortbenton.com: p. 70

Rodger Touchie has written, edited, and published books on western Canadian history intermittently over the past 35 years. Born in Hamilton, Ontario, he came west to attend graduate school at the University of British Columbia and was first attracted to writing when his MBA thesis was published in three parts by *Canadian Business Magazine*. While enjoying a diverse business career, primarily as a consultant and entrepreneur, Rodger continued to write on B.C.

history and travel, publishing *Vancouver Island: Portrait of a Past* with Douglas & McIntyre and *Preparing a Successful Business Plan* with Self-Counsel Press.

In 1995, with his wife, Patricia, Rodger purchased Heritage House Publishing Company and has now published in excess of 100 titles that celebrate the cultural heritage and many attributes of the West. Having edited a number of books about the original Mounties and repeatedly finding reference to the superhuman deeds of Jerry Potts, Rodger embarked on a plan three years ago to research the subject, sort out the various discrepancies that he found in print, and write his own account of the man and his times.

Rodger and Pat now divide their time between Nanoose Bay and Victoria, B.C., while overseeing their Heritage Group publishing interests that, in addition to Heritage House, include TouchWood Editions and Rocky Mountain Books.